Modern Security Analysis 2nd Edition

Simple & Effective

Tony Pow

Why you invest

You will need to learn about investing sooner or later in your life. You also need to take some calculated risks.

Compare the returns of the following assets: cash, CDs, treasury bills, bonds, real estate and stocks. We start with the risk-free investments and end with the riskiest. It turns out that the average returns are in the opposite order. Cash and CDs are not risk-free as inflation eats our profits. For example, the real return is negative for the 2% return in a CD and a 3% inflation rate. In addition, you have to pay taxes for the 'returns'. <u>Our capitalist system punishes us for not taking risks</u>. However, protect your portfolio such as using stop orders and not using leverages including options for beginners. Start being a turtle investor rather than a trader that could <u>lose</u> all your money.

There are two kinds of risk: blind risk and calculated risk. If you buy a stock due to a recommendation from a commentator on TV or a tip, most likely you are taking a blind risk. It would be the same in buying a house without thoroughly evaluating the house and its neighborhood. When you buy stocks with a proven strategy (i.e., when/what stocks to buy and when/what stocks to sell), you are taking a calculated risk. In the long run, stocks with calculated and educated risks are profitable.

Be a turtle investor by investing in value stocks and holding for longer time periods (a year or more). "Buy and Monitor" is a better approach than "Buy and Hold" as some could lose all the stocks' value such as in the failure of Enron.

For experienced investors, shorting, short-term trading and covered calls would make you good profits. Simple market timing would reduce your losses during market downturns. If you buy a market ETF and use my simple market timing, you should have beaten the market by a wide margin from 2000 to 2019.

With so many fraudulent and poor managed hedge funds (but many exceptions), do not trust anyone with your investing. Do not buy investing instruments that are highly marketed such as annuity and term insurance.

If you are a handy man and do not mind to satisfy the constant requests of your tenants, buy real estate in growing areas that could be very profitable in the long run. Take advantage of the tax laws such as investing in a 401K especially the part that is matched by your company and/or a Roth IRA.

Why you trust me

This book represents my years of investing experience, the hundreds of investing books I read and thousands of simulations. Hopefully this book will improve your financial health substantially as it has one to mine. I also hope that by reading this book you can become a better investor no matter if you are a **beginner or a fund manager**.

My children have no interest in investing, so I do not hold back anything. I expect my readers will do better financially if they can avoid my mistakes that I will point out in this book. Today and at my age I am a very conservative investor and am doing well with my investments. I wish I could have tried out many of my strategies earlier in my investing life.

- I had a 50% return in one month in 2018 by using my year-end strategy. I would challenge any investor with this type of monthly return in a diversified portfolio of 8 stocks or more.

- I recommended 20 stocks in an article titled Amazing Return in Seeking Alpha. If you bought them on the published date, you would have beaten the S&P 500 index by more than 100% in a year without considering dividends as demonstrated in my other article A Tale of Two Portfolios.

   I challenge anyone who has a better one-year performance by recommending a diversified portfolio of 15 or more stocks in any publication.

- In 01/2016, I recommended buying OIL in my posts in Seeking Alpha's Wall Street Breakfast and my blog when oil was less than $30 per barrel.
http://tonyp4idea.blogspot.com/2016/01/oil-price.html.

- Recommended Apple at $55.72 (1-7 split adjusted) on April 19, 2013 as the only example in my book Scoring Stocks and I recommended selling it at $132 in 2/2015 with valid arguments described in this link.
http://tonyp4idea.blogspot.com/2015/02/dump-apple.html

Outline on how to start

1. First determine your risk tolerance, how much time you have for investing, your knowledge in investing and your portfolio size. When the market is risky (Chapter 2), do not buy any stock. After the

plunge, we need to find the reentry point as illustrated in the same chapter.
2. Ensure the screened stocks are fundamentally sound (Chapter 9).
3. Sell the stock when it fulfills your objective, the fundamentals deteriorate or the market is plunging (Chapter 1 and 17).
4. Paper test your strategy.
5. When it is thoroughly tested out and the result is good, use real money slowly and gradually. Monitor your performance.

While most of my predictions are materialized, some are not. Learn from the arguments for the predictions, not the predictions themselves. When the predictions are based on educated guesses, more of them will be materialized in the long run. I do not use predictions after-the-fact as many authors do.

#Filler:

I was deeply moved by the family members of the church victims forgiving the shooter. At SeekingAlpha, I wrote a brief post: "Forgive" is the most powerful word in every language and in every culture. I forgot it until I received a response today from Jim.

"Tony,

Without even knowing it, you made the greatest comment I have seen on Seeking Alpha--and it had nothing to do with investing. You mentioned somewhere that "Forgive" is the most powerful word in every language. Wow.
I shared that with my children. Financial commentary is easily forgotten, but that will stay with me forever. Thank you for that.
Jim"
Jim, forgive me to publicize your email as I hope to spread the word to others.

I cannot take any credit as it is just common sense except for those who do not go to church. The credit should be given to the forgiving family members and to the preaching of the church. With the power of forgiveness, we should not have the wars in the Middle East, past, present and future.

Contents

Why you invest 2
Why you trust me 3
Outline on how to start 3
Highlights 9
    Amazing returns in my portfolio 9
    A Tale of Two Portfolios 15
Introduction 20
        Disclaimer 24
        How the rate of return is calculated 25
*** First Part of this book – The basics *** 25
I Market Timing 27
    1   The power of market timing 27
    2   Simplest market timing 31
II Finding Stocks 34
    Performance of my screens 34
    3   Finviz's parameters 38
        Your broker's website 46
        Other sources 46
        Gurus 47
        Quick and dirty 47
        5-minute stock evaluation 48
    Common parameters 50
    4   Sectors to be cautious 54
    5   Tutorial on screening stocks 57
        Nasdaq 59
III Evaluating Stocks 60
    6   Simplest ways to evaluate stocks 60
    7   Manipulators and bankruptcy 64
        Mergers 65

- 8 Intangibles 66
- 9 Qualitative analysis 70

IV Technical Analysis 74
- 10 Simplest technical analysis 79
- 11 Technical Analysis example 80
- 12 Our window to the investing world 84
- 13 ETFs / Mutual Funds 86
  - Quick analysis of ETFs 91
  - Rotation of 4 ETFs 94
- 14 Order prices 95
- 15 Stop loss & flash crash 101

*** Second part of this book: The advanced *** 104

VI Market timing 104
- 16 Market cycle 105
- 17 *Spotting big market plunges* 111
  - Using VIX as a timing model 119
  - Other technical indicators 120
  - Fear and Greed 120
  - Other related hints on value 121
- 18 Actions for different stages of a market cycle 122
  - Metric performances & market cycle 124

VII Market timing by calendar 125
- 19 Market timing by calendar 125
- 20 Summary 129

VIII Evaluating Stocks 131
- 21 *Fundamental metrics* 131
- 22 Mysteries of P/E 141
- 23 Score your stocks 148
- 24 *Adaptive Stock Scoring System* 148
  - My recent performance monitor on metrics 152

IX Technical Analysis ... 155
- 25 More on technical analysis ... 155
- 26 Examples on using technical analysis ... 158

X Tools ... 162
- 27 Covered calls ... 162
  - Buyback, Diluting and Spinoff ... 164
- 28 Diversification ... 165
- 29 Trade plan ... 169
- 30 Tax avoidance ... 174

XI Strategies ... 178
- *31 When to sell a stock* ... 179
  - Selling a winner ... 183
  - Examples of overpriced stocks ... 185
- 32 Define Swing trading ... 187
- 33 Tom's conservative strategy ... 193
- 34 Top-Down investing in a nutshell ... 195
- 35 Sector Rotation ... 197
  - Sectors ... 199
- 36 Dividend investing ... 200

XII Investment advice ... 201
- 37 Newsletters and subscriptions ... 201
- 38 Retirees, take notice ... 207
- 39 The advantages of a retail investor ... 208

XIII The economy ... 211
- 40 The evils of printing money ... 211
- 41 Low interest rate ... 213
- 42 Inflation and deflation ... 214
- 43 The states of the United States ... 218

XIV Two industries ... 223
- 44 Airlines ... 223
- 45 Apple ... 229

XV Bonus 234

- 46 *Monitor my big gainers* 234
- 47 Monitor my big losses 240
- 48 Performance monitor example 243
- 49 Debunk the myths 246
- 50 Preaching that works 253
  - Search value stocks like Buffett 257
- 51 Newsletters and subscriptions 258
  - Making full use of a subscription 263
- 52 This time is different 266
- 53 Hedge fund 101 270
- 54 Modern portfolio theory MPT 274
- 55 2011, the year stock pickers died 275
- 56 Seeking Alpha 276
- 57 Fidelity stock research 277
- 58 Institutional investors 278
- 59 The scents of a winner 279
  - Common hints of a winner beside the above 282
- 60 CALM, a short squeeze candidate 282
- 61 Politics and investing 286
- 62 GuruFocus 290
- 63 Piotroski's F-Score 291

Epilogue 294

Bonus: Simple Techniques 295

- How to start 296
- 1 Sample portfolio 297
- 2 Investing for 'lazy' folks 299
- 3 Simplest analysis of ETFs 301
- An example 304
- 4 Simplest ways to evaluate stocks 305
- 5 Simplest market timing 309

6	Rotate four ETFs	313
7	Simplest technical analysis	315
8	The best strategy	315
9	Don'ts for beginners	316
10	Summary	317

Appendix 1 – All my books 319

    Best stocks to buy for 2023 319

    Sector Rotation: 21 Strategies 320

    Shorting Stocks and ETFs 321

Appendix 2 – Art of Investing 321

    Your choice for your next book 325

Appendix 3 - Our window to the investing world 325

Appendix 4 - ETFs / Mutual Funds 327

Highlights

Amazing returns in my portfolio

To achieve a consistent 10% return above the S&P 500 over many years is every fund manager's dream. To double one's investment above the S&P500 return is amazing while tripling it is unheard of. I beat the S&P500 by 700% and I can detail the history of my transactions.

Many analysts show their average yearly returns and/or their returns of their top 10 stocks this time of the year. The market is closed early today on Christmas Eve, so I have the time to check my recent performance. As a trader with many trades, it would be far too complicated for me to do the same for the entire year. I selected all the stocks I purchased in the last 90 days. Most of them are deeply-valued stocks. Let's check how I perform so far on these stocks.

Whenever you have achieved a high return such as this one, take profit as it may have reached its peaks. To me, most profits are made in swing trades with an average holding period of 90 days.

Stocks bought and their returns as of 12/25/12

Stocks	Date Bought	Return	SPY Return
BANR	12/07/12	3%	-.13%
KTCC	12/06/12	0%	.7%
QCOR	12/07/12	15%	-.1%
KTCC	12/06/12	-1%	.7%
ACTV	12/05/12	-5%	.7%
IAG	12/05/12	-1%	.7%
ADES	12/04/12	6%	.6%
NC	12/03/12	15%	-.3%
VELT	12/03/12	64%	-.3%
ANR	11/28/12	33%	4.8%
AAPL	11/16/12	1%	4.8%
C	11/14/12	13%	3.0%
DECK	11/13/12	16%	2.7%
MSFT	11/13/12	0%	2.7%
ALU	11/13/12	38%	2.7%
DLTR	11/09/12	7%	3.4%
CAT	11/08/12	4%	1.9%
MSFT	11/07/12	-8%	.5%
BSX	10/24/12	14%	.3%
BSX	10/19/12	7%	.3%
20			
AVG:		11%	1.35%

Beat SPY (in %) = (11%-1.35%)/1.35% = 716% or 7 times

Average Return = averaging each return of 20 stocks = 11%
Average Annualized Return = 148% or 122% (= 11% *365 / avg. holding period)
Average Return = Profit / Capitalization　　　　　= 10%[1]

How returns are calculated

Using BANR to illustrate how the return and SPY return are calculated.

BANR	12/07/12	3%	-.13%

BANR was bought on 12/07/12 (17 days from 12/24/12) at 27.93 and it was at 30.43 on 12/24/12.
Rate of Return = (30.43 – 27.93) / 27.93 = 3%

SPY was at 142.53 on 12/07/12 and at 142.35 on 12/24/12.
Rate of Return = (142.35-142.53) / 142.53 = -.13%

Commissions and dividends are not included for simplicity. Commissions are negligible and dividends could add about another 2% for the annual return.

Interpreting the performance result

The quantity of each stock bought is not important as I am comparing the return of the stock. However, a few stocks have been listed twice as I bought two times usually on separate dates. If I chose them as one purchase instead of two, my return would appear even better. The purchases are real, so the amount of each stock is not identical to each other.

I'm not too excited yet. This phenomenal return could be just this one time only. 90 days is a short period. Consistency could be achieved with an improved stock picking technique, plain luck or a combination. By any measure, it is an extremely decent return. However, I do not expect beating the S&P 500 by 7 times again.

My best return is from 2009 in my largest taxable account. It is over 80% beating SPY by about 3 times. 2003 is another good year for profit. These two years are defined by me as the Early Recovery stage in a market cycle and the market provides the best profit opportunity.

The four losers are MSFT (-8%), ACTV (-5%), KTCC (-1%) and IAG (-1%). The best winners are: VELT (64%), ALU (38%), ANR (33%) and QCOR (19%). The following are in 14% to 16% range: DECK, NC and BSX (2 purchases). Click here for the entire list.

Cheating the results
I could 'cheat' for better results by doing the following, but I did not:

1. Exclude stocks only purchased in last 20 days (instead of 15).

2. If my purchases of CSCO were included, the result would be even better. CSCO has been bought three times on 7/24/12 and it has

gained 31% as of 12/25/12. I still have CSCO, but it is not included as it just the 90-days requirement.
3. I could include those buy orders that had not been executed due to their fast appreciation.

Hence, there are many ways to cheat and you should read others' results carefully. For me, 7 times better is the same 2 times better, so why cheat?

What stocks were included

There are 20 purchases. I bought some stocks twice and counted as two purchases. None of the stocks have been sold as of 12/25/12.
I have excluded the stocks that I bought in the last 15 days (too early for meaningful performance results) and the stocks that I am testing a strategy by trading them every month and most are in a separate account that I do not have to pay commissions.

This strategy so far looks promising with good gains and requiring almost no effort on my part. I will include the result in my blog for this book if it proves itself to be consistently profitable. It is based on common stocks of two subscription services both seeking momentum stocks.

How the stocks were picked
The majority of the stocks were screened by my selected screens that had been proven profitable in the last 3 to 6 months or are historically profitable at this stage of the market cycle. I also analyzed most of the screened stocks and assigned a score (15 and higher is a buy) based on the metrics that had reliable prediction recently. I do not stick with the scoring system 100%, but most stocks I purchased twice have high scores.

The poor performers were scored as: MSFT with a score of 13, ACTV 16, KTCC 27 and IAG 23. The scoring system is OK. MSFT should not be bought judging from its low score. However, I believe MSFT has a long-term appreciation potential. The other three are the latest purchases in this portfolio and they may perform better in longer period.

The winners were scored as: VELT 34, ALU not scored, ANR not scored and QCOR 30. The scoring system is great for this group. ALU and ANR were selected from two Seeking Alpha articles and their selections were not based on scores. I read several Wall Street Journal articles on ALU and CSCO to convince me to buy both.

The average winners were scored as: DECK 9, NC 26 and BSX not scored. DECK was selected based on an article from Seeking Alpha and it seemed DECK was experiencing the same short squeeze as CROX once did. BSX was selected from a Sunday paper article.

Observations

1. I notice that most big winners (ALU is $1) have a stock price less than $10. The myth of holding quality stocks with prices higher than $15 is not true here as most of my big winners are below $10 including ALU.

2. I did not double bet on VELT and ALU, which both turn out to be my best performers. VELT scored high in my analysis. ALU was very convincing but it seemed to be risky. 'Nothing risk and nothing gain' applies here. I did triple bet on CSCO, which is a large company with good fundamentals that were not 'discovered' by the market.

    Both AAPL and DECK gained more than 25% and then lost most of their gains during my short holding period. I should have sold AAPL as many of my fellow investors sold the winners expecting higher capital gain taxes next year. The myth of 'buy and hold' does not work here.

3. During this period, I had several buy orders not executed due to their stock prices had been sky rocketed. Market orders could be the solution. It is another example of pennies smart and pound foolish.

4. It will be interesting to check the results again in 6 and 12 months. Except ALU, all are in my taxable accounts and I usually keep them for a year to qualify for the lower tax rates for capital gains.

5. I have not described any specific method, but concepts to build better strategies to customize to your individual situations and/or market conditions. Bet the money you can afford to lose. Past performance does not guarantee future results.

6. Reading articles such as Seeking Alpha is beneficial. However, you need to do your own analysis.

7. The market has been up by .8% in last 90 days and this portfolio increases by 11%. If my portfolio amplifies the market, I wonder whether it will be down by the same rate in a down market.

8. This portfolio is quite diversified even I have not planned that way except weighing more with high tech companies. There are not big winners and big losers that could change the average return.

9. I tried not to include emerging countries such as China as I do not trust their balance sheets.

10. I have never achieved such an amazing return. I'm emotionally detached to big wins and big losses. It could be plain luck. Even the best strategy will have its "black swan" moment eventually.

11. To achieve over 100% annualized return is not sustainable by checking the top performers of S&P 500 and their returns. However, it is possible but not likely if you churn your portfolio more than once and you time the market correctly.

12. Time to take profit as most have achieved my objectives. Use the cash to buy stocks with similar appreciation potentials. You will never go broke for taking profits.

Conclusion

My three steps of making stock purchase are: 1. Market timing, 2. Screening stocks, 3. Stock Analysis and 4. When and what to sell. They have all been discussed throughout the book. Market timing and strategy (#2 and #3) does not always work, but it will be better with using them than without.

I am the living proof *against* the Efficiency Theory and the claims that stock picking does not work. It may not work from time to time, but in the long run it works.

Footnote

[1] Profit / Capitalization could be wrong. It could be 20% but actually a little less than 20%.

The original 10% is correct when you invest all the 20 stocks at the start of the beginning of the investment period. I bought these stocks in different dates. If I assume the average time of all the stock purchases is at mid-point, then my average capitalization is only half and hence giving a 20% return.

It is slightly less than 20% as I did not include the stocks that I bought in last 15 days.

Use the number for comparison and that's why we have to be concerned on the performance from most investment subscriptions.

A Tale of Two Portfolios

The first portfolio (20 stocks) was described in my SA article Amazing Returns more than a year ago and the second portfolio (15 stocks) was described in my book, Best Stocks 2014, According to Me, and was also mentioned in one of my comments in the article.

The first portfolio consists of Banner (NASDAQ:BANR), Key Tronic (NASDAQ:KTCC) (2 times), Questcor Pharmaceuticals (NASDAQ:QCOR), The Active Network (NYSE:ACTV) (acquired), Iamgold (NYSE:IAG), Advanced Emissions Solutions (NASDAQ:ADES), Nacco Industries (NYSE:NC), Velti (VELT, delisted), Alpha Natural Resources (NYSE:ANR), Apple (NASDAQ:AAPL), Citigroup (NYSE:C), Deckers Outdoor (NYSE:DECK), Microsoft (NASDAQ:MSFT) (2 purchases), Alcatel-Lucent, S.A. (NYSE:ALU), Dollar Tree (NASDAQ:DLTR), Caterpillar (NYSE:CAT) and Boston Scientific (NYSE:BSX) (2 purchases).

The second portfolio consists of Universal Insurance Holdings (NYSE:UVE), Gray Television (NYSE:GTN), Esterline Technologies (NYSE:ESL), Johnson Controls (NYSE:JCI), Nexstar Broadcasting Group (NASDAQ:NXST), Pozen (NASDAQ:POZN), China Lodging Group (NASDAQ:HTHT), CVS Caremark (NYSE:CVS), Home Inns & Hotels Management Inc. (NASDAQ:HMIN), Arotech Corporation (NASDAQ:ARTX), Canadian Solar (NASDAQ:CSIQ), Jazz Pharmaceuticals Public (NASDAQ:JAZZ), Motorcar Parts of America (NASDAQ:MPAA), Micron Technology (NASDAQ:MU) and Och-Ziff Capital Management Group (NYSE:OZM).

The first one has an average return of 53% beating SPY's (an ETF simulating S&P 500) 25% by 112% from 1-4-2013 (the publish date of the article) to 1-4-2014, a year later.

The annualized return of the second portfolio is 31% beating SPY's 16% by 94% from 12/16/13 (the publish date for the book) to

2/15/14 (2 months later). The choice of the end date will be explained later. Dividends are not considered in all calculations.

The second portfolio is one of several short lists from the 135 stocks recommended in the book. The best short list is Small Cap which has an annualized return of 98% beating SPY by 512% for the same period. It consists of the following nine stocks: Arotech, Consumer Portfolio Services (NASDAQ:CPSS), Entravision Communications (NYSE:EVC), Gastar Exploration (NYSEMKT:GST), Dot Hill Systems (NASDAQ:HILL), Lee Enterprises (NYSE:LEE), MTR Gaming Group (NASDAQ:MNTG), RAIT Financial Trust (NYSE:RAS) and Star Gas Partners (NYSE:SGU). Recently, small stocks are not doing as good as before.

The returns are pretty good, but they are not the discussion here. I would like to see what we can learn in investing.

You cannot learn from someone you do not respect

There were a lot of criticisms and doubts in my original article. I welcome all of them as I can learn from the comments and how I should be more defensive in writing. However, some do not make a lot of sense.

- The short duration would boost my annualized returns. Yes, the annualized return of a week is not meaningful, but a month is, at least for 20 stocks. The annualized return is a two-edged sword and it can amplify the losses too.
- Sometimes I do not have a choice such as comparing the performance of my momentum portfolio. It has an average holding period of one month. Now, I compare the performance of the 20 stocks for one full year.
- I could have skipped my losers. They were all real trades within the specified period in my largest taxable account. Actually, I skipped some huge winners that missed my criteria by days. Now, I use the publish date of the article as the start date.
- Today's low commission should not be a concern even for 20 stocks. My commission is $5 per trade and it represents a negligible percent of the trade.

- I did have a loss at one time on my second portfolio. There was nothing to be concerned with. If you believe you never want a loss, do not invest and let inflation eat up your investment. The yardstick is whether you can beat an index such as S&P500.

Survivor Bias

VELT was delisted and ACTV was acquired. I used my sold price for VELT and the proceed I received from ACTV to calculate my return. Hence, the return is not precise for simplicity.

When you test a strategy, your return could appear better than the reality. In this case, VELT and ACTV are not selected in your test as they've been taken out from your historical database; few handle this bias.

Usually, the delisted stocks lose a lot of value and the stocks being acquired gain a lot of value, so they would balance out the effect. In reality it is not. There are more stocks delisted and/or bankrupted than the stocks being acquired. In addition, usually their average loss is more than the average gain of the stocks being acquired.

Countries and sectors

Usually, I do not trust the foreign countries that do not have a regulator similar to our SEC, especially on small stocks. VELT, a loser here, could be one.

I outlined in my books several sectors to be cautious of, including miners and ANR and IAG belong to this sector.

Size of bet

I had double bet on BSX and a low position on VELT. I did not place a large bet on ALU, a winner but risky at the time of evaluation. Gained some and lost some. In general, you want to double or increase the bet when the appreciation potential is good with acceptable risk.

Fundamental analysis works

Most of the 20 stocks scored high in my two scoring systems (one using simple metrics available to all). Value stocks need time for the market to realize their values as they're swimming against the tide. The short-term return usually does not mean anything, though it does this time.

The second portfolio is intended for short-term swings (3 months to me).

Fundamental analysis does not work

It is not contradictory. It depends on what the stocks are intended for. The second portfolio is for short-term swing. I used fundamental analysis to the minimum. There were about 135 stocks recommended in the book and I did not have time to evaluate each stock fundamentally in detail. If I did, the information would be obsolete. I provided a simple method in my book on how to do fundamental analysis.

These stocks are selected from the strategies (screens, subscriptions and screening recommended stocks from the subscriptions) that have been proven recently. They're described in my book The Art of Investing which covers most of my investing ideas. When you select the stocks based on momentum, do not hold them too long, as momentum usually does not last longer than 3 months.

Account
I have all the 20 stocks in the first portfolio in my taxable account and most of the stocks in the second portfolio in my retirement accounts.

I placed ARTX in a taxable account by mistake. I did not sell it when it gained more than 50% in one day due to the tax consideration.

Holding period

It is targeted to over one year for the first portfolio so they are eligible to the low tax treatment on long-term capital gains. For one year or two, my Federal tax on a huge capital gain was virtually zero taking advantage of a provision in the tax law.

I use two months for the second portfolio, as this is the time I start to sell the stocks for the short-swing portfolio. I compare different periods and this is the choice. In actual trading, I take advantage of their weekly fluctuations using technical indicators such as Bollinger Bands.

"Buy and hold" is not for me
Before 2000, market timing was waste of time. Since 2000, we had two market plunges with the average loss of about 45%. I have a simple chart to detect market plunges. It will not catch the peak and bottom as it depends on the falling/rising market. Hopefully, it will give us plenty of time to prepare as the last two.

The second reason I churn my portfolio is improving the appreciation potential. It is just my preference. When I sell a stock, it does not mean I'm not buying it back.

Risk tolerance. I am more conservative as a retiree. However, I was more than 'all in' (using my equity credit) in 2009. It depends on individual risk tolerance and situation.
Conclusion

Using these two portfolios, I have covered a lot of my ideas in investing. Implement the ideas that make sense to you and your requirements.

We need to have a trade plan to find stocks, analyze them, order them in the right account and sell them. Enhance your trade plan and stick to it. In addition to the described portfolios, I have one for momentum where I keep stocks for a month or less. I have other strategies such as Top Down and Sector Rotation. When the market is risky, I sell more stocks than I buy. Today I'm taking a break.

There will not be a book titled "Best Stocks for 2015". I find stocks almost once every month so it does not take too much effort to document my selections in a book. The window to sell the book is too short and it does not make it financially rewarding. But, never say 'never'.

I may have another article on my next 20 stocks in the future. The market is risky by any yardstick. Excessive printing of money causes the current non-correlation of the market and the economy. The government eventually has to reduce the money supply and they will correlate again. Until then, I am investing more conservatively.

Introduction

This book is modern compared to similar books written 20 years ago. At that time, they did not have free internet sites providing all kinds of financial ratios such as P/E. The need to examine the financial statements was substantially reduced. The 1 billion earnings do not tell you much, but the P/E and other fundamental metrics that are readily available to you via many free websites.

In addition, they did not have technical analysis (or charts) to detect market plunges. We have lost an average of 45% in the last two market plunges and hence 'buy-and-hold' is not a good strategy since 2000. This book uses simple techniques with or without charts to detect market plunges that work for the last two major ones.

We do have our challenges. Sometimes we are overloaded with information. Some articles in the free web sites are written with hidden agenda that could cost you lots of money. We need to select the relevant data and ignore traps and garbage.

I make it easy by splitting this book into two parts: Basic and Advanced (from Chapter 16 and on). Even for the basics I try to implement the advanced concepts using simple and free information from the internet. Even if you are an advanced investor, try to glance it through the first part to review anything you may have missed.

This book helps someone looking for simple but profitable strategies in investing. The swing strategy only takes about half an hour a month to monitor the market and decide what stocks to buy and sell.

I selected Finviz.com, a free financial site for most of my investing techniques and it is supplemented by other sites (some free and most requiring small fees).

I start with market timing. You should not buy any stocks when the market is plunging. Actually you should sell most of the stocks you own when the market is plunging. I have a simple way to spot market plunges.

It is based on charts. However, you can obtain similar info without creating charts and there is nothing to subscribe to.

The chart tells us when to reenter the market for the best opportunity to make money. It worked very well in the last two market plunges. It may not give us ample time as the last two. I have not tested the market plunges before 2000 as they were quite different from today's market.

For starters, just trade ETFs and you can skip the latter chapters in evaluating stocks if you are a beginner investor.

In the simplest terms, I discussed how to evaluate stocks fundamentally and technically. Use the research available in the free sites such as finviz.com. Instead of spending hours researching one stock, you can do the same in a few minutes as others have done the research for you.

Some of the strategies described here have been used in my book Best Stocks 2014, According to Me. From 12/16/13 (the publish date) to 3/4/14, the list of all 135 selected stocks beat SPY (an ETF simulating the S&P 500) by 103% and the list of 9 small cap stocks beat SPY by 500% without considering dividends and compounding. This performance is not sustainable.

Retail investors have a lot of advantages over fund managers. However, I advise not to be a trader, especially day traders for beginners. Statistically most amateur traders lose money as they cannot compete with experienced, disciplined traders. Even if you study several good books by great traders, you will still lose money initially. No books can replace the actual trading experience.

My books do not teach you to be a trader but a 'turtle' investor. Buy value stocks that are fundamentally sound and re-evaluate them in six months to determine to keep or sell.

For beginner investors

Both Fidelity and AAII (both require being a client or a member) have excellent articles for beginners. Alternatively, buy a book for beginners. To include all the basic terms and concepts, I have to double the size of this book which is already lengthy and bore most readers who already have the basic knowledge.

Click here for Morningstar classroom.

http://morningstar.com/cover/classroom.html

Click here for Fidelity basic in investing.
https://www.fidelity.com/investment-guidance/investing-basics

For starters

Follow the following steps if you have never invested.

- Set up an emergency fund, at least 3 months of your salary.
- Save. Do not spend over your limit. Eliminate credit card debts.
- Buy a house if you're married with two jobs.
- Invest in Roth IRAs if you're qualified.
- Invest in retirement accounts.
- Read one or two of the above links for beginners. Alternatively buy a book for beginners.
- Read this book. Learn market timing.
- Buy an ETF that simulates the S&P 500 index or the total market. If the chart described in this book tells you to exit the market, do so. It may not be right all the time, but hopefully in the long term, it works.
- Read this book again and paper test how to analyze stocks.
- Study the advanced techniques described in this book. You cannot learn by reading only but by paper testing your techniques.

How this book is organized

Most graphs and tables are in landscape orientation for both paperback and e-readers. Some graphs may not be displayed adequately on a small screen of an e-reader. E-readers may be available in the current version of Windows, so you can read e-books on the larger screen of your PC. For better orientation, just flip the e-readers 90 degrees.

A link is usually included for these screens. Copy it to your browser to display the graphs on your PC if desirable. Instructions on how to produce some graphs are provided as you should try them out. One example is how to produce a chart on detecting market crashes.

It is easier to display some tables in landscape mode. Select a table or a graph via your e-reader to display it to fit the screen.

The font size and page size of most e-book formats can be adjusted. The unknown, special character is the "smiling face" that the current Kindle does not convert correctly as of this writing.

There are clickable links to web articles. Most of them are from my own web sites and public web sites such as Wikipedia. Some public links may not be available in the future as they are not under my control and my book offerings may change.

Fidelity Video provides video clips to explain some basic terms and it may require Fidelity customers to sign on in order to view them. Check the trial offer from Fidelity. YouTube offers similar video lessons.

These links extend the usefulness of this book by making available specific topics that may not be interesting to every reader. It also provides articles (most are not written by me) for more in-depth analyzes.

The current version provides most of the links the paperback readers can enter into your browser. Get the same information by entering a search in Wikipedia such as Dogs of Dow.

Investopedia is another source beside Wikipedia.
http://www.investopedia.com/

'Afterthoughts' includes my additional comments and comments from others. Readers can make comments in this book's website. These comments may be included in the Afterthoughts in subsequent revisions, with the commenter's last name redacted. It is the section of the article for freer and informal discussion. It also contains some political and social issues.

There are fillers with tips and jokes (most original) to fill up the empty space of the printed book. Fillers, links and afterthoughts may disrupt the flow of reading this book. However, no readers so far ask me to take them out.

For convenience, this book uses SPY, an Exchange Traded Fund (ETF) simulating the S&P 500, as the benchmark for the market.

Annualized returns (Return * 365 / (Days between)) are used where appropriate for more meaningful comparison. To illustrate, I have a 10% return in 6 months, a 10% in a year and a 10% in 2 years. It is more meaningful to use annualized returns of 20%, 10% and 5% respectively for the 6-month return, the one-year return and the 2-year return in this example.

Usually I do not include the dividend, so you can add an estimated 1.5% to the annualized return. In addition, compound interest is not used for easier calculation, so the actual return could be even better.

Fast track

Read the following chapters first: Chapter 2, 3 and 7.

You should do pretty well by trading ETFs with market timing. It would also be minimal effort by taking out the complicated stock analysis that is also included in this book for future references.

About the author
I graduated from Cal. State University at San Jose in Industrial Engineering and University of Mass. in Amherst with a MS in Industrial Engineering. I have retired from a job in IT. I have been an investor for over 30 years.

Dedication
To all retail investors and future retail investors including my grandchildren.

Acknowledgement

Thanks to Seeking Alpha, Wikipedia and Investopedia for the many helpful links to enrich this book. Yahoo!Finance and Finviz.com for the tools and charts used in this book.

Important notices
© 2022-2023 Tony Pow. Version 1.0 4/2022. 1.1 02/2023

J
No part of this book can be reproduced in any form without the written approval of the author. Fidelity is my primary broker. I retired from Fidelity from their IT department. Several vendors supply me their products free for evaluation but I do not accept money for endorsing their products.

Disclaimer
Do not gamble with money that you cannot afford to lose. Past performance is a guideline and is not necessarily indicative of future results. All information is believed to be accurate, but there is not a guarantee. All the strategies including

charts to detect market plunges described have no guarantee that they will make money and they may lose money. Do not trade without doing due diligence and be warned that most data may be obsolete. All my articles and the associated data are for informational and illustration purposes only. I'm not a professional investment counselor, a tax professional or any other field. Seek one before you make any investment decisions. Remember to consult with a registered financial adviser before making any investment decisions. The above mentioned also applies for all other advice such as on accounting, taxes, health and any topic mentioned in this book. Tax laws change all the time, so talk to your tax advisors before taking any action. Some articles may offend some one or some organization unintentionally. If I did, I'm sorry about that. I am politically and religiously neutral. I have provided my best efforts to ensure the accuracy of my articles. Data also from different sources was believed to be accurate. However, there is no guarantee that they are accurate and suitable for the current market conditions and /or your individual situations. The values of some parameters such as RSI(14) are arbitrarily set by me. I have made a lot of predictions that may not materialize. My publisher and I are not liable for any damages in using this book or its contents.

How the rate of return is calculated

They are for education purposes only, and do not make your investing decisions based on them. I usually use annualized for better comparisons; 4% in a month is more than 5% in a year for example. For short-term strategies including momentum, shorting and year-end strategy, I use the returns for a month, and sometimes including returns for 2 months for comparison. Annualized returns are usually used for long-term strategies. The holding periods may have a few days off due to holidays and weekends. For simplicity, most of my returns do not include commissions, exchange fees, order spread and dividends. Most numbers have been rounded up for better readability. The return = profit / investment. I and my publisher are not liable for any error. I use SPY and sometimes RSP as a yardstick; RSP and SPY have the same S&P 500 stocks, but the stocks are weighed evenly in RSP. However, many readers do not know RSP.

#Filler: One way to evaluate a company
https://www.youtube.com/watch?v=fGVtypWv04Y

*** First Part of this book – The basics ***

The basic concepts and basic procedures are described to reduce the complexity of the topic. If you already have the basic knowledge, ensure you do not miss anything.

We start with Market Timing (Section I), Finding Stocks (Sector II) and Evaluating Stocks (Section III).

The basic technical analysis is quite easy to implement. In a sentence, you do not want to buy stocks with downward trend. Early Recovery after the plunge (detected by our simple technique) is an example.

Section V gives you some tools and information.

I Market Timing

The first chapter should convince you how important is market timing and the second chapter tells you how to detect market plunges. These chapters are critical to your financial health.

1   The power of market timing

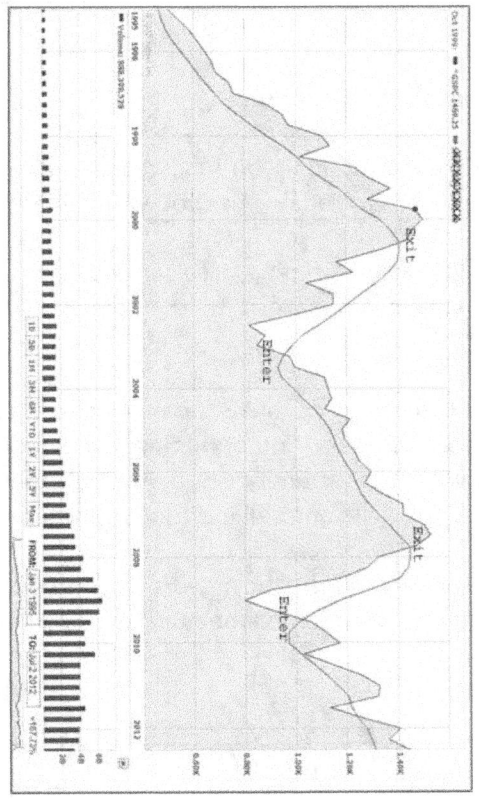

Most e-book readers allow you to select the graph to make it fit entirely to your screen. Detecting market plunges indicates the exit points and reentry points from 2000 to 9-2009 as follows.

Table: Vital Dates

Market Plunge	Peak	Bottom	Indicator Exit	Indicator Reenter
2000	08/28/00	09/20/02	10/01/00	06/01/03
2007	10/12/07	03/06/09	02/01/08	09/01/09
			08/01/11	11/01/11

As of 04/2014, my chart (from Yahoo!Finance) still indicates to invest fully in the market. For simplicity I skip a few brief exits and reentries since 2011. Run the simple chart once a month. When it indicates a potential market plunge is closer, run the chart once a week.

It is based on stock prices so it may not identify the peaks and bottoms precisely, but so far it has never failed to avoid big losses and ensure big gains by reentering the market. Hope it will give us enough time to act in the next market plunge as the last two did.

Unbelievable return with market timing

Calculate how much you made if you followed the above exit points and reenter points from 2000 to today. I bet you would make a good fortune.

To test the effect of market timing, I calculated the return of S&P 500 with market timing and compare it to the return of S&P 500 without market timing from 1-2000 to 9-2013.

There are many assumptions to make the calculations easier. In general, dividends are not considered. Compounding is not considered in most cases. The return with market timing should be substantially better if we buy a contra ETF during exits and sell it during reentries.

I was shocked by the incredible return by using simple market timing and the chart tells us to exit and reenter the market only 3 times from 2000 to 2013.
Summary info:

S&P 500 1-2000 to 9-2013	With Market Timing	Without Market Timing
Better	500%	
Gain	1,000	167
Gain %	68%	11%
Annualized gained	5%	1%
Days	4,959	4,959

Calculations:

S & P 500	With Market Timing	Without Market Timing
1-2000	1,469[1]	1,469[1]
Exit 10/01/00	1,041[2]	1,041
Enter 06/01/03	1,041	964[4]
Exit 02/01/08	1,489[3]	1,379[4]

Enter 09/01/09	1489	1,020[5]
Exit 08/01/11	1,888	1,293
Enter 11/01/11	1,888	1,251
09/03/13	2,469	1.638
Gained	2,469 – 1,469=1,000	1,638-1,469=167
Gain %	1000/1469 = 68%	167/1469 = 11%
Annualized gained	68% * 365/4959=5%	11%*365/4959=1%
Better	(1,000-167)/167 = 500%	

Portfolio with Market Timing:

[1] Both start with S&P 500 of 1,469 on 1-3-2000.

[2] 10/01/00
The market timing portfolio exits the market and remains same value of 1,041 until 6/1/00.

[3] 02/01/08
The market timing portfolio exits the market and remains same value of 1,489 until 9/1/09.

'1,489' is calculated as follows:
1,041 * (1 + Rate) = 1,041 * (1 + 1,379-964)/964) = 1,489
where S&P 500 is 964 on 6/1/00 and 1,379 on 2/1/08.

The other calculations are based on S&P 500 is 1,020 on 9/1/9, 1,293 on 8/1/11, 1,251 on 11/1/11 and 1,636 on 9/3/13.

Portfolio without Market Timing:

[1] Both starts with S&P 500 of 1,469 on 1-3-2000. We could use the 9/3/13 S&P 500 value, but it will not account on some compounded interest consideration.

[4] S&P 500 is 964 in 6/1/00 and 1,379 on 2/1/08.

[5] 02/01/08. The portfolio value is calculated to be 1,020 as follows:
1,379 * (1 + Rate) = 1,379 * (1 + (1020-1379)/1379) = 1,020
where S&P 500 is 1,379 on 2/1/08 and 1,020 on 9/1/09.

The other calculations are based on S&P 500 is 1,293 on 8/1/11, 1,251 on 11/1/11 and 1,636 on 9/3/13.

I cannot believe the shocking return with market timing. I checked my calculation and there was nothing wrong but do not hold me on this. Ignoring the compound rate of return should be minor. If you have time, send me your e-mail address to pow_tony@yahoo.com, so I can send you the spreadsheet to check out any error.

Even if I made a mistake somehow and got 100% instead of 500%, it still doubles the return without market timing! Ask any fund manager what it means to his or her fund performance and his / her career.

It will detect the next market plunges, but it may not give us ample of time to react as the last two did. It will not detect the precise bottoms and peaks as they depend on the stock price of an ETF representing the market. I have separate statistics on market peaks and bottoms but they have not been proven. The above may not work as effectively if there are too many followers. On the contrary it may work as it could be a self-fulfilling prophesy.

Filler:

Poor Lochte

Lochte was born in the wrong time and wrong place. Without Phelps he could make top money in endorsements. Now, they are all gone for making a simple lie on a very minor situation. He is NOT a role model anymore! That's what happened when the family (most likely) did not give him a decent education on honesty and be careful on drinks and drugs. It will not be the last time as we're in a permissive culture. All the politicians think they can fool us all the time and they should learn it from Lochte.

2 Simplest market timing

Why market timing
Before 2000, market timing was a waste of time. However, after that, we have had two market plunges with the average loss of about 45%. It sounds harder to time the market than it actually is. We have a simple technique to detect market plunges and when to reenter the market. Our objective is reducing the loss to 25%.

Market timing depends on charts; the following describes how to use chart information without creating charts. Most charts will not identify the peaks and bottoms of the market as they depend on data (i.e., the stock prices). However, it would reduce further losses. It is simpler than it sounds. Just follow the procedure below.

The first part of this technique detects potential market plunges, and the second part advises you when to start reentering the market. It applies to individual stocks too. It also works to detect the trend of a sector (entering an ETF for the specific sector instead of SPY) and a specific stock.

Step-by-step procedure
When the market timer indicator (Death Cross) described next tells you to exit the market, sell SPY (an ETF simulating S&P 500). Do not forget to buy back SPY or similar ETF such as RSP, when the indicator, (Golden Cross) tells you to return.

My experiences in 2000s
Basically I did the same as the above with some adaptations. I worked for a mutual fund company and they did not allow me to trade stocks effectively. However, I was allowed to trade sector funds offered by the company. Every two months, I switched to the sectors with the best performances for the last month. When most sectors were down for the last month, I rotated them to the money market fund. In March or April, 2000, I switched to traditional sectors from high-tech sectors (better to switch to market money fund). During the time, I bought those stocks that had cash enough to last more than two years judging by their burn rates. The indicators should do a better job.

How to detect market plunges without charts (similar to **Death Cross**)
1. Bring up Finviz.com.

2. Enter SPY (or any ETF that simulates the market) or RSP for equally weighed SPY.
3. If SMA-200% is positive, it indicates that the market plunge has not been detected and you can skip the following steps.
4. The market is plunging if SMA-50% is more negative than SMA-200%. To illustrate this condition, SMA-200% is -2% and SMA-50% is -5%.
5. Conservative investors should sell most stocks starting with the riskiest ones first such as the ones with negative earnings, high P/Es and/or high Debt/Equity. Obtain this info from Finviz.com by entering the symbol of the stock you own.
6. Aggressive investors should sell all stocks. Extremely aggressive investors should sell all stocks, buy contra ETFs, and even short stocks. I do not recommend beginners to be aggressive.

Example
As of 2/12/2022, the following are from Finviz.com.

ETF	SMA-200	SMA-50	SMA-20	Death Cross?
SPY	-0.8%	-4.2%	-1.7%	Yes (Step #4)
RSP	-0.5%	-1.9%	0.4%	Yes (Step #4)

Both ETFs indicate the market is a confirmed crash from my indications using a technique similar to Death Cross. However, they are quite close, and we should keep an eye on these numbers. In this case, SMA-20 has not been used. If it is a false alarm, the Golden Cross would indicate it and you should return to equity; it could be quite common in volatile markets. The futures indicate that on Monday (2/14/22) the market would plunge further.

Another test is using SMA-350: When the current price is below SMA-300, it is a crash. SMA-20 has to be more negative than SMA-50 and it has not been used here.

When to return to the market (similar to Golden Cross)

Use the above in a reversed sense to detect whether the market has been recovering. However, when the SMA-200% turns positive, I would start buying value stocks (low P/E but the 'E' has to be positive, and/or low Debt/Equity).

1. Bring up Finviz.com.
2. Enter SPY (or any ETF that simulates the market).
3. If SMA-200% is negative, the market is not recovering, and you can skip the following steps.
4. Sell all contra ETFs and close all shorts if you have any.

5. Market recovery is confirmed when SMA-50% is more positive than SMA-200%. To illustrate this condition, SMA-200% is 2% and SMA-50% is 5%. Commit a large percent of cash (or all cash for aggressive investors) to stocks. If you do not know what to buy, buy SPY or an ETF that simulates the market.

How often should you check the market timing indicators?

Do the above once a month. When the SPY price is closer to SMA actions percentage, perform the above once a week. The charts and data for market timing described in this book are based on SMA-350 (Simple Moving Average) that is more preferable than this simple procedure, but it requires some simple charting.

Nothing is perfect

If the market timing is perfect, there would be no poor folks. The major 'defects' are:
- It does not detect the peak / bottom as it depends on past data. However, it would save you a lot during the crash.
- It is hard to determine whether it is a correction or a crash.
- From 2000 to 2010, there was only one false signal. The indicator tells you to exit and then tells you to reenter the market shortly. In most cases, you do not lose a lot. After 2010, we have more false signals.
- The market may not be rational or may be influenced due to specific conditions such as excessive printing of USD. If you do not mind charting, use SMA 350 (or 400) using SPY. Buy when the price is above SMA-350 (or SMA-400), and sell otherwise. SMA-400 reduces the number of false signals, but it is not nimble.

#Filler: Glad to be an investor

After watching the following YouTube video, I am glad my parents did not push me to play piano and also glad I do not have any musical gene. How can I compete with this kid?

https://www.youtube.com/watch?v=yf0B4rVoq44

Also, glad not into some life-threatening professions such as surgical doctors, soldiers, fire fighters, etc. I can make mistakes in investing from time to time without suffering from the consequences.

II Finding Stocks

The worst way to find stocks is via TV. Many analysts have hidden agenda. More than one time, a fund manager or an analyst recommended a stock while his company was unloading it. Many have conflicting interests. Some may buy the stock before they recommend it. Unless you have reliable insider information (be warned that it is illegal to use insider information), trust your own research.

Performance of my screens

I monitor the performance of my top screens every 6 months or so. Here is my September, 2013 summary. The purpose is identifying the screens that perform well recently. It is for illustration purpose only. All returns are annualized. They are sorted by Grand Avg. in descending order.

Screen	Last Monitor 2/13	Current Test Avg.	Long-term Avg.	Short-term Avg.	Grand Avg.	Avail.
EP	39%	66%			59%	75%
BB3	35%	70%			53%	25%
LPSER	-21%	72%			49%	75%
MN	19%	53%			45%	75%
CW	54%	49%	39%	20%	38%	100%
LR	30%	37%			35%	100%
TT	30%	26%	71%	8%	35%	100%
TV2	50%	76%	14%	19%	35%	100%
BFSCB	5%	38%			31%	100%
DO	29%	24%	30%		28%	100%
AR	56%	53%	23%	6%	28%	100%
BE	81%	44%	10%	13%	25%	100%
FA	16%	27%			25%	100%
BS5BV	21%	25%			24%	100%
SE		53%	20%	-3%	23%	100%
CAO	-3%	17%	37%	12%	21%	100%
...	...	...	---	...	...	
Avg.	34%	19%	23%	5%	19%	

Screen. They are the abbreviations. To illustrate, CAO is the screen looking for candidates for acquisition with low market caps. I have about 25 production screens. They have been selected among over 100 screens.

Last Monitor 2/2013. Copied from the "Current Test Avg." from my last monitor in 2/2013.

Current Test Avg. It is the average of the four tests in recent months. The four test dates are: 03/11/13 to 7/9/13, 4/9/13 to 8/7/13, 5/9/13 to 8/17/13 and 6/8/13 to 9/6/13. They are about 4 months apart. It is the most important average to reflect what screens work recently.

Long-term Avg. It is the long-term performance (about 12 months) of the actual, screened stocks. Some have been purchased after evaluation.

Short-term Avg. It is the short-term performance (about 6 months) of the actual, screened stocks.

Grand Avg. It is a weighted average of the above 4 return categories (Last Monitor, Current Test Avg., Long-Term Avg. and Short-Term Avg.) and they're sorted in descending order.

Run the top screens first as they have given me better return before. It does not guarantee that they will perform well as before, but they have better chance to perform well than the screens scored below the average.

Availability. To illustrate, if the screen found stocks 1 out of the 4 tests, it is 25% available. These screens may not have enough data for prediction on future results and there is higher chance I do not find stocks using these screens with low availability.

Observations
The following are my personal findings on my own screens. You can do something similar to separate your top screens from the rest of your screens. Test and monitor the performances of your own screens.

- Usually the top half of the screens from the last monitor show up in this monitor though their ranks may vary.
- CAO in the last monitor should be better than it indicates. At least two companies had been acquired and they had very good returns and one I actually owned. These two companies did not show up in the test as they've been taken off from the historical database termed as survivorship bias.
- CW is quite consistent to the last monitor.
- EP and BB3 have not found any stocks in actual usage. MN proves to be a good screen in these two performance monitors. I missed the opportunities to make good money from this screen – my mistake.

- LPSER is a risky screen demonstrated here and from the previous monitors. Prefer not to take unnecessary risk even the profit may be great. I should include a column of maximum drawdown to avoid risky screens.
- LR was below the average and that's why it had not been used. It is above the average in this monitor, so it will be used.
- TT is above the average in these two monitors. The returns of screened stocks during this monitor are better in both long term and short term and hence it will be used.
- The original table (not shown here) has comparisons to SPY (an ETF simulating the market). Beating the market could be a better yardstick. If most of your screens beat the market, most likely they will beat the market again.

  The market during my last monitor is better than the current monitor. If the SPY is negative in the last three months, there is a good chance that the market is trending down.
- There are some screens just do not perform for a long while. They will not even be monitored next time. However, when the phase of the market cycle changes, the performances of these screens may respond differently.
- The test results are not always consistent but they are good guidelines. It could be due to my limited data.

Filler: Happy Mother's Day Poem

The following is my translation from poet Yu's work in Chinese. I changed some words as some could not be translated effectively. I added the title "Two Cries".

-------- Two Cries -----------
I cried at two unforgettable times in my life.

The first time when I came to this world.
The second time when you left this world.

The first time I did not know but from your mouth.
The second time you did not know but from my heart.

Between these two crises, we had endless laughs.
For the last 30 years, we had joyful laughs that had been repeated, repeated...

You treasured every laugh.

I cherish every laugh for the rest of my life.

3   Finviz's parameters

Most metrics are described in Finviz (via Help), Investopedia and/or Wikipedia and my articles on P/E and fundamental metrics if available. We use the metrics for screening stocks and then evaluating the screened stocks.

The following are my personal comments and why I feel some metrics are more important than the others. Personally, I divide the metrics into fundamentals and technical, which are more important for long-term investors and short-term investors respectively.

Compare the ratios to the companies in the same sector (industry) and also its averages from the last few years (5 preferable) from many other websites such as Fidelity.

From your browser, enter Finviz.com. Enter a symbol (I used ABEO for discussion). A chart is displayed with the prices and volumes for the last eleven months. SMAs (Single Moving Average) are displayed sometimes with other technical indicators. Intraday, Daily and Weekly options are available for day traders, short-term traders and long-term traders respectively. I prefer Candle – Advanced for drawing charts.

Besides the chart and the metrics described next, it describes what the company does, analysts' recommendations (I prefer Fidelity's Equity Summary Score), insiders' trading and articles that are good for intangible and qualitative analysis. Many free websites such as Yahoo!Finance provide a list of articles about the company.

"Financial Highlights and Statements" are materials for more in-depth analysis and they were more important decades ago when most financial ratios had not been calculated for you. It is important for investors with good knowledge in financial accounting. The current version also includes the basic balance sheet, income statement and cash flow for the current (TTM) and the last two years. Click on the following YouTube links for more detail.

Balance: https://www.youtube.com/watch?v=DMv9JC_K37Y
Income: https://www.youtube.com/watch?v=0--AvwZablQ
Cash flow: https://www.youtube.com/watch?v=hMBN6yTIDb0

A section on Insider Trading is also included. Do not be alarmed when insiders dump small quantities of the stocks. Buying large quantities (e.g., insider transaction more than 5%) at prices close to the market price could be favorable news.

The following metrics are roughly based on the flow of Finviz from top to bottom and left to right. I skip those metrics that I believe are not too important. You can also place your cursor on the metric to retrieve the description from Finviz or via Finviz's Help. Some metrics are left blank to indicate they are not applicable (for example, zero, negative or not available). For example, the Debt/Equity of YRCW in 1/2019 is blank (same as null) due to its negative Equity. From Yahoo!Finance at the time of writing, it has a total debt of 888M.

- **Index**. Most of us trade stocks in the three major exchanges in the USA. Stocks listed over-the-counter are too risky for most of us. Skip the stocks in local exchanges and foreign exchanges unless you are an expert on these stocks and/or have insightful (not illegal info from insiders) information. I screen the stocks and then ignore the stocks that are not in the Dow, NASDAQ and Amex. Other screeners may let you select a group of exchanges.
- **Market Cap** (MC). To me, stocks below 50M are risky even though they could be very profitable. Ensure the Avg. Volume is at least 10,000 shares and / or your order is less than 1% of the average volume. Some small stocks are controlled by the owners and have small volumes. You cannot trade these stocks easily.

  Float = Outstanding shares – Insider shares

  Usually, Float does not matter as they are typically the same. However, it does for small companies with large insider shares. Most of these owners do not want to sell their family businesses and hence they reduce the chance of being acquired entirely or partially for good prices. In this case, you may have to hold this kind of stock for a long time or you may have to sell it at a very unfavorable price.
- If **Forward P/E** (a.k.a. Expected P/E) is not provided, use the P/E which is based on the trailing last 12 months (TTM). Alternatively, calculate the E by using the E from P/E and multiplying it by its growth rate. It may not be seasonally adjusted. I prefer using Forward P/E as it provides a better predictability power to me. Successful investing is usually a result of correct guessing the future earnings.

Finviz.com leaves the P/E blank (same as null) if the earnings are negative. In this case, I would check out Yahoo!Finance's EV / EBITDA, which also considers taxes, cash and interests. The blank condition also happens in some other metrics such as negative assets (very seldom).

Earnings Yield is equal to E/P. I call it 'True Earnings Yield' for EBITDA / EV. It is easier to understand. Compare Earnings Yield or True Yield to the annual dividend yield of a 10-year Treasury – with the low interest rate in 2021, skip this comparison for this year.

E/P is easier in screening and sorting the screened stocks. If you use P/E instead of E/P, you need to screen or sort stocks with a clause "P/E > 0".

When the P/E is less than 5, be careful and there may be a reason why it is so low. Many bankrupting companies have low P/Es at one time before their stock prices go to zero..

Compare the P/E or Forward P/E with the average P/E for the sector (such as high tech) and its average P/E for the last 5 years that are currently available from Fidelity.com. Some sectors such as technology have high P/Es (such as 25 for me). If the sector is cyclical, the earnings could be affected.

Do not solely use P/E to determine the value of a stock. The other metrics are P/E Growth (PEG), P/B, Debt/Equity to name a few.

When the prospect of the company is good such as Tesla in 2020, ignore P/E. Investors are betting on the future. Do not short these rocket stocks.

- **Cash / share**. It is used to calculate Pow P/E and Pow EY when EV/EBITDA for the stock is not available. To illustrate, if the stock is $10 and it has $10 cash / share without debt (i.e., Debt/Equity = 0), most likely it is underpriced as you can get the whole company for nothing. You should find out why the price is so low. It could be the market ignoring the stock, or there is a serious event happening such as a major lawsuit. P/C is a better choice than Cash/Share; the lower the better.
- **Dividend %** is useful for income investors. The payout ratio should not be more than 30% except for matured companies. Most

developing companies and tech companies plough back the profits into research and development, and hence they do not pay dividends.
- **Recs**. Select stocks with 1 or 2. Do not base your stock selection on this recommendation alone. There have been many bad recommendations that could cost you a fortune in losses. Use Fidelity's Equity Summary Score instead.
- **PEG** is a measure of the growth of P/E and hence a growth metric (the other ones are Sales Growth Q-Q and Earnings Growth Q-Q). It is similar to P/E, but it takes the expected earnings growth rate into account. The lower value is better as long as earnings is positive. If earnings is negative, then the reverse is true. It is a defect in using P/E and PEG and that's why I recommend EY (Earnings Yield) and EYG, Earnings Yield Growth. The chance of appreciation of the stock is high when the PEG is less than 1.

If there are two companies with the same P/E, the one with a better PEG ratio is better. For similar logic, if two companies have the same E/P, the company with higher Earnings Growth (EPS Q/Q) would be better.
- **P/B**. Book value or Asset (= Total Assets – Total Liabilities) may not include intangible assets such as patents. Do not trust it 100%, so is ROE and other metrics which are based on the book value. Negative equity is possible when Total Liabilities is more than Total Assets. This popular metric is outdated for most matured companies as it is now made up of more intangible assets including patents, management, the quality of their employees, brand names, market share, partners, free cash flow and customer base to name a few. Some assets such as gold mines and real estates can be easily calculated. To illustrate, when gold price is falling, the P/B of a company's stock could be less than 1. It could be a good buy, but it is not if the trend continues downward.
- **P/S**. If two companies are unprofitable, this ratio could be more useful. A retail company such as Walmart is very different from a research company in P/S. This metric is only meaningful for stocks within the same sector or related sectors.
- **P/FCF**. I prefer it to be greater than 0 and less than 50 for value investors. Most metrics can be manipulated easily, but not this one. This is a major metric to avoid bankrupting companies.
- **Sales Q/Q** reduces the seasonal deviation. To illustrate, retail sales for the Christmas season should be compared to the same season in the prior year.

- **EPS Q/Q**. Same as above. I prefer the growth of EPS over Sales. Both of these Q/Q ratios are growth metrics. When a company terminates its unprofitable product(s), its Sales Q/Q could be down but its EPS Q/Q could be up. In 2000, many internet companies had great Sales Q/Qs but negative EPS Q/Qs.

  Q/Q comparison (quarter to quarter) takes out the seasonal variations as Sales Q/Q. I prefer both Sales Q/Q and EPS Q/Q increase. When EPS Q/Q increases far higher than Sales Q/Q, it could mean the EPS Q/Q could be temporary such as the oil company when the oil price rockets.

  When the company buys its own shares, EPS could be misleading as E is fixed and the number of shares is reduced. In most cases, the fundamentals of the company have not changed.

  In 2021, many companies such as many energy stocks have incredible EPS Q-Q and most of their Forward P/E are better than the P/E. They could be momentum play unless they are sustainable.

- Positive **Insider** Transactions are favorable. Sometimes, they are misleading. Need to scroll to the end of the screen and check out more info there. If the transactions are outdated such as 3 months or so ago, and or they are purchases in a similar amount than the sales a while ago, they are not important. Insiders know the company better than us.

  So is **Institutional Transactions** as institutional investors move the market. Most institutional investors do not trade small stocks, and hence this metric is not important for small cap stocks.

- Insider Own, Shares Outstanding and Shares **Float** determine the number of shares that are available for trading. The stock with a small Float and a high Insider Own limits trading and the stock, and hence it should be avoided in most cases. Also, compare your trade positions for this kind of stock to their Avg. Volumes.

- **Profit Margin**. I prefer it over Gross Margin and Oper. Margin which does not include interest expenses and taxes. When you sell software, the Gross Margin is high as it does not include development, support and marketing, etc. A retail store has low Gross Margin. It all depends on the industry, and hence it is better to compare companies in the same industry.

- **Short Float**. I prefer it to be less than 10%. If it is greater than 10%, the shorters could find something wrong with the company. If it is over 25%, I would check the fundamentals and any important events such as a major lawsuit. If they are good, I would buy it expecting a

short squeeze potential. It is risky but it has been proven profitable in some of my trades.
- Technical metrics: SMA-20, SMA-50 and SMA-200. Finviz expresses them in convenient percentages. If they are all positive, it means the trend is up. SMA-20 and SMA-50 are a short-term trend indicator and SMA-200 is a long-term trend indicator. If you are a short-term swing investor, stick with the short-term trend and vice versa. The first two are also used as momentum grades. Many long-term investors do not buy stocks when the SMA-200% is negative. Some buy stocks when both SMA-20 and SMA-50 are positive and SMA-20 crosses SMA-50,. Some sell the owned stocks when both SMA-20 and SMA-50 are negative and SMA-20 crosses SMA-50. Some use SMA-50 and SMA-200 instead. They are called the Golden Cross and the Death Cross.
- **RSI(14)**. If it is greater than 65%, it is overbought to me. If it is under 30%, it is under-bought for me to me. Some use 5% up or down than my percentages. Use it as a reference. Most stocks making new heights are always overbought, and many of these stocks keep on rising. I recommend using trailing stops to protect your profits on rising stocks.
- **Beta**. A volatile stock fluctuates a lot. Higher beta stocks are good for short-term traders. A beta of 1 means the stock would fluctuate with the market, and it is more volatile if it is higher than 1. For volatile stocks (higher than 1), the stops should be higher. For example, if your stops are normally 10%, you may want to use 15% or even higher for volatile stocks.
- **Perf**. If the stock lost more than 50%, there is a good chance it could be a candidate for bottom fishing, or it could be heading to bankruptcy. Need more research if you want to buy these risky stocks.
- Management performance is measured by **ROE**. It is also judged by **Analysts' Rec.** and Institutional Ownership (except for small companies). The confidence of their own ability, the company and its sector are measured by Insider Ownership and Insider Purchases.
ROE = Net Income / Average Shareholder's Equity

According to Investopedia, a normal ROE for utilities should be 10% while high tech companies should be 15%. Compare this ratio and many other ratios with its peers that are available from many sites including Fidelity.
- Avoid all companies that are going to bankrupt at all costs. Debt/Equity, P/FCF, Cash/Sh., P/B, Profit Margin, Forward P/E, Short Float, RSI(14), SMA20% and SMA50 would give us some hints. Need

to summarize all the info and study many other factors such as obsoleting products (including drugs going to be generic). Study articles which are available from Finviz and many other sites.
- Unless you have concrete information, do not buy stocks a week or so before the Earnings Date (available in Finviz). It is seldom to make great profits when the announcement is better than the expected as the stock price is usually priced in, and the reverse could hurt the stock price a lot.

More useful information:
- **Equity** = Total Asset – Total Liability. When the Equity (Book) is negative, many of the metrics based on Equity would not be displayed. In May 5, 2022, TUP has Equity of -207M (from Finviz's Balance Sheet reported on 12/25/21). The related metrics are blank or null such as P/B, Debt/Eq, LT Debt/Eq in Finviz, and so is EV/EVITDA (from Yahoo!Finace). However, the P/E is less than 4. It could be a buy.
- The price chart. It has a lot of features such as the resistance line. Some charts include technical indicators such as double top (a bearish warning) and double bottom (a bullish sign).
- Description under the symbol. It briefly describes what the company (sector and industry) does and its country of registration. You want to buy a stock within a sector that is trending up. For example, according to Finviz Apple is in the Consumer Goods sector and the Electronic Equipment industry.

  If you do not want to buy foreign stocks, skip it if it is not listed in the US exchange or headquartered in a foreign country. Buying a foreign stock could be profitable, but risky due to the currency fluctuation, lack of regulations, and politics (such as Russia in 2022 and China in 2021). Some foreign stocks ask you to pay additional taxes when you sell them. Some foreign companies listed in the U.S. exchanges take out a good portion of the dividends.
- Articles on the company for qualitative analysis.
- Insider trading. Pay more attention to the insider purchases at market prices. Use common sense.
- The last line lets you open Yahoo!Finance and other sites.
- There are many ways to calculate intrinsic value of a stock. Many web sites (most require subscriptions) include this information. Use it as reference only, and evaluate the stock your yourself. Buy it when the intrinsic value is below the stock price, and sell it otherwise. It is "Buy Low and Sell High" concept. They work in general and in the long run.

Need to consider other intangibles. Many stocks such as Tesla and Amazon had low intrinsic values, but they kept on rising.

Other important sites

Yahoo!Finance.

From Statistics, you can find Enterprise Value / EBITDA. I call it True Yield when I flip them to EBITDA / Enterprise Value. In case it is not available, I use Earnings Yield. In my spreadsheet without considering the cell designations,
=IF (Earnings Yield = "", True Yield, Earnings Yield)

Fidelity

Compare the P/E of the average PE of the last 5 years by using spreadsheets.
Cheaper By Historically =IF(PE="","",(Avg. of 5-year PE -PE)/Avg. of 5-year PE)

Compare the P/E of companies in the same sector. In my spreadsheet for demonstration,
Cheaper By To the peers =IF(PE="","",(Industry PE - PE)/Industry PE)

Your broker's website

Your broker website should have plenty of tools to analyze stocks. As of Dec., 2018, Fidelity lets you use their extensive research free by opening an account with no position restriction. I describe some of their metrics that should be beneficial to your research.

- Equity Summary Score. Potentially good buy when it is 7 (8 for conservative investors) or higher. With some exceptions, you should avoid buy or short stocks if the score is 3 or below. The stocks ranking from 4 to 6 could be turnaround candidates if they are supported by good Q/Q Earnings and/or good news. The above are my suggestions.

- The 5-year averages are good yardsticks. For example, in Dec., 2018, C's P/E is about 9 and the average for the last 5 years is 14. Hence it is a value buy.

Other sources

If you have other sources (most require a subscription or being a customer), skip the stocks that have one of the failing grades. The exceptions are a new positive development and increased insider purchases.

Vendor	Grade	Fail
Fidelity	Equity Summary Score	< 7
IBD	Composite grade	< 50
Value Line	Proj. 3-5 yr. return. Also, its composite rating	< 3%
Zacks	Rank	5
VectorVest	VST	< 0.7

You may be able to find Value Line and IBD in your local library. Try out the free stock reports from your broker first. Finviz and Seeking Alpha should have articles (now fewer free articles from Seeking Alpha) on stocks and earnings conferences, which could have important information after separating from the "welcome" and garbage talks.

Yahoo!Finance has good info. "EV/EBITDA" is better than "P/E" as it considers debts and cash. Most use Earnings from the last 12 months, which has poorer predictability than Forward Earnings to me.

When negative values such as Equity in Finviz.com, we need to adjust many related metrics or do not use them at all.

MarketWatch.com has many articles on the market in general and personal investing.

If the stock is close to the Earnings Date (found in Finviz.com), you should avoid trading the stock; as earnings could have a big swing for the stock price. Consult Zacks' ranking which is currently free for individual stocks.

Gurus

It is nice to know how gurus would rate the interested stocks. GuruFocus is a good source but requires subscription. NASDAQ is a simplified version. Bring up Nasdaq.com from your browser. Select "Investing" and then "Guru Screeners". On the third selection, enter the stock symbol such as THO. Click "Go". You will find how 10 or so gurus would evaluate this stock in theory. Click "Detailed Analysis" for each guru.

Quick and dirty

Many times we need to evaluate a stock fast such as taking action due to some development. Or, when you have over 30 stocks from your screen, you may want to reduce the number by using the following two methods.

Refer to my other article "Simplest way to evaluate stocks". The following should take a few minutes. Bring up Finviz.com and enter the stock symbol.

Using SWKS on 6/10/16 to illustrate, Forward P/E is about 11 (fine between 3 and 25), Debt/Eq. is 0 (fine less than .5), ROE is 30% (fine greater than 5%) and P/PCF is 31 (fine if not negative).

Also, check out Market Cap, Avg. Volume, Dividend, Short Float (fine between 0% and 10%), Country and Industry. Judging from the above, it is a buy.

If you have more time, check out the following: Recom. (Ok if less than 2.5), P/B (fine between .5 and 4), Sales Q/Q (fine if not negative), EPS Q/Q (fine if not negative), Cash/Sh (compare it to Debt/Sh) and Profit Margin (fine >5%). Check some articles described for this stock.

5-minute stock evaluation

It takes even less time than the above "Quick and Dirty". However, I recommend you should spend more time researching stocks.

- From Finviz.com, enter the stock or ETF symbol. Look at the number of reds in metrics. If there are more than greens, most likely it is not a good stock.

- It should be fine if Fidelity's Equity Summary Score is greater than 8.

If you have more time, I recommend you to check the following:

- Check out Forward P/E (E>0 and P/E < 20), Debut / Equity (< 50%) and P/FCF (not in red color).

  If time is allowed, replace Forward P/E with True P/E (same as "EV/EBITDA"), which is available from Yahoo!Finance and other sources.
- SMA20 (or SMA50 for longer holding period). If SMA20 is > 10%, it is trending up.
- It is fine if the Insider Transaction is positive.
- Be cautious on foreign stocks and low-volume stocks.
- If most of the above are positive, it is likely a buy. As in life, nothing is 100% certain.

Links

PEG: http://en.wikipedia.org/wiki/PEG_ratio
Short %: http://www.investopedia.com/university/shortselling/shortselling1.asp#axzz2LNDvpemo
Openinsider: http://www.openinsider.com/
Finviz: http://Finviz.com/
terms: http://www.Finviz.com/help/screener.ashx
Insider Cow: http://www.insidercow.com/
Current Ratio: http://en.wikipedia.org/wiki/Current_ratio
Cash Flow: https://www.youtube.com/watch?v=1v8hRZ36--c
How to find quality stocks.
http://seekingalpha.com/article/2381395-how-to-identify-quality-stocks-and-is-there-really-alpha-to-be-had
Over-priced stock: https://www.youtube.com/watch?v=VeMr0n4pvtM:
Outperform the market
https://www.youtube.com/watch?v=3DdY0JdUilM
Balance sheet: https://www.youtube.com/watch?v=DZjU0CHKyV4
Reading financial sheet.
https://www.youtube.com/watch?v=DMv9JC_K37Y&t=954s
https://www.youtube.com/watch?v=8NelYFn07jg
Intrinsic Value: https://www.youtube.com/watch?v=l-T-Vyk2txc

Common parameters

Different styles of investing use different parameters for screening stocks. Here is my summary/guideline on parameters in using Finviz.com. Finviz.com is not complete in functions but it is the best free screener that incorporates both the fundamental and the technical criteria. The first table is for Value and the next one for Growth. The last one is for finding stocks the institution investors are trading.

Value Screens	Common	Penny	Micro Cap	Dividend
General				
Market Cap (M)	>500	<50	50-200	+Mid(>2B)
Price	>5	<5	1-15	>5
Exchanges (Major 3)	In	Not In	In	In
Avg. Volume	>100K	>5K	>10K	>100K
Country	USA		USA	USA
Dividend%				>3%
Float Short	<10%	<10%	<10%	<10%
Analyst Rec	Buy or +	Buy or +	Buy or +	Buy or +
Fundamental				
Forward P/E	<20	<20	<20	<25
ROE	>10	>10	>5	>15
QQ earning	>0			>0
QQ sales	>0			>0
PEG	<1	<1	<1	<1.2
Payout%				20-50%
P/S	<10	<10	<10	<10
Technical				
Price above 200 SMA	Yes	Yes	Yes	Yes
RSI(14)	Not Over	Not Over	Not Over	Not Over

There may be no or very few analysts following penny stocks and micro-cap stocks.

Growth

Growth Screen	Common	Technical	Momentum
General			
Market Cap (M)	>50	>1,000	>500
Price	>1	>10	>5
Exchanges (Major 3)	In	In	In

	>50K	>200K	>100K
Avg. Volume			
Fundamental			
Forward P/E	<30	<30	<30
Return of Equity	>5	>0	>0
QQ earning	>10%	>15%	>20%
QQ sales	>5%	> 5%	>10%
PEG	<1	<1	<1
Analyst recs.	Buy or +		
Technical			
Price above 200 SMA	Yes	Yes	
50 SMA	Yes	Yes	Yes
RSI	< 75	< 75	

Short-term trends are important for momentum stocks.

Explanation

The above are suggestions only. Adjust them to your personal preferences and risk tolerance.

- Finviz screener lacks ranges, such as market cap range and multiple of exchanges. To get around, deselect the stocks that do not fit your requirements.

- Average Volume. When the price of the stock is less than $3, double the average volume requirement. In most cases, 10K is quite acceptable to me. When the volume is small, you may have to pay more (a.k.a. spread) to trade.

- There are many fundamental metrics such as Debt/Equity and Price/Free Cash Flow not included here and they should be included in your further evaluation. Each industry sector has different thresholds. For example, the P/S is very different for a supermarket than a high-tech company. Compare the company to the average value of the companies in the same sector. Many sites including GuruFocus.com and Fidelity.com have the average values.

- For momentum stock, you ignore most fundamentals and concentrate on price trend such as SMA-20% and SMA-50%. The higher the percent, the higher it is away from its own average. SMA-20 is the Single Moving Average for the last 20 trade sessions.

- For growth stocks, ensure the PEG (P/E growth), quarter-to-quarter earnings and quarter-to-quarter sales are above the averages in its own sector and/or the market.

- Technical analysis favors large cap stocks with large volumes. I prefer stocks with positive earnings and fundamentally sound.
- Include 3 basic technical indicators here. When they're all positive, they should be in uptrend.
- RSI(14) indicates whether the stock is oversold (>60) or under bought (<35).
- You may want to check out your strategies using a virtual account from your broker or a simulator.

A general guideline for Institution investors

Criteria	Value
Description	
Relative Volume	Over 2 M
Country	USA
Institution Ownership	Over 50%
Technical	
20-Day Simple Moving Avg.	>10%
Volatility	Week – Over 3%
RSI(14)	>40%
Fundamental	
Market Cap	>1B
ROE	>10%

- These are my suggested metrics and you may want to vary the parameters. I prefer USA companies. If you use foreign countries, ensure larger companies and/or in countries that has regulator similar to our SEC.
- For value investors, select Forward P/E less than 20 and Earning is positive.
- Check out how many analysts following the stock.

To illustrate, I find 12 stocks for that time. I narrow them to 3. First, I skip all stocks that already have more than 10% rise recently. They may have risen too high already.

Select profitable stocks with forward P/E less than 25. "Debt/Equity" is less than .5 (50%). Then, ROI is higher than 25%. Stop when you have reached the optimal number of stocks (2 for me in this example).

If you find too many stocks, tighten the criteria and vice versa. Save the criteria and the selected stocks in a portfolio for paper testing.

4 Sectors to be cautious

There are many reasons to be very cautious when investing in the following sectors. However, Technical Analysis (a.k.a. charting) would give you more hints than the fundamentals for stocks in these sectors. The following sectors should be cautious.

Loan companies/banks

The financial statements do not show the quality of their loan portfolios. Following this advice, you may be able to skip the banks that melt down in 2007. The peak of Citigroup is $550 and several banks bankrupted that was quite "impossible" before 2007.

Drug (generic is ok)

Understanding the complexities of the drug pipelines, its potential profits for new drugs and the expiration of its current drugs may not be worth the effort for most retail investors. In addition, a serious lawsuit and / or a serious problem of a drug could wipe out a good percentage of the stock price. When a drug shows unpromising sign(s) in any trial phase, the stock could plunge and vice versa.

Miners

It is extremely difficult to estimate the value of ore the company has. Some miners own several different ores of different grades in same or different mines. It is further complicated by the complexities to extract and transport them. When the total of these costs is greater than its production price, the company will not be profitable. Understanding the market for ore futures is another discipline.

Many mining companies are in foreign countries such as Canada, Australia and countries in South America. Their financial statements of Canada and Australia are more trustworthy than those from most other emerging countries. One potential problem of mining companies from many emerging countries is nationalization.

Mining rare earth ore is extremely risky when the profit depends on how China, a major producer of these ores, will price its ores. After China announced the export restrictions on rare earth elements, several non-Chinese companies announced to reopen their mines for rare earths but few make any profits as of 2013 and as of 2016 most are not profitable in this venture.

Developed countries have stricter environmental regulations. Coal suffers from the cleaner oil and gas. China will still depend a lot of their energy from coal even with most of their new nuclear generators on-line by 2020.

Insurance companies
Insurance companies profit by:

1. The difference between the total premiums received and the total claims minus expenses in running the company.
2. How well they invest your premiums (you pay your premiums earlier than you may collect the claims).

They can protect the profits in #1 by restricting claims by natural disasters such as earthquakes and by re-insuring. However, a bad disaster could wipe out a lot of their profits.

Even if the insurance company shows you its investment portfolio, most of us, the retail investors, do not have the time and expertise to analyze it.

Emerging countries (not a sector)
Their financial statements especially from small companies cannot be trusted and many countries use different accounting standards. However, emerging countries are where the economic growth is. I trade FXI, an ETF, rather than individual Chinese companies. I have lost a lot in small Chinese companies due to frauds. To check out whether the stock is an ADR, try ADR.COM.
https://www.adr.com/

Stocks with low volumes (not a sector)
Most likely you pay a high spread to trade these stocks. They can be manipulated easier. I remember I have a hard time to sell a stock of this kind. The majority of this company is owned by one person or one family.

For simplicity, I trade stocks with the average daily trade volume over 6,000 shares (double it if the price is $2 or less). The better way could be calculating the percent of your trade quantity / average daily trade volume to reduce the effect of penny stocks that have larger volumes due to the lower prices. You need special skill to trade these stocks but it could be very profitable.

Good business and bad business
Banking is a good business. My deposit to them makes virtually zero interest, and they loan the same money making 3% for illustration. If they are more selective in loaning my money, they should make good profits.

Restaurant is an easy business to open/run, but it is very hard to make good money. With the rising of minimal wages, it will get even tougher. That could be the reason of so many coupons today. The high-end restaurants are doing better due to the rising stock market. As of 8/2014, the new comers Noodles & Company (NDLS) and Potbelly (PBPB) are not doing well.

Retailing is a tough business. Looking at the top 10 retailers 15 years ago, I can only find two that are still surviving. Most are either bankrupted or being acquired. Even Macy's was at one time in financial trouble.

Airline is a tough business. You can tell by the average increase in fare in the last 10 years. It cannot even beat inflation. They have to charge you everything. The next frontier charge is the rest room (especially for long-distance flights). Now I understand why they call themselves "Frontier Air". As of 2014, it is quite profitable due to mergers, charging everything they can and the low fuel cost.

There are several software companies that produce software such as the virus detecting programs and tax preparation software. The customers faithfully buy new versions every year. That's great business. Links:

Nationalization: http://en.wikipedia.org/wiki/Nationalization
Spread: http://en.wikipedia.org/wiki/Bid-offer_spread
Insurance: http://seekingalpha.com/article/1239671-property-casualty-insurance-and-reinsurance-what-you-need-to-know

5 Tutorial on screening stocks

If you do not use finviz.com, try Yahoo!Finance. From your browser, bring up Yahoo!Finance's screener by clicking here or
type http://screener.finance.yahoo.com/stocks.html

Select the following to select stocks with share price > $5, market cap > 250 mil, P/E < 15, Est. Earning Growths up to 20% for 1 year and up to 5% for 5 years, and Buy Rating = 1.

Screener Settings

Search for stocks by selecting from the criteria below. Click on the "Find Stocks" button to view th

Category

Industry:	Any / Accident & Health Insurance (Financial) / Advertising Agencies (Services) / Aerospace/Defense - Major Diversified (Industrial Goods) / Aerospace/Defense Products & Services (Industrial Goods)
Index Membership	Any

Share Data

Share Price:	$5	Min	Any	Max
Market Cap:	250 mil	Min	Any	Max
Dividend Yield:	Any	Min	Any	Max
Beta (Volatility):	Any	Min	Any	Max

Sales and Profitability

Sales Revenue:	Any	Min	Any	Max
Profit Margin	Any	Min	Any	Max

Valuation Ratios

Price/Earnings Ratio:	Any	Min	15	Max
Price/Book Ratio:	Any	Min	Any	Max
Price/Sales Ratio:	Any	Min	Any	Max
PEG Ratio:	Any	Min	Any	Max

Analyst Estimates

Est. 1 Yr EPS Growth:	Up more than 20%
Est. 5 Yr EPS Growth:	Up more than 5%
Avg Analyst Rec: (1=Buy, 5=Sell)	Buy Rating (1)

Results Display Setting

Click on Find Stocks. As of 9/21/2013, you cannot find any stocks based on these criteria. Relax the filter by taking out the Est. 1-Yr Growth and the 5-Yr Growth. Click on Find Stocks again. You should find several stocks. The stocks with '.xx' at the end could be the stocks you may not want to consider. They could be foreign stocks in foreign exchanges, listed in pink sheets, etc.

My common filter criteria besides avoiding some specific sectors:

These are my personal choice. Adjust them to your preferences.

1. Traded in one of the three major exchanges, or specific exchange(s) for your country.

2. Market cap > 200 million.

3. Price > 2.

4. Average daily volume > 8,000 (6,000 if stock price > 200) shares.

Ensure positive earnings in using P/E (by specifying E > 0) or use E/P instead if available. Sorting on P/E will not be in the right order as intended for stocks with negative earnings.

If you only want to deal with large companies, use Market Cap > 1 billion (many use 10 B) and Price > 10 (many exceptions for price).

Small stocks (with prices between $1 and $2 and market caps between 100M to 300M) may have the best performances but at higher risk. Most analysts and institutional investors do not consider them, so a thorough analysis could find some gems.

There are many exceptions. At one time ALU was a $1 stock but it had a market cap of 2 B.

Do not trade stocks with minimal volume as the spread (between ask price and bid price) is high. Expect to pay more for their trades. I traded one stock with the owner and his family as the major stock owners. It took me a long time to sell this stock at a far lower price than I asked for.

The number of shares traded is a very rough estimate to determine the daily average volume. The correct calculation is the ratio of No. of Shares of your order / Average Daily Volume to adjust for the price difference (a small stock price has higher volume logically). You can buy the stock easier when this ratio is 1% than the ratio of 50% for example.

Nasdaq

It is similar to GuruFocus's screens in some aspects but quite simplified. Currently it is free. Bring up Nasqaq.com from your browser. Select "Investing" and then "Guru Screeners".

Learn how it works and its features from the following illustration. Select "P/E Growth Investors" and change "Some" to "Strong". Click on "Go".

As of 6/9/2016, I have about 14 screens with about 20 stocks in each screen. It is too many stocks to evaluate. Sort "Guru(s) Strong" in descending order; each "strong" is usually based on a fundamental metric defined in this specific search.

I have 5 stocks with 3 "Strong": THO, MPX, GGAL (ADR), BRDCY (ADR) and BMA (ADR). If you prefer U.S. companies only, you only have THO and MPX and both have desirable "Proj. P/E" under 20.

Alternatively to reduce the number of screened stocks, include stocks with "Some Strong". Sort the "Proj. P/E" in ascending order. If it is blank, most likely it is losing money or there is no estimate for this stock. Use Finviz.com or Yahoo!Finance to confirm.

PEG (P/E growth) is a growth metric and it is available for sorting. Need to evaluate each screened stock. For example, a low P/E stock may not be good if it has excessive debts, pending lawsuits...

Click on the stock THO. It explains how Peter and other gurus score this stock. If you use 70% as a passing grade, 7 gurus rate it passed and 3 gurus rate it failed.

Click on "Detailed Analysis". Peter rates 4 "Pass" and 2 "Neutral" together with the description.

III Evaluating Stocks

6   Simplest ways to evaluate stocks

Beginners should trade ETFs only. This chapter is for the readers who are ready or getting ready to trade stocks. In general, ETFs are diversified, less volatile than trading stocks. However, stocks offer higher profit but higher risk.

Many stock researches have already been done recently and some are available free of charge. I have no affiliation with Fidelity except I retired from it. You can open an account with them with no balance. Their Equity Summary Score is one of the best indicators; I check out **value** stocks with scores higher than 8. Concentrate on fundamental metrics such as P/E for long-term holds, and momentum metrics for short-term holds. Add criteria to limit the number of screened stocks. Finviz.com is a free screener.

Several sources

The popular ones are Morningstar, Value Line, The Street and Zacks (currently free for rankings of individual stocks). If they are not free, check out whether they are available from your local library. I have 3 simple ways to evaluate stocks starting with the simplest. In addition, read the articles on the selected stocks from Fidelity, Finviz, Seeking Alpha and many other sources for further evaluation.

Fidelity

Select only stocks that have Fidelity's Equity Summary Score 8 or higher. There are tons of information about a stock. Once in a while I did not agree with this score such as SHOP and ZM that scored high in August, 2020. Include the following for your analysis.

A modified stock selection based on a magazine article

Most metrics are available from Finviz except EV/EBITDA.

1. Forward P/E (expected earnings and not based on the last twelve months). It should range from 5 to 15 (10 to 25 for high tech stocks). EV/EBITDA (from Yahoo!Finance) is a better choice as it includes the

debts and cash than P/E; it would be more effective if it uses forward earnings. If you do not use EV/EBITDA, ensure Debt/Equity is less than 0.5 except for the debt-intensive industries.

2. ROE (Return of Equity) measures how well the company uses the capital. I prefer stocks with ROE greater than 5%.

3. Volatility. Conservative investors should select stocks with a beta of less than one (i.e., less volatile).

4. Insider Transactions for sales (i.e., negative) should be less than 5%. If it is -5%, most likely the insiders are dumping it.

5. Compare the metrics such as P/E and Debt/Equity to its five-year average and its competitors (available in Fidelity).

6. Momentum. Check out the SMA-50 (actually SMA-50%) and SMA-200. Ideally, they should be positive. SMA-50% is especially important for stocks you do not want to keep for a long time.

7. Check out articles on the stock as some recent events (for example a new lawsuit) have not been included in the metrics.

8. Compare the trend of the sector this stock is in. Under Finviz, enter the related sector ETF.

Summary
The sources are Fidelity (Equity Summary Score and various comparisons), Finviz and Yahoo!Finance (for EV/EBITDA). Value stocks should be held longer.

Category	Score / Metric	Value /Momentum
Score	Fidelity's Equity Summary Score	Both
Value	EV/EBITDA	Value
	P/E cheaper compared to 5-year avg.	Value
	P/E cheaper compared to its sector.	Value
	Insider Purchases	Both
Safety	Debt/Equity	Value
	Compare it to its sector.	Value

Momentum	50-SMA%		Momentum
	200-SMA% (for long term holds).		Value
Articles	Check out latest events		Both
Market	No purchase if market is risky.		Momentum

A simple scoring system using Finviz
Bring up Finviz.com and then enter the stock symbol.

No.	Metric	Good	Bad	Score
1	Forward P/E[1]	Between 2.5 and 12.5, Score = 2	> 50 or < 0, Score = -1	
2	P/ FCF[1]	< 12, Score = 1	>30 or < 0, Score = -1	
3	P/S[1]	< 0.8, Score = 1	< 0, Score = -1	
4	P/ B[1]	< 1, Score = 1	< 0, Score = -1	
5	Compare quarter to quarter of last year Sales Q/Q	> 15%, Score = 1	< 0, Score = -1	
6	EPS Q/Q	> 20%, Score = 1	< 0, Score = -1	
			Grand Score	
	Stock Symbol Date[2]	Current Price	SPY	

Footnote

[1] Negative values for Sales (due to accounting adjustments), Equity and Book are possible but not likely.

[2] The last row is for your information only. SPY is used to measure whether it will beat the market by comparing the return of this stock to the return of SPY.

The Score
Score each metric and sum up all the scores giving the Grand Score. If the Grand Score is 3, the stock passes this scoring system. Even if it is a 2, it still deserves further analysis if you have time. You may want to add scores from other vendors. To illustrate on using Fidelity, add 1 to the score if Fidelity's Equity Summary score is 8 or higher. Monitor the

performance after every 6 months or so to see whether this scoring system beats the market.

Very basic advice for beginners
Beginners should stick with U.S. stocks with Market Cap greater than 800 M (million), Debt/Equity less than .25 (25%) except for debt-intensive industries such as utilities and airlines and Forward P/E between 5 to 20 (25 for high-tech companies). These metrics are all available from Finviz.com, which is free.

Do not have more than 20% of your portfolio in one stock (unless it is an ETF or mutual fund) and do not have more than 30% of your portfolio in one sector.

For more conservative investors, buy non-volatile stocks whose beta (available from Yahoo!Finance) is less than 1. Beta of 1 represents the market (the S&P 500 index). For example, a stock with beta 1.5 statistically fluctuates more than 50% of the market and hence it is very volatile.

Try paper trading to check out your strategy and your skill in trading stocks. If your broker does not provide one, use a spreadsheet to record your trades or check the availability of simulator.investopedia.com.

#Filler: Silence is golden

I am glad I did not give advice to a friend who had to decide whether to take a lump sum payment or an annuity. The correction in March, 2020 would wipe out a lot of his portfolio if he took the lump sum payment. No one would share his profits when the predictions are correct, but the blame if it does not materialize.

It is the same in investing that nothing is certain. With educated guesses, we should have more rights than wrongs especially in the long run.

7   Manipulators and bankruptcy

If we can avoid bankrupting companies and/or companies losing most of their stock values, our portfolio would be improved substantially. Some companies make bad bets and lose, such as Enron betting on energy futures. Here are some signs of bad situations.

- Foreign companies. I do not have too much luck in developing countries, especially their stocks of small companies. They include China, Ireland and Israel to name a few. However, as of 2019, many large Chinese companies are doing very well.
- When the P/E is too good, find out why. If the P/E is too bad, stay away.
- P/PFC should be greater than 0 and less than 50. Even a healthy cash flow may not be able to service the debt if it is huge. Hence, compare the cash flow to Debt/Equity.
- Altman Z-Score. I prefer a score above 3, a sign not to be bankrupt. However, Z-Score is not designed for financial sectors.
- Beneish M-Score. I prefer a score less than -2.22, a sign that the earnings are not manipulated. Both Z-Score and M-Score are available from GuruFocus.com for a fee.
- Z-Score metrics are: "Working Capital / Total Assets" (A), "Retained Earnings / Total Assets" (B), "Earnings Before Interest & Taxes / Total Assets" (C), "Market Cap / Total Liabilities" (D) and "Sales / Total Assets" (E).
  Z-Score = 1.2 A + 1.4 B + 3.3 C + .6 D + E
- Skip companies with bond ratings less than B.
- New government regulations such as taking out the credit for solar panels.
- Extraordinary profits such as Timber Liquidator and many banks in 2007-2008.
- Accounting manipulation: Excessive buying of stocks to boost Earnings per Share, excessive loans to officers, companies betting on futures such as Enron, too many one-time charges and reinstating the previous earnings.
- Skip thinly-traded stocks especially those stocks with the majority owned by a few owners.

The current financial statements could be the best source to look for them. If you read something you do not understand, be cautious.

We need to consistently monitor our stock holdings and sell them before they lose most of their value. I Recommend use stops.

This is why we need to have a focused investment portfolio of about 10 stocks; the number depends on your time available for investing. To illustrate, I have about 10 stocks with larger investments and about 100 stocks in smaller purchases. I would likely spend more time in monitoring the 10 stocks than the rest.

Mergers

Mergers are usually good for the merging companies to eliminate duplicate corporate functions such as payroll administration and researching on similar subjects.

The company being acquired usually has a high appreciation. I have a screen to search for the potential candidates. The Early Recovery (a phase of the market cycle defined by me) has more of these candidates. Big companies know their values and see good values when these stocks have been beaten in the market.

Then I do an intangible analysis on items that are not available from the financial statements and/or cannot be quantified. They are patents, technologies, research, customer base, the brand name, the barriers to entry, the distribution channels, the competition, the product cycle, the management and the pension obligations.

In 2003 I bought stock in a software company that was acquired by IBM profiting more than double. In the 2008 cycle, I bought ALU at $1 and sold it shortly at 40% profit. I expected Cisco would acquire it as Cisco did not build a network. Cisco and the U.S. did not acquire this valuable technology. In two years, it was acquired by another competitor for more than $3. I need patience.

The company going to be acquired tries to make the financial statements look very rosy. A Chinese company tricked Caterpillar in acquiring it and Caterpillar lost huge in this deal. Even big companies can be fooled. The record mergers in 2015 may not be good for the companies involved judging from the past history. When two losing companies merge, there will be one big loser.

#Filler: Why do poor countries remain poor?

One reason is suffering from repeated natural disasters such as earthquakes and hurricanes.

Even though the U.S. has been spending a lot of resources on Puerto Rico, some politicians want to be kings and queens as they do not care about their citizens.

8   Intangibles

I give a score for each stock I evaluate. Occasionally some stocks with poor scores have great returns and vice versa. In general, the scoring system works. It has been proven statistically and repeatedly from my limited data.
I stick with high-score stocks with some exceptions.

Once in a while I change my scoring system to adapt to the current market conditions. To illustrate, the market bottom phase and early recovery phase of the market cycle favor value more than momentum/growth. Here are some of my recent experiences and strategies:

- I double or even triple my stake on stocks with high scores. In the longer term, they are consistently better winners than the average with some minor exceptions. Besides the score, look at the intangibles described in this article.

- Watch out for the stocks with outrageous metrics such as P/E of 4 or less. It could be a big lawsuit pending, an expiration of some important drugs, etc. Also, be careful with scores in the top 5%. From my statistics they do worse than the average. Their problems may not show up in the current financial statements.

- The technology of a tech company cannot be ignored even though the company's P/E is high, that I set a limit of 25 instead of 20 for other stocks. The value of the company's technology and patents will not be shown in the fundamental metrics except from the insiders' purchases at market prices.

    For example, IDCC rose about 40% in 2 days. There was a rumor that Google was buying the company and/or Apple was bidding on it too for its mobile technology. Charts usually would flag this kind of event. For non-charters, use the SMA-20% from Finviz.com. They could be a little late as the charts depend on rising prices.

- There are more acquisitions during a market bottom (same as early recovery). The companies with good technologies are bargains and the larger companies especially those in the same sector understand their values better than most of us. These potentially profitable companies will not be shown by their scores explicitly. When corporations have a lot of cash or the credit is cheap, they are looking for smaller companies to acquire or invest in. The candidates are usually small, beaten up, low-priced and having valuable intangible assets such as technologies, customer base and/or market share of the industry segment. 2009-2012 was just the perfect environment and the before that was 2003. I had at least one stock in each of these periods and they appreciated a lot.

- The opposite is Netflix, Chipotle in 1/2012 and Amazon in 1/2013. They are overpriced by any measure. However, the mentioned companies are investing in the future. The shorters (not for beginners) are having a tough time making money on them. When their P/Es are higher than 40, watch out. Some could be OK in the mentioned companies, but usually they are not. Do not follow the herd and your due diligence will verify whether they will still go up.

  Use reward/risk ratio. It is based on experiences. To illustrate, if the company has the equal chance to go up 50% and go down 25%, then it is a buy and the reverse is a sell.

- The retail investor just cannot possibly know about some events until they actually happen. For example, ATSC dropped 15% due to losing its second primary customer. Fundamentals cannot predict this kind of event. Charts can signal this event, but usually they are too late unless you watch the chart all day long.

- After a quick run up, TZOO plunged due to missing some negligible earning expectations. It seems the original climbing prices already had the perfect earnings growth built-in.

  I do not understand why a company loses 10% of its market cap when it missed by 1% of the expected earnings. It could be driven up and down by the institutional investors. Evaluate the stock before you act. Acting opposite to the institutional investors could be very profitable for the right stocks. Avoid trading before the earnings announcement dates (about 4 times a year for most stocks).

- The following are not easily found in financial statements: industry outlook, patents, good will, market share, competition, product margins, management quality, lawsuits pending, potential acquisition, pension obligations, advertising icons, etc. That is why we need to read articles on the stocks in our buy list or our purchased stocks.

- The financial data could be fraudulent or manipulated. I do not trust small companies in emerging markets. I have been burned too many times. Check the company names such as foreign names, ADR and their headquarter addresses (from the company profile in most investing sites).

   Earnings can be manipulated with many accounting tricks. A jump in earnings from last year may not be as rosy as it looks. Check the footnotes in the accounting statements. I usually skip financial statements unless I have big purchases in mind as my time in investing is limited.

- Cash flow cannot be easily manipulated. It is good information whether the company will survive or not, but to me it does not prove to be a consistent predictor in my tests, but an important red flag for companies on their way to bankruptcy. Examples abound.
- Repeated one-time, non-recurring and extraordinary charges are red flags.
- Stay away from the companies where the CEOs are over-compensated. As of 7- 2013, Activision's CEO raised his salary by more than 600%, while the stock lost its value in double digits.
- Value stocks. Need to know why they become value stocks (i.e., fewer investors want to own them) even if they are fundamentally sound. For example, there are two primary reasons for the downfall of a supplier to Apple: 1. Apple is declining in sales and 2. Apple is switching suppliers to replace their product. Technology companies are continually building better mouse traps. They could turn around in a year or so with better products.

Conclusion

Buying a stock is an educated guess that its stock price will rise. Fundamentals do not always work, but they work most of the time:

1. When we buy a value stock, we're swimming against the tide. Hence, we need to wait longer (usually more than 6 months) for the market to realize its value. The exception is the Early Recovery phase (see the Market Cycle chapter) and it has faster and larger returns than most other stocks from most other stages of the market cycle.

2. Some metrics are misleading. Book value could be misleading for an established company such as IBM. The image of the cowboy in a tobacco company could be a very important asset that is not included in its financial statement.

3. The market is not always rational.

Afterthoughts

- Brand names of big companies are one of the most important intangibles. Here is a strategy to buy big companies in a down market. It has been proven that it works. However, do not just buy these companies without analysis.
http://seekingalpha.com/article/1324041-buying-brand-names-in-a-bear-market-can-make-you-rich

- The reputation of a company takes a long time to build but a bad incident to destroy in the case of GM such as the delay in recalling the killer switches.

#Filler: Carrie Fisher, another sad American story

Unless drug addiction is part of the culture now as evidenced from the legalization of certain drugs, we're in a permissive society! Brits pushed opium as a nation when they had nothing better to trade. Opium killed millions of Chinese and bankrupted China. When we do not learn from history, we will repeat history. It is another sad story of fame and money and then losing it all. I bet she would be happier in a normal life instead of being born in a privileged class. Same can be said for many celebrities such as Presley, Houston and her daughter. RIP.

9   Qualitative analysis

This is the last analysis to evaluate a stock fundamentally. Then the next is technical analysis which is used to find an entry point (also the exit point) for the stock. The market is not always rational. It also depends on the available of money such as easy credit to pump up the market.

Where quantitative analysis fails and why

I find that some stocks with high scores fail and some stocks with low scores succeed as indicated by my performance monitor. The scoring system still works statistically for the majority of my stocks.

- Reasons why stocks with low scores perform:

    o   Oversold. The institutional investors (fund managers and pension managers) dump them first, and then followed by the retail investors. These big boys will buy these stocks back when they reach a certain price range. RSI(14), a technical indicator described in the Technical Analysis article and is available from many sites including Finviz, is useful to detect these oversold stocks.

    o   The falling price (P) improves all fundamental metrics that have the stock price such as P/E and P/Sales. However, the trend of the price is down. Improving Forward P/E is usually a good hint.

    o   The company has turned around after fixing its problems and/or the market has changed for the better. A new management team could improve profitability such as recalling Steve Jobs for Apple.

    o   The current problems have been resolved but not known to the public that could be evidenced by the increase in Insiders' Purchases (from Finviz to start). It includes resolving a lawsuit, a new product, a new drug, or a new big order, etc.

    o   Heavy purchases by insiders. The company's outlook is not shown in its financial statements. Sometimes the insiders hide them so they can buy more of their companies' stocks for themselves.

- Reasons why stocks with high scores plunge in addition to the described in the previous discussion:
    - The company's fundamentals and its prices have reached or closed to the maximum heights. They have no way to go but down. It is particularly true when the stock's timing rating is at or close to the highest point. TTWO that I gifted to my grandchildren had been 5-baggers in the last few years before it plunged in 2018.
    - It has reached its potential value (or a target price) and it is time for many investors to take profits.
    - Sector (or finding another stock or sector with better appreciation potential)) rotation, particularly by institutional investors who drive the market.

        - The outlook of the company, its sector and/or the market is deteriorating. Most companies with P/E less than 5 have problems, and you need to find out the reasons why the stocks are so cheap. Via Finviz, check out debt / share (more than 0.5), negative Q-Q Sales, negative Q-Q Profits, and/or outdated products like typewriters.

    - The stock price may be manipulated. There are many reasons to pump and dump the stock. Shorting is not recommended for most investors. However, some experienced shorters make money consistently when they find valid reasons to short stocks.
    - It could be due to a new serious lawsuit, a new competing product or drug, canceling a major order, etc.
    - Downgrade by analysts. They could spot some bad events such as product defects, violations of regulations or accounting errors / frauds. The downgrades are more important than the upgrades that could have conflict of interest.
    - The financial statement had been manipulated. The SEC may ask for an investigation.
    - Does not meet the consensus in earnings announcements, which have been over-acted by many investors.

Qualitative Analysis

We need to do further analysis after the quantitative analysis and the intangible analysis. Check out the company's prospects. Check out the date of the article and any potential hidden agenda items from the author. Older articles may not have much value.

Be careful on 'pump-and-dump' manipulation written by authors with a hidden agenda. It has happened especially on small companies before even SeekingAlpha.com has its share. Here was an article that tells you to sell NHTC. There was another article to tell you to buy ARTX. They fit into this category.

The sources are:

1. Seeking Alpha.
   Type the symbol of the company to read as many articles on the company as you have time for. Today this site and many other similar sites require you to be a paid member. If you cannot find too many good articles, check out the articles from Finviz.com.

   Recently, I read an article on AMD and it said it may have good profits in the next two years with the game consoles. The outlook of a company is not shown by any fundamental metric which are far from favorable.

   Following a well-known writer, I bought IBM without doing my due diligence (my fault). It went down more than 15% quickly. You can learn from my mistakes.
2. Research reports from your broker. If you do not find many, open an account with one that provides such reports. Some subscription services such as Value Line provide such reports.
3. Yahoo!Finance board. Most comments are garbage. However, once in a while you find some great insights. Usually, you cannot find any info from other sources on tiny companies.
4. The most recent company's financial statements. They are usually available from the company's website.
5. 10-Ks from Edgar database (www.sec.gov/edgar). Check out new products and its potential competition, key customers, order backlog, research and development and pending lawsuits.
6. Check out the outlook of the sector the company is in and the company itself.
7. Check out its competitors.
8. Some companies are run by stupid people. I received information via my email saying that my mutual fund account could be treated as an abandoned property. I have been cashing dividend checks every year and why it would be considered as an abandoned property. I called them right away to close my account.

The tall and handsome guy presented articulately how he would turn around JC Penny on TV. I could tell you right away that all his tricks had been tried by other companies such as Sears, and most did not work. The intelligent investor does not care about how handsome, how articulate, how rich his family is and how many advanced degrees from prestigious colleges he possesses. If he does not make sense, do not buy his preaching and his company's stock. [Update. As of 5/2020, J.C. Penny filed for bankruptcy protection. If you had this stock and my book, you would have saved a lot of money minus $10 for my book!]

9. Check out its business model. Some business models do not make business sense and some do. Here are some samples.
- Giving razors makes sense, as the customers have to buy the blades eventually and keep on buying blades for life.
- Supermarket M lowers prices on common merchandise such as Coke and it works. They make money by providing inferior (but profitable to them) products that you cannot compare prices easily such as meat and seafood.

Eventually there will be a supermarket in my area to satisfy me both in price and quality or at least make a good tradeoff.
- Last week it had been brutally hot. I went to a Barnes & Noble's bookstore to enjoy reading the updated books and enjoyed the air conditioning. When there are more free loaders like me than customers, this business model does not work.
- Market dumping works to capture the market. Microsoft used to do it with their new Office and Mail products that could not compete with the established products at the time. Google is following the same model to dump its equivalent products to compete with Office. Now, Microsoft is taking a dose of the same medicine. As of 2015, Google is not winning.

Amazon.com gives writers (like myself) great deals if you only sell your digital books via them. This model will work so far, as it has captured the self-publishing market today.

IV Technical Analysis

The basics

Technical analysis (a.k.a. charting) is easier to learn than expected. It represents the trend of the market (a stock or a group of stocks) graphically. If more investors are in the market (a stock or a group of stocks), the trend is up until it changes. We divide the trends into short-term, intermediate-term and long-term.

The chartists usually do not consider fundamentals as they believe they have already been priced in the stock price and some fundamentals are not available. To illustrate, a new drug has been discovered, the stock price of the company jumps. Its fundamental metrics do not show right away but many are buying to boost up the stock price.

The volume is a confirmation. When the stock moves up or down by 10% with a low volume, the trend is not confirmed.

The trend of the stock price is not straight line in most cases. Hence a trend line is usually drawn to indicate the direction of the stock. Many believe the stocks fluctuate in certain range (or channels) and the chart draws the upper value (the resistance line) and the lower value (the support line).

When the price passes the channel, it is called a breakout. Darvas, one of the oldest and successful chartists, profited from the breakouts of the resistance line and believed the stock is close to the support line of the new channel. Hence it has a long way for profit.

If it is so simple, there will be no poor folks

It works most of the time, but do not bet all your money on it. For chartists, 51% is great (it is too for playing Black Jack). Some trends reverse very fast such as the bio drug stocks in 2015. You need to hedge your bets such as placing stop orders. Most do not want to spend their lives in watching the trend from a big screen. Most novices use too many indicators and lose to the professionals.

Simple Moving Average
The basic technical indicator is SMA. It is the average of the last N trade sessions. When N is 20 (or SMA-20), we classify it as short-term. Similarly,

SMA-50 is intermediate-term and SMA-200 is long-term. This trend duration is important: You do not want to place long-term bets using SMA-50 uptrend for example. There are many modifications that I do not find them better such as giving more weights to recent data. Finviz.com includes this information without charting.

Defining the trend periods is arbitrary. I use SMA-350 to detect market plunges and SMA-100 for stocks.

Trend is your best friend
Most use TA for trending for short durations. Value investors can also use TA to time the entry and exit points for better potential profits. Value investors usually are patient and they do bottom fishing. They treat 'oversold' as value. TA does have indicators for detecting the bottom of the stock such as RSI(14) described next.

When the market is overbought, the technical indicator would indicate the market is peaking. Many indicators do not indicate market bottom and market peak as it depends on the market data. If the volume is low (compared to its average), the indicator may be too weak to be considered.

Many sites provide charting free of charge such as Yahoo!Finance. Finviz.com provides a lot of technical indicators without charting such as SMA% and RSI(14). It also provides screen searching for stocks that meet your technical analysis criteria.

Beginners make a common mistake by using too many technical indicators. Start with SMA (Single Moving Average). The parameter for SMA is "days", which are actually trade sessions.

TA patterns
There are many TA patterns such as Bollinger Bands and MACD. The patterns are based on the stock prices indicate the trend of the stock. Many times history repeats itself.

Sites for TA

There are many free sites for charts with explanation of the technical indicators. Popular ones include BigCharts.com, SmallCharts.com and Yahoo!Finance. Fidelity includes some unique features such as P/E.

Technical analysis depends on charts and its practitioners are called chartists, technical analysts or technicians.

Why I do not use TA for as a primary tool for stock picking

My investing style is different from a day trader. I prefer to 'Buy Low and Sell High' instead of 'Buy High and Sell Higher'. I try to find the real bottom price. TA will not find the bottom easily but it racks the trend better. As a bargain hunter, I do not expect the stock will rise fast as I'm swimming against the tide.

For some strange reason beyond my reasoning, a lot of times I placed buy orders on stocks that appreciate very fast. This is not good for me as my buy orders are usually not market orders, so I miss many big gainers.

I have many stocks losing 25% in one day. TA will not help me to sell these stocks, but stop orders might. However, a bad pattern would identify most of the coming falls.

My opinion

I do not want to argue whether TA is good for you or not. You need to find it out. Most likely, the day traders and short-term swingers will profit more from TA than the investors seeking for value for long-term gain.

Most should benefit to study the fundamentals of a stock and then use TA to enter and exit on the trade.

My current situation does not allow me to use TA extensively due to evaluating and maintaining a large number of stocks in a limited time. Most likely I am the exception. However, I do have a TA parameter in my scoring system that helps me to determine the trade decision. My investment subscription services and my personal metrics in my momentum strategy use TA more than my evaluation for bargain stocks.

Random remarks

Even if you do not use technical analysis, you should spend some time in learning it. It is better to marry fundamentals and TA. My random remarks are:

- The Institution investors (insurance companies, pension funds, mutual funds, etc.) use TA and they MOVE the market. A lot of times it becomes a self-fulfilling prophecy. It is better to join them as most of us cannot beat them.

- Day traders take advantage of the institution investors by spotting their trends.

- Most TA stocks should be good sizes and have large average daily volumes. I prefer to use TA on sound fundamental stocks.

- I do know some folks making big money using TA, but I know more making good money using fundamentals. If you marry the two disciplines, you should be a better investor. Since TA predicts the market better in shorter term, its practitioners may have to pay higher taxes (in today's tax laws) in taxable accounts.

- Our objective should be making money at the least risk. Once you claim to belong to a certain group of either Fundamental or TA, you will be biased and forget your primary objective in investing.

- The price movement usually tells the hidden reasons why it moves and its volume confirms it.

    There are many factors not shown in the financial statement such as serious lawsuits pending, market trend, insiders' purchases (based on legal or illegal information), a new product, a clinical outcome of a drug, competition, etc., but TA spots them all.

- It tracks the last two big market plunges (2000 and 2007) pretty well. The chart will not warn you right away for the upcoming plunge (as it depends on past data) to avoid the initial losses, but they will warn you to avoid bigger losses.

    I use it to track the market more than on specific stocks (you can use it for both purposes).

Afterthoughts

- Steps in buying a stock. Screen stocks, perform quantitative analysis, perform qualitative analysis and lastly perform technical analysis.

Today it is possible to do the technical analysis first to screen stocks as many web sites provide technical parameters in screening such as Finviz.com.

- Besides searching for stocks that have potential breakouts according to specific patterns, we should check the stocks we owned for potential breakdowns.

  Technical Analysis tutorial.
  https://www.youtube.com/watch?v=GENBVwV8PMs

  SMA tutorial.
  https://www.youtube.com/watch?v=Na-ctpPsnks

Links
Fidelity video: Technical Analysis
https://www.fidelity.com/learning-center/technical-analysis/chart-types-video

10   Simplest technical analysis

When the stock, the sector that the stock is in and the market both are above its SMA-n averages (Single Moving Average for n days), it is a buy.

1. Bring up finviz.com from your browser.

2. Enter SPY. Write down the SMA-200 (Single Moving Average for 200 days). Positive numbers indicate the trend for the market is good.

   However, the market could be peaking or overbought. Do not buy stocks when SMA-200 is over 5% and / or RSI(14) is over 65%. RSI is a metric in the same screen.

3. Enter the sector ETF (check ETF in Chapter 14) the stock is in. Write down the SMA-50. Positive numbers indicate trend for the sector is good.

   However, the sector could be peaking or overbought. Do not buy stocks when SMA-200 is over 10% and / or RSI(14) is over 65%. RSI is a metric in the same screen.

4. Enter the stock symbol. If your average holding period of the stocks is 50, use SMA-50 and so on. I recommend SMA-200 for holding stocks long term. Write down the SMA-n for your stock. Positive numbers indicate the trend is good.

   However, the market could be peaking or overbought. Do not buy stocks when SMA-200 is over 25% and / or RSI(14) is over 70%. RSI is a metric in the same screen.

If the above three criteria and the fundamental criteria are satisfied, most likely it is a good buy.

11   Technical Analysis example

The easiest way to find its trend is using Finviz.com. Enter the stock symbol and look at the SMA50 and SMA 200 (Single Moving Average). If it is 10% plus, the trend is good. The difference between 50 days and 200 days depends on how long you keep the stock and how frequent you trade.

You may want to enter SMA yourself via Yahoo!Finance. Here is an example of using SMA to trade CSCO.

I have outlined how we can spot market plunge using TA and I use it to monitor the market every three months or so (recommend to do it every month).

Here is an example on how to use it to trade individual stocks. I have to admit I do not use TA that much on individual stocks and clearly I am not an expert in TA. If this article and the last two stir up your interest, read more books or attend seminars / classes on TA. Personally I prefer to seek fundamentally sound companies at bargain prices and wait for their full appreciation. It is only me.

TA is very useful for momentum and day traders. With the rising volume, you can detect while stocks are traded by managers of mutual funds, hedge funds, insurance companies and pension funds, and profit by riding on their wagons.

Some stocks are good for TA. Usually they are larger companies with above-average volumes. Let me pick CSCO (a cyclical stock) for illustration. I bought it several times in 2012 but save it for the long term. This is quite different from what traders would use the following information for.

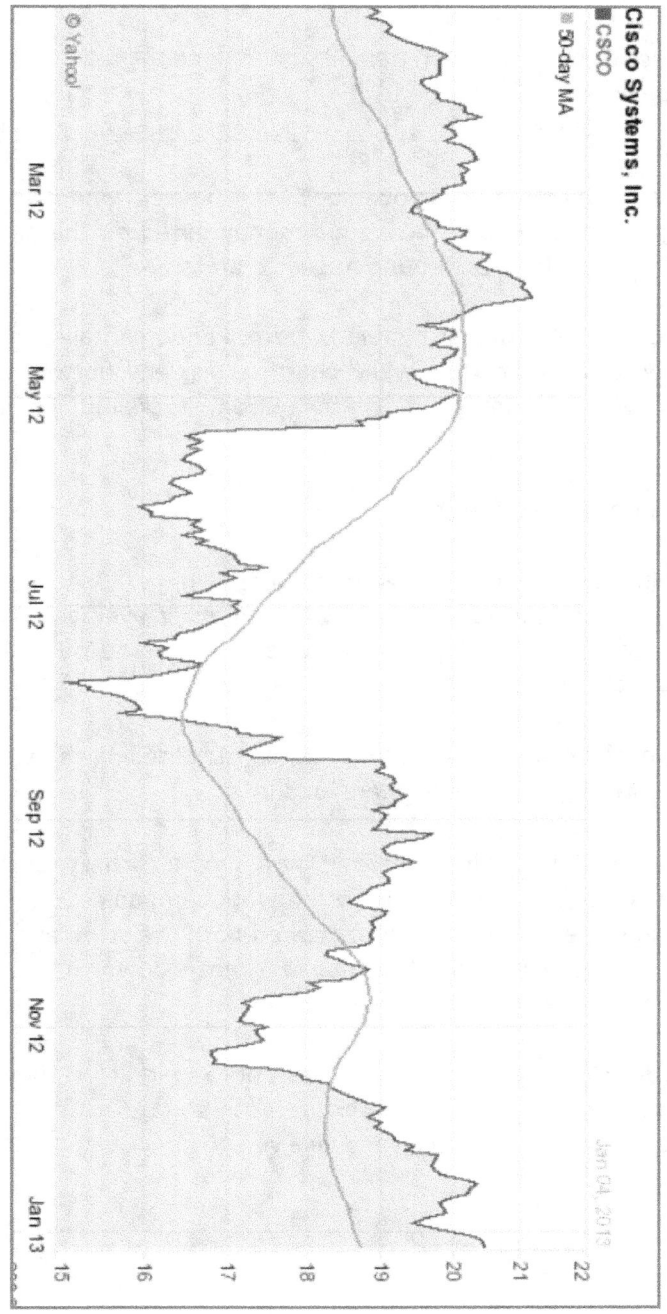

CSCO Stock Price and 50-day SMA   Source: Yahoo!Finance

The green line is 50-day simple moving average (SMA). The above is the stock prices for one year.

If it does not display clearly on a small screen, type the following on the browser on your PC.
http://ebmyth.blogspot.com/2013/05/chart-for-ta-example.html

Buy the stock when it is above its SMA and sell when it is below. Following the chart would make good money based on this simple rule. Sell on May 1, buy back on around August 1, and so on.

Not all stocks follow this profitable pattern. Fundamentalists may try to pick the bottom in late July while chartists pick the bottom later. The chartists have an advantage to stay away from stocks in their downward trend.

We can improve the trades by:

- Use different moving average in number of days (50 in this example) and other indicators such as EMA (a moving average that weighs higher with recent data). It may prove accuracy and/or cut down the number of trades.

- Instead of selling the stock for cash, consider selling the stock short. Selling short is not for beginners for sure.

- The accuracy is usually improved by a separate chart for its sector. For CSCO, you can use an ETF for network companies (or S&P 500 to represent the market). In theory, when both the stock and its sector (and optionally including the market) move down, it has a higher chance to move down, and vice versa.

  Optionally, include the SMA for the entire market. In theory, if the market, the sector and the stock are all in an uptrend, the chance of the stock to move up is high and vice versa.

TA is not for most fundamentalists but it should be used

For a bargain hunter like me, TA would not benefit me for picking stocks. I would try to pick up CSCO with prices ranging from 15-17 and all below the moving average line that TA would not show me a Buy signal. However, for very short-term swing trader TA is a Godsend.

To me, TA is good indicator for growth and momentum for short-term traders. Some fundamentalists may use TA for entry and exit point. It is good for 'Buy High and Sell Higher'.

In selecting a tool, you have to understand how, why to use it and whether it fits your investing style. I use TA for market timing for the entire market rather than on individual stocks.

TA is good indicator when a value stock is trending up in a rising market and a rising sector that the stock is in. Most of us cannot spot the bottom of a stock; I had but most likely they were due to luck. When a stock is moving up from the bottom, there is a good chance it will move further up. TA shows it and its volume confirms it.

Conclusion

Even a fundamentalist like me can benefit by using TA. This book touches the very basics of TA but the most useful TA indicators.

Filler:

In any business, we can learn a lot from Bill Belichick.
http://www.espn.com/espn/feature/story/_/id/17703210/new-england-patriots-coach-bill-belichick-greatest-enigma-sports

It is the same for stock research, we need to have knowledge, leave no stone unturned, work hard... Luck has nothing to do with success for most successful folks.

12   Our window to the investing world

This is a summary of the web sites described in this book and the web sites you may want to refer to. Click on the sites and a brief comment may be included. The paperback version of this chapter can be found in the following link.

http://ebmyth.blogspot.com/2013/11/web-sites.html

- **General**
  Wikipedia / Investopedia /Yahoo!Finance / MarketWatch / Cnnfn / Morningstar /

  CNBC / Bloomberg / WSJ / Barron's / Motley Fool / TheStreet

  Understanding the news is fine but most likely you will not profit directly from the news. Read the chapter on Headlines to interpret the news and profit from it.

- **Evaluate stocks**
  Finviz / SeekingAlpha / MSN Money / Zacks / Daily Finance / ADR / Fidelity / BlueChipGrowth / Earnings Impact / OpenInsider / NYSE / NASDAQ / SEC /

  SEC for 10K and 10Q (quarterly) reports required to file for listed stocks in major exchanges.

- **Charts**
  BigCharts / FreeStockCharts / StockCharts /

- **Screens**
  Yahoo!Finance / Finviz / CNBC / Morningstar /

- **Besides stocks**
  123Jump / Hoover's Online / FINRA Bond Market Data / REIT / Commodity Futures /

  Option Industry

- **Vendors**

AAII / Zacks / IBD / GuruFocus / Vector Vest /

Fidelity / Interactive Brokers / Merrill Lynch /

Fidelity has extensive research and I feel they have excellent executions in trades. Interactive Brokers is least expensive to trade options and their interest rates are low. Merrill Lynch provides 30-commission free trades per month for a deposit requirement in the bank; check their current offer.

- **Economy.**
  Econday / EcoconStats / Federal Reserve / Economist /

- **Misc.**
  Dow Jones Indices / Russell / Wilshire /

  IRS / Wikinvest /

  ETF Database / ETF Trends /

  Nolo (estate planning) / AARP /

I prefer to use a spreadsheet to maintain my portfolio instead of using Wikinvest or one of the many web sites that have this function. My broker has done a good job in tracking the profit/loss and performance. I use Yahoo!Finance to update the stock prices in my portfolio. This also helps me to monitor the performances of individual fundamental metrics and the screens I use. AARP is a good site for retirees. However, they are more interested to sell you Medicare supplement insurance.

13   ETFs / Mutual Funds

What is an ETF

Fidelity: Index ETFs (https://www.fidelity.com/etfs/overview).

Wikipedia on ETF (http://en.wikipedia.org/wiki/Exchange-traded_fund).

List of ETFs
ETF Bloomberg
http://www.bloomberg.com/markets/etfs/
ETF data base
http://etfdb.com/
ETF Trends
http://www.etftrends.com/
A list of ETFs. Seeking Alpha.
(http://etf.stock-encyclopedia.com/category/)

Fidelity's commission-free ETFs. Check current offering and whether they are still commission-free.
(https://www.fidelity.com/etfs/ishares)

Fidelity Annuity funds with performance data.
http://fundresearch.fidelity.com/annuities/category-performance-annual-total-returns-quarterly/FPRAI?refann=005

A list of contra ETFs (or bear ETFs)
http://www.tradermike.net/inverse-short-etfs-bearish-etf-funds/
Misc.: ETFGuide, ETFReplay (highly recommended).

Other resources
Your broker should have a lot of information on ETFs and many offer commission-free ETFs.

Most subscription services offer research on ETFs. IBD has a strategy dedicated to ETFs and so is AAII to name a couple.

Seeking Alpha has extensive resources for ETF including an ETF screener and investing ideas.

Not all ETFs are created equal
Check their performances and their expenses.

Small but well-performed ETFs
Here is a list.
http://finance.yahoo.com/news/small-etfs-pack-big-punch-195430875.html

Guggenheim Spin-Off ETF (CSD) looks interesting. The ETF tracks corporate spinoffs. It has beaten SPY for a long while; check the current performance. Not a recommendation.

When not to use ETFs
I prefer sector mutual funds in some industries that need to extensive research. They are drug industry, banks, miners and insurers.

Half ETF
Taking out half of the stocks that score below the average in an index ETF could beat the same full ETF itself. I call it HETF (half the ETF). You hear it here first. I hope all the fund creators of HETF (trademark pending ☺) will donate to my secret retiring fund for using the name and my concept.

To illustrate, sort the expected P/E (not including stocks with negative earnings) in ascending order and only include the stocks on the first half. Add more fundamental metrics. It will take minutes.

Disadvantages of ETFs
- When you have two stocks in a sector ETF one good one and one bad one, the ETF treats them the same. Stock pickers would buy the one with better appreciation potential.
- The return is better than the actual return due to stock rotation. To illustrate, on August 29, 2012, SHLD was replaced by LYB in a sector fund. SHLD was down by 4% and LYB was up by 4% primarily due to the switch. Unless you sell and buy at the right time (that's impossible), your return would not match with the ETF's return due to the replacement.
- Ensure the performance matches the corresponding index, which is most likely does not include dividends.

Advantages of ETFs
- We have demonstrated you can beat the market by using market timing. Between 2000 and Nov., 2013, you only exit and reenter the market 3 times and the result is astonishing.

- It is easy to rotate a sector vs. buying/selling all stocks in this sector. It makes sector rotation the same as trading a stock.
- The risk is spread out and your portfolio is diversified especially for a market ETF or buying three or more ETFs in different sectors.
- Eliminate the time in researching stocks.

Leveraged ETFs

I do not recommend them. Some are 2x, 3x and even higher. They're too risky. However, when you are very sure or your strategy has very low drawdown, you may want to use them to improve performance. I recommend skipping all leveraged ETFs.

My basic ETF tables

I use a list of selected ETFs and commission-free (check details) ETFs from Fidelity for my purpose. I include some mutual funds and mutual funds for Fidelity's annuity. Some may be interesting to you. I use ETFs for sector rotation and parking my cash when the market is favorable and I do not have stocks I want to buy.

ETFs and funds come and go. Some ideas and classifications are my interpretation.

Table by market cap:

Category	ETF	Fidelity ETF	Mutual Funds	Fidelity's Annuity	Contra ETF
Size:					
Large Cap	DOW		See Blend		DOG
	SPY				SH
	QQQ	ONEQ			PSQ
	RYH				
Blend	IWD	IVV	BEQGX		
Growth	SPYG	IVW	FBGRX		
Value	SPYV		DOGGX		
Dividend	NOBL	DVY	FRDPX		
	VYM				
Mid Cap				FNBSC	MYY
Blend	MDY	JJH	VSEQX		
Growth		IJK	STDIX		
			BPTRX		
Value		IJJ	FSMVX		

				FPRGC	SBB
Small Cap					
Blend	IWM	IJR	HDPSX		
Growth		IJT	PRDSX		
Value		IJS	SKSEX		
Micro	IWC				
Multi					
Blend			VDEOX		
Growth			VHCOX		
Value			TCLCX		
Bond					
Long Term (20)	VLV		BTTTX		TBF
Mid Term (7 – 10)	VCIT		FSTGX		
Short Term (1 – 3 yrs.)	VCSH		THOPX		
Total	BOND		PONDX		
Corp Invest Grade	VCIT		NTHEX		
High Yield (junk)	PHB		SPHIX		
Muni	MUB		Check state		
Special situation					
Buy back	PKW				

Table by sectors:

Sector	ETF	Fidelity ETF	Mutual Funds	Fidelity's Annuity
Banking[1]			FSRBK	
Regional	IAT			
Bio	IBB		FBIOX	
	XBI		Large	
Consumer Dis.	XLY	FDIS	FSCPX	FVHAC
Consumer Staple	XLP	FSTA	FDFAX	FCSAC
Finance	KIE	FNCL	FIDSX	FONNC
	IYF			
Energy	XLE	FENY	FSENX	FJLLC
Energy Service			FSESX	

Gold	GLD		FSAGX	
Gold Miner	GDX		VGPMX	
Health Care	IYH	FHLC	FSPHX	FPDRC
	VHT		VGHCX	
House Builder	ITB		FSHOX	
	ITB		Perform	
Industrial	IYJ	FIDU	FCYIX	FBALC
Material	VAW	FMAT	FSDPX	
	IYM			
Oil	USO			
Oil Service	OIH		FSESX	
Oil Exploration	XOP			
Real Estate	VNQ		FRIFX	FFWLC
REIT	VNQ			
Retail	RTH		FSRPX	
	XRT			
Regional bank	KRE		FSRBX	
Semi Conduct	SMH			
Software	XSW		FSCSX	
	IGV			
Technology	XLK	FTEC	FSPTX	FYENC
	FDN		FBSOX	
			ROGSX	
Telecomm.	VOX	FCOM	FSTCX	FVTAC
Transport	XTN			
	IYT			
Utilities	XLU	FUTY	FSUTX	FKMSC
Wireless			FWRLX	

Footnote. [1] Also check Finance.

Table by countries:

Country	ETF	Fidelity ETF	Mutual Funds	Fidelity's Annuity
Australia	EWA			
Brazil	EWZ			
Canada	EWC		FICDX	
China	FXI		FHKCX	
EAFE	EFA			
Emerging	VWO		FEMEX	FEMAC
Europe	VGK		FIEUX	
Global	KXI		PGVFX	
Greece	GREK			

India	INDY		MINDX		
Indonesia	EIDO				
Latin America	ILF		FLATX		
Nordic			FNORX		
Hong Kong	EWH				
Japan	EWJ		FJPNX		
S. Africa	EZA				
S. Korea	EWY		MAKOX		
Singapore	EWS				
Taiwan	EWT				
Turkey	TUR				
United Kingdom	EWU				
Foreign:					
Combination	1	2	3	4	
Intern. Div.	IDV	DWX			
Small Cap	SCZ	GWX			
Value	EFV				
Europe	VGK				

Quick analysis of ETFs

ETF is a basket of stocks according to a specific sector, country or a theme. I use different yardsticks to evaluate ETFs.

From Yahoo!Finance, enter the symbol of the ETF. It displays its historical P/E (last twelve months). If it is below 15 and above zero, it could be valued. Also, if the current price is lower than its NAV, it is sold with discount (or premium vice versa). Compare its YTD Return to SPY's.

From Finviz.com, enter the ETF symbol. If SMA-20%, SMA-50% and SMA-200% are all positive, most likely the ETF is in uptrend. If your average holding period is about 50 days, SMA-50% is more meaningful to you. If RSI(14) > 70, it is probably over-sold; if it is < 35, it is probably under-sold (i.e. value).

In addition, ensure the average volume is high (more than 10,000 shares to me), market cap is more than 200 M, and it has low fee... Most popular ETFs have these characteristics.

How to determine the sector has been recovered

It is easier to profit by following the uptrend (or downtrend for shorting and/or contra ETFs) of an ETF using the above info. It is hard to detect when the bottom of an ETF has been reached. If SMA-20%, SMA-50% and

SMA-200% are all positive, most likely the ETF is in uptrend or it has recovered. It did not happen for some ETFs in 2015.

An example

This example illustrates how to evaluate ETFs. First, determine whether the market is risky. If it is risky and you're more risk tolerant, you can buy contra ETF(s) betting the market or the specific sector will go further down. Most investors should not invest in a risky market.

Next, you want to limit the number of sector ETFs by selecting those that are either trending up or hitting bottom. Personally I prefer sectors with long-term uptrend (indicated by cnnfn.com). Seeking Alpha has many current articles on ETFs.

Today's market (as of 2/5/2015) is risky. For illustration only, I select the following ETFs: SPY (simulating the market based on large companies), XLP (consumer staples) and XLY (consumer discretionary). XLP should perform better than XLY during a recession as those products are the necessities.

Technical indicators such as SMA-50 (Simple Moving Average for the last 50 sessions), SMA-200 and RSI(14) are from finviz.com and the rest are from Yahoo!Finance.com. After you buy the ETF, use stop loss to protect your investment. Bio tech sector moved up for many months until it crashed later in 2015.

As of 2/5/2015	SPY	XLP (staples)	XLY (discret.)
Price	190	50	71
NAV	192	50	73
• Technical			
SMA-50	-4%	0%	-7%
SMA-200	-6%	2%	-7%
RSI(14)	44	50	36
Other	Double bottom		
• Fundamental			
P/E	17	20	19
Yield	2.1%	2.5%	1.5%
YTD return	-5%	0.5%	-5%
Net asset	174 B	9 B	10 B

Explanation
- The figures may not be the same from the two web sites due to the date they use.

- XLY has better discount among the 3 ETFs as most investors believe a recession is coming.
- XLP is less down trend among the 3 ETFs as expected.
- XLY is more undersold among the 3 as expected.
- Double bottom is a technical pattern that indicates the stock would surge.
- SPY has better valued according to P/E.
- XLY's dividend is the least among the 3 as they have more tech companies. They have to plow back the profits to research and development.
- XLP has the best YTD return among the 3.
- As long as the asset is above 500 M, it is fine and all three pass this mark.

Rotation of 4 ETFs

We can beat the market by rotating one ETF that represents the market such as SPY and cash (or short-term bond ETF) via market timing.

During market uptrend, rotate the following four ETFs could be more profitable. Be warned that short-term capital gain in taxable accounts is not treated as favorably as the long-term capital gain; check current tax laws.

The allocation percentages depend on individual risk tolerance. You can use indexed mutual funds. Compare their expenses and restrictions. Some mutual funds charge you if you withdraw within a specific period.

Select the best performer of last month (from Seeking Alpha, cnnFn, or the ETF/mutual fund site). Add a contra ETF such as SH to take advantage of a falling market for more aggressive investors. Add sector ETFs to the four ETFs such as XLY, XLP, XLE, XLF, XLU, IYW, XHB, IYM, OIL and XLU to expand your selection.

ETFs	Money Market	US	International	Bond
Fidelity		Spartan Total Market	Spartan Global Market	Spartan US Bond
Vanguard		Total Stock Market	Total International Market	Total Bond Market
My choice	Fidelity	SPY	Vanguard	Fidelity
Suggest %				
During Market plunge	90%	0%	0%	10%
After plunge	10%	60%	10%	20%

Explanation

- The above are suggestions only. If your broker offers similar ETFs, consider using them.
- Check out any restrictions of the ETFs.
- 4 ETFs (one actually is a money market fund) are enough for most starters. They are diversified, low-cost and you do not need balancing

except during market plunge (refer the chapter on Detecting Market Plunges).
- The percentages are suggestion only. If you are less risk tolerance, allocate more on money market fund and/or bond ETF.
- Have at least 10% allocated to the money market fund. When there is a mild market dip, move the money market fund to the US equity fund. Move it back to money market when there is a mild market upsurge. If you do not have time to check the market, allocate this 10% to the bond ETF.
- When the market is risky, reduce stock equities (i.e. increase money market and bond allocations).
- The symbols for Fidelity ETFs are FSTMX, FSGDX and FBIDX.
- The symbols for Vanguard ETFs are VTSMX, VGTSX and VBMFX.

If you are more advanced, use additional sector ETFs to rotate. Find out the current winners from many sources including CNNfn.com. Also buy long-term bond funds (such as 30-year Treasury) when the interest rate is 10% or more. I have covered the basics in sector rotation.

14   Order prices

Market orders

Use market orders only when it is necessary (more later) as stocks prices can easily be manipulated especially on stocks with low trading volumes.

However, in a rising market, many fast rising stocks can only be bought via market orders. Many winners never take a breather on its way up.

In my momentum portfolio on 11/2013, I placed a sell price for GERN far higher than the market price. Surprisingly I sold it for this price making an annualized return of 1,176% for holding it for 21 days. When there are few or no other sellers for the stock, the market price would be the price you set. If I cannot sell it in the next 9 days (30 days is my holding period for momentum stocks), I would set it lower. Update: One year later, GERN lost 29%.

Sensible discounts

I prefer to buy the stock at the price closest to the last trade price (to most it is the market price). I seldom lose buying these orders. Sometimes

I use the day's lowest price to buy (or the highest to sell) plus a penny (or minus a penny for sell prices to sell).

My other purchase strategy is using 0.15% or 0.25% less than the current prices for stocks I really want. For some promising stocks, I buy them at almost the market price and then place another order on the same stock at 0.5% less than the last trade price (and sometimes 2% depending on the current market trend).

We all want to pay less and sell at higher prices. However, if the market price is too far away from the market price (such as 5% from the market price), these trades may never be executed. I have a long list of buy orders that are not executed and turn out to be big gainers. Learn from my bad experiences.

Use a good discount (such as 10% from the market price) if you believe the market, the sector or the stock will dip by 10%. After you bought the stock, you place a sell order 10% more than the price you paid for hoping the stock return to the original price and you pocket 10%. Wishful thinking! However, it has happened to me several times primarily due to temporary market dips.

It works when there is a correction and/or the stock is very volatile. It is usually within the 5% range to take advantage of these situations, not the 10% described. For 10% plunge, it usually is due to some serious problem of the company surfacing. One common reason is not meeting its earnings expectation and in this case it usually continues its downward trend.

Larger discounts on a falling market
During a falling market (or a mild correction), 3% less than the current prices for buy orders may be fine for some stocks (use 5% for volatile stocks). To illustrate, I placed about 10 of such orders over the last two months during a market dip. Most of the orders were filled. When the market is plunging, do not buy any stock.

Caterpillar and Cisco are some of my buys at these discounts. They are in my watch list to buy. Initially these shares often fall even lower as the trend was downward. As of 12/18/12, CAT earned me from 3% and 14% (bought in 6/12 and 7/12) and CSCO bought in 7/14/12 returned about 34%. My original objective: Buy deeply-valued stocks, wait and sell when the economy returns.

When you predict the market to dip by 5%, set your buy orders accordingly. Again, predictions are just educated guesses. From my experience, they work most of the time but not all of the time.

On the day of the earnings announcement, the fluctuation of the stock is usually high. Check any change in the earnings estimate before the announcement and act accordingly. Zacks is supposed to be a useful tool to predict earnings estimates. Do not place orders before the earnings announcement dates. When the earning turns out to be good, the stock price surges and your order will not be executed. When the earning is bad, the stock price will plunge usually and you most likely overpay.

Option expiration dates usually cause more volatility. Retail investors do not have to concern except using wider stops. In theory, dividend days have little effect on the stock price as it will be lowered by the dividend amount.

High volume of a stock could mean opportunity

High volume usually increases the stock price volatility. If the volatility of a stock increases substantially (such as doubling its average daily volume), there could be important news on the company, recommendation changes from a major analyst or trading by the institution investors. It usually takes the institution investors a week to trade a stock with their sizable positions.

Many times it is started by the insiders who know about the breaking news of a stock before it is publicized. Some investment services / sites specialize in identifying the increasing volumes of stocks.

Because day traders do not want to leave any open positions overnight, higher volatility occurs at the end of the day. It is the same on the day (usually on Friday) when the options are expiring.

Monitor your trade prices

You cannot tell whether you are paying a fair price without keeping a record. To illustrate, you're paying 1% less than the market prices in buying stocks. You may have missed buying some winners. If the 1% you saved is smaller than the appreciation of the stocks you would have bought at market prices, then you should adjust the buy prices to 0.5% less than the market price and monitor again.

Market trend makes a difference too. When the market is trending up, buying any stock would most likely be profitable and usually the purchase orders with high discounts will not be executed.

Follow the same logic on sell orders. Need to have at least 25 stock purchases (and potential purchases) to make the conclusion meaningful. If you do not trade a lot, you do not have enough data to verify.

Good prospects

When you find gems especially those stocks that are followed by analysts, buy them even at market prices and consider doubling the bet if you are really sure you have a winner. From my super stock screens, I spotted NHTC. I placed several bets and one market order. All of them have NOT been executed except the market order. At the end of the day NHTC is up 18% and my executed order is up 14%. I did not have the best buy but made a good profit. NHTC was on its way to huge appreciation and I sold it too early. Learned not to sell a winner and protect the profit with a stop.

Lower the bet for risky stocks even they have good fundamentals.

Quality over quantity

I prefer to research a stock thoroughly than buying several stocks not thoroughly researched just for better diversification.

Double the bet on stocks that look great after the research. For risky stocks that look good, you may want to halve your normal bet to cut down the risk. If you are less risk tolerant, do not buy risky stocks at all. My results are not conclusive on risky stocks but I do have a good sleep.

A recent example
Recently I sold EA with $1 more than my order price but $2 less than the current price of the day, which was the earnings announcement day. I recommend not placing orders right before the earnings announcement day for the stock. If the earnings is good, you do not get all the profit as in this real example; my broker did get me $1 more. If the earnings is bad, you will not sell it any way. It is the same for buying stocks.

Afterthoughts

- Besides luck, the smart investor never sells at the peak but usually within 10% of the peak. No one can predict the peaks consistently.
- I made mistakes like most of you. One time my buy price was higher than the last price executed. Luckily my broker adjusted it to the right price and I would not be that lucky next time. Several times I switched the buy price and sell price by mistake. One time it was due to my boss was coming that forced me to enter my order hastily.
- Some experts do not suggest their clients to buy stocks on the way down. With respect, I offer opposing arguments.

    - It is fine to buy them on the way down, if you have the conviction that the company or the economy will recover.
    - No one knows where the bottom is, but averaging down could be beneficial if the company or the economy can recover. Check why its stock price is falling and whether the company can fix its problems. Some major problems are only temporary or easy to fix.
    - Most of my big profits are made by buying close to the bottom prices on stocks that have good potential to recover.
    - Many value stocks are on sale when the market dips. The most favorable time is in the Early Recovery, a phase in the market cycle defined by me.
    - Most experts agree that: The best time to buy is when there is blood in the street. It is demonstrated by the year 2003 and 2009.
    - Contrarians never follow the herd, but you need to have a good reason to be contrary. I recommended Apple in 2013 when every institution investor was dumping Apple.
    - Stocks are manipulated via selling shorts. When the shares of a stock to short (like over 30% of shorts) are running out, there is a good chance for a short squeeze. Ensure the company being shorted heavily is not heading to bankruptcy.
- Make good money when you are right only 45% by: 1. Limit your losses via stops and 2. Place higher stakes on stocks with higher appreciation potential.
- Some make money on earnings announcement (found in Finviz.com). Earnings would amplify the stock price by at least 5%. Once a while, there are exceptions. In the last quarter of 2015, Disney posted great results, but the stock dropped. It could be the market even expected better results or the market is not rational. I believe the later in this case.

Links

Selling short:
http://en.wikipedia.org/wiki/Short_%28finance%29
Short squeeze:
http://en.wikipedia.org/wiki/Short_squeeze
Fidelity Video: Stop Loss.
https://www.fidelity.com/learning-center/trading/trailing-stops-video

15 Stop loss & flash crash

You can limit your stock loss with stops. There are some incidents that you do not always want to use stop loss.

- <u>Flash crash</u> (May 6, 2010 also August 2015).
  It would turn your stops into market orders that could be substantially lower than your stop prices. Some brokers offer stop limits, but they do not guarantee the orders will be executed.

  The better way is "mental stop" (my term). You do not place a stop order but place a market order to sell when your stock falls below a pre-defined price. During flash crashes, you do not want to place the market orders to sell but place orders to buy from your watch list.

  I bought some stocks at more than 10% discount during the flash crash (actually I could buy them even at better discounts) and within a week most returned to the prices before the flash crash.

  Placing buy orders with huge discounts to the market prices works better for volatile stocks. However, I did buy some of these stocks due to bad news such as unfavorable earnings announcements. The strategy of always leaving some buy orders at huge discounts is not perfect. However, I should say from my experiences I won more than I lost.

  Avoid trading drug and bio companies with huge differences to the market prices. High tech is a good sector for this purpose and fluctuating 10% in this sector is more a norm than an exception. Buying an ETF at 5% discount is a better bet than buying specific stocks from my experience.

- My experience with 911.
  I sold many stocks due to stop orders during 911. The market came back in the next three days and I missed the recovery from the stocks that were sold and did not buy back in time.

- If your stocks are rising, you need adjust the stop loss prices accordingly. To illustrate in maintaining a 10% stop loss, your stop is at 90 when the current price is 100. When the stock price rises to

200, it should be adjusted to $180 (10% less than the current price). It is also called as trailing stop.

Some brokers automatically delete the stock orders over a certain period of time (1 month, 3 months…) even on 'Terminate until Cancel' orders, and these stop loss orders should be re-entered at the end of the period. Check your broker's policy.

- Risky market.
  When the market is risky, you may want to use stop loss. To prevent another flash crash, you may want to use 'mental' market order. It is not perfect, as it requires constant watching of the market.

  There are many investing services and sites that give you the 'right' prices for stop loss. Basically it depends on how volatile are the specific stocks. The chartists will tell you under normal conditions stocks are trading between the resistance line and the support line. Use the stop loss just below the resistance line to avoid the stop order being executed due to the volatility of the stock.

  For simplicity as I have too many stocks in my portfolio, I use a percent. In the old days, it is recommended 8% or so below the prices you paid for. In today's volatile market, I recommend 12%.

- Risky stocks.
  Stop loss is the only way that can limit your loss for big drop (such as 25%).
- Low-volume stocks.
  The market order could drive the prices right down as there are few buyers in low-volume stocks. If there is only one buyer, he will buy the best price for him (or the worst price to the seller).

  Unless I have good reasons, I would skip the low-volume stocks. I define low-volume: If my buy amount is higher than 1% of the average daily amount (= average daily volume * stock price).

- Beta.
  Stocks may be more volatile than the market. Beta is used to measure its volatility. The market can be measured by S&P500 index. If the beta of a stock is 1, its volatility is the same as the market. If it is 1.2, it is 20% more volatile.

Set a lower stop loss for volatile stocks to prevent stocks from selling due to regular fluctuations.

Afterthoughts

Let me show you my bitter experience. The following are 5 stocks I wanted to buy and the average return is quite good.

Stocks	Ann. Return
URI	63%
GMCR	572%
MTW	186%
PII	-74%
TSCO	-127%
Avg.	124%

I placed buy orders at 5% less than the market prices as most 'bargain' investors do. I bought all the two losers but no winner. The winners never took a breather on its way up, but the losers went down. I did buy GMCR via a market order in my momentum strategy in a separate account.

Filler:

Tip

As of 3/2014, TSLA, AMAZ, NFLX and AAPL are all over-priced by most fundamental metrics. However, they are the darlings of institution investors. My advice is not to do anything (not to buy and not to short them) as we cannot fight the city hall and the momentum.

*** Second part of this book: The advanced ***

VI Market timing

The apples you picked are sour but some other times are tasty from the same tree. You just pick them in the wrong time or in the right time. It is nothing wrong with the tree but timing.

Market timing is about educated guesses unless you have a time machine ☺. Hopefully we will have more rights than wrongs when we follow general guidelines. It would reduce risk and could benefit us financially in the long run.

I divide the market timing in three categories by durations as follows. All time durations are estimates.

1. Secular Cycle.   Duration: 20 years.
2. Market Cycle.   Duration: 5 years.
3. Correction.   Duration: 1/2 for 5% and 1 yr. for 10%.

If SMA-350% (Simple Moving Average for last 350 trade sessions) is zero, exit the market. It means the market (represented by SPY, an ETF for S&P 500) moves below its moving average (350 days). Afterwards, when it is above zero, reenter the market.

We use SMA-200 as it is readily available from finviz.com.

	SMA-350	SMA-50	SMA-200	SMA50/SMA200	RSI (14)
Market					
Peak	9%		5%	101%	65%
Bottom	-31%		-32%	78%	25%
Correction					
Peak	8%	3%	4%	102%	68%
Bottom	-7%	-5%	-8%	97%	26%
Stock					
Peak					70%
Bottom					30%

16   Market cycle

"Bull markets are born on pessimism, grow on skepticism, mature on optimism, and die on euphoria" - Sir John Templeton

The stock market has cycles as our practical interpretation of the above. It is about five years apart, but it fluctuates widely. I divide it into four stages: Bottom, Early Recovery, Up and Peak.

My defined four stages of a market cycle

We need to apply the right investing strategies to each of the four stages of the cycle.

- **Bottom**

    I would not invest for at least the first six months (or even a year) after the big plunge starts, which could lose over 25% in a few months. The exceptions are investing in contra ETFs and selling short for aggressive investors.

    I estimate it will take a year from the start of the plunge to the bottom, so I will normally sell stocks early in the plunge and do not buy stocks that are in the sector (sometimes sectors) that causes the bubble for about two years after the plunge. Do not buy the stocks even they do not have a chance to recover.

    At the bottom, the high-yield corporate bonds (i.e. junk bonds) would prosper when the interest rate is decreasing to simulate the economy.

    From mid-2007 to mid-2008, bonds suffered as the investors thought the sky was falling down - it was to those who lost the jobs and/or their houses. After that, some bonds especially the long-term bonds appreciated about 50% for the following year.

    The government lowered the interest rate and these bond prices with high interest rate surged. Correct timing in buying bonds could be very profitable.

    Long-term bonds have more impact by the interest rate: The lower the interest rate, the higher the bond prices of higher-yield bonds.

The older bonds with higher interest rates are more valuable to the newer bonds with lower interest rates.

I define this period of the bottom from the start of the plunge to the start of Early Recovery.

- **Early Recovery**

    It usually starts after one year from the plunge; no one can pin point the exact time consistently. By this time preferably earlier, we should have closed out all positions in contra ETFs and shorts.

    Roughly speaking, October, 2007 (some use 2008) is the start of the market plunge. March, 2009 is the end of the bottom stage and the start of the early recovery stage of the 2007 cycle. However, every market cycle is different in where it starts and ends.

    The one-year gain from the bottom is most profitable. It usually gains over 25% in a year from the market bottom. I, a conservative investor, had huge gain using some leverage in my largest taxable account in 2009. I recalled I had a similar return in 2003 from my memory.

    In this phase, value is a better parameter than growth in searching stocks. If your investment subscription provides a composite value score and a composite timing score, the sort parameter of your screened stocks could be "Composite Value / Composite Timing" in descending order. Select the top stocks in this order. Still have to analyze the top-screened stocks.

    Expected P/E is a good metric. However, most companies may be losing money at this stage. Those companies that can last for more than one year with its cash reserve are potential good buys. The best appreciated stocks are beaten companies that have precious technologies and good customer bases. They could be candidates to be acquired if they are small enough.

- **Up**

    Usually the growth metrics such as PEG could be better than the value metrics such as expected P/E during this phase. Most stocks are winners except contra ETFs and shorting stocks. When the growth stocks are making headlines and the defensive stocks are being dumped, this is the hint that we're well into the Up phase of the market cycle.

Locate stocks with growth metrics such as favorable PEG and high SMA-200% (from Finviz.com). Do not be scared on how much they have already appreciated. The strategy "Buy High and Sell Higher" works in this phase. Protect your profits with stops.

Ensure they have value too. Skip the stocks with expected P/Es higher than 35 unless there are good reasons. Most stocks will gain due to the tide of the market. However, when they're overbought (RSI(14) over 60), be careful. When institutional investors sell these stocks, they will crash.

- **Peak**

    When everyone makes easy money and the interest rate is high, watch out. Stop loss and/or stop limit should be used to protect your investment. Check out whether there is any bubble that would be burst like the internet in 2000 and the finance (and housing) in 2007.

    Internet crisis is easy to spot, but not the financial crisis. In 2007 we had a cycle longer than the average which is about 5 years. The plunge is very fast and very steep – thanks to the institution investors who drive the market down.

    Run the technical analysis chart described in the Chapter on Spotting Big Market Plunges at least monthly (weekly if you have time). Protect your investment. Do not fall in love with any stock (you can buy it back later at a deep discount). Making the last buck is a fool's game.

    Accumulate cash according to your risk tolerance. A retiree or a conservative investor would accumulate from 25% to 50% and should be ready to move to all cash when the plunge starts.

    We can lower the cash percent if we use enough stop loss protection. Be psychologically prepared that the stock market may still rise for a while. There is no perfect market timing.

The 2007 Cycle

The market plunged starting in 10-2007 and ending in 3-2009 (bottom), started to recover in 3-2009 (early recover), and trended up from 2010 to 1-2013 (the up phase of the market cycle). As of 3/2016, it is the peak phase defined by me.

As of 1/2013, we have recovered all the market losses since 2007. However, as of 7/2014, the economy has not fully recovered compared to the economy before the plunge. The employment judging by the medium salary has not fully recovered and the economy is not expanding. It is uncommon that the economy does not follow the market. It is due to the excessive supply of money by the government and partly due to globalization to allow companies hire overseas.

Although a W-shaped recession seldom happens, we have a chance today. We hope we do not have a depression and/or the similar lost decades that Japan has been experiencing. Some may conclude we are close to complete a market cycle from 2007 to 2016. As of 2016, the economy is recovering slowly and we're better than most other global economies.

Again, market timing is not an exact science as it involves irrational human beings and government interventions. The timing using market cycle described here is a guideline as it is hard to time it exactly.

The average market cycle is about 5 years, but they fluctuate. If we consider 2007 as the plunge, we have about 8 years of this cycle as of 2015.

In a typical cycle (few are typical), we have about one year in each of the 4 phases I defined (plunge, early recovery, up and peak).

Events/Triggers

There are financial events and triggers that cause the transition of one phase of the market cycle to another. They usually do not change the sequence of the phases (say not from Peak to Early Recovery), but they may change the duration of the phase. Examples are:

- The government announcing change of the interest rate,
- Change of employment, and
- Change of GNP.

Sectors in a market cycle (my suggestion)

Market Phase	Favorable	Unfavorable
Early Recovery	Financial, Technology, Industrial	Energy, Telecom, Utilities
Up	Technology, Industrial, Housing	
Peak	Mineral, Health Care, Energy, Long-Term Bond, Consumer Discretionary	
Bottom	Consumer Staples, Utilities	Consumer Discretionary, Technology, Industrial, Long-Term & high-yield Bond

The sectors that cause the recession usually take longer time to recover. In 2000, the technology sector was not favorable in the Early Recovery phase, contrary to the above table. In 2007, the financial sector was not favorable in the Early Recovery phase. These are the "offending" sectors that cause the plunges.

In a recession, we usually cannot cut down on consumer staples and utilities, but we can cut down buying consumer gadgets. Companies usually postpone investing in equipment and systems during a recession and expand when the economy is humming. The government usually lowers the interest rate right after the plunge to stimulate the economy.

Conclusion

When the market is about to plunge or change from one stage to another, run the described chart more frequently and read more articles written by the experts. In 2000, one article described that it could fit all the employees of a specific high-tech company into a conference room of any major corporation and the two companies had similar market cap. This article drove me to unload all of my stocks in high tech.

Again, market timing is not an exact science but it is based on educated guesses. The better guesses should have more rights than wrongs in the long term. Our actions depend on our risk tolerance. Be careful on using any new strategy that has not been fully understood and proven. Since

2000, market timing is very important to your financial health with two market plunges with an average of about 45% loss.

Afterthoughts

- The Dow Theory has a lot of followers in detecting market directions. In a nutshell, the market heading upwards is confirmed by the Industrial Index and the Transportation Index (less important in today's market especially with internet sales such as songs and movies), and vice versa. As of 4/2014, the two indexes are not in uniform.
http://finance.yahoo.com/blogs/talking-numbers/this-is-a-130-year-old-warning-sign-for-stocks-231901097.html

- The bear market has the following three phases.

    1. The market is over-valued.
    2. Corporations are not doing well with decreasing earnings and sales.
    3. Investors are selling due to fears.

    It is the reverse for a bull market: 1.The market is under-valued. 2. The market increases due to increasing corporate profits/sales and 3. Investors are buying due to greed.

- Investopedia has several articles on this topic.
http://www.investopedia.com/terms/b/businesscycle.asp

- The yield curve could predict the interest rate change and hence the economy. There are three main types of yield curve shapes: normal, flat and inverted.

    A normal yield curve is one in which longer maturity bonds have a higher yield. It is similar that the long-term CD should have a higher interest rate than the short-term CD.

    When the shorter-term yields are higher than the longer-term yields, it indicates an upcoming recession. A flat yield curve indicates the economy is transiting. Now, you've read the essence of a book on this topic costing about $50 to buy.

However especially today, it does not mean anything as the government supplies too much money to stimulate the economy unsuccessfully. My simple chart described using SMA-350 (Simple Moving Average for 350 trade sessions) which depends on the stock price works better. Click here for The dynamic yield curve.

The interest rate plays a role too. The easy money encourages folks to borrow money to buy stocks and companies to acquire other companies.

- As of Feb., 2013, I believe we're in the Up stage of the market cycle. I checked the performances of my top screens from each stage (a.k.a. phase) of the market cycle for the last 60 days. The best performance as a group belongs to the screens for the Up stage. Controversial! Always use the screens (same as searches) that perform well recently.

  In addition, the market has recovered 120% of the loss of 2007-2008. Hence the duration for an average Up stage of the market is quite close.

- Total Market Cap / GNP ratio is hotly debated on the market value. Different from the traditional 100%, I would suggest that the boundary ratio should be 130%. If it is over 130%, the market is over-valued and vice versa.
  http://www.investopedia.com/terms/m/marketcapgdp.asp

17 Spotting big market plunges

This chapter is lengthy, complicated in some concepts and requiring you to try it yourself. Make your market decision by combining all the hints described in this article.

No one can consistently predict the correct stages of the market cycle. This chapter is intended for educational purpose only. However, if we have more rights than wrongs with our calculated and educated guesses, we should do well. As in everything in life, there is no guarantee.

There are my nine hints to identify a market plunge. The average loss of market plunges from top to bottom for the last two crashes is about 45%. It could wipe out most gains for the entire market cycle. We target to avoid half of the loss.

Do not buy stocks during market plunge that could last for more than a year, which is defined by me from the market peak to the market bottom.

It is a million dollar decision for many including myself. This low-cost book serves as a reference and past performances do not guarantee future performances.

From 2000 to 2008, we only have one false signal for our SMA-350 out of 3 signals. Since then, we have more false signals. To adjust to this volatility, do not move everything to cash on an exit signal. Adjust the amount of cash according to your own risk tolerance. Usually we do not lose much (sometimes we gain some) as another signal tells us to return to the market shortly. They only have tax consequences in taxable accounts.

Ten hints of a market plunge

1. Technical analysis (TA).

    The following chart is created by Yahoo!Finance. If it does not display well on a small screen, copy the following link to your browser to display it on your PC.
    http://ebmyth.blogspot.com/2013/05/ta-graph-for-spotting-plunges-chapter.html

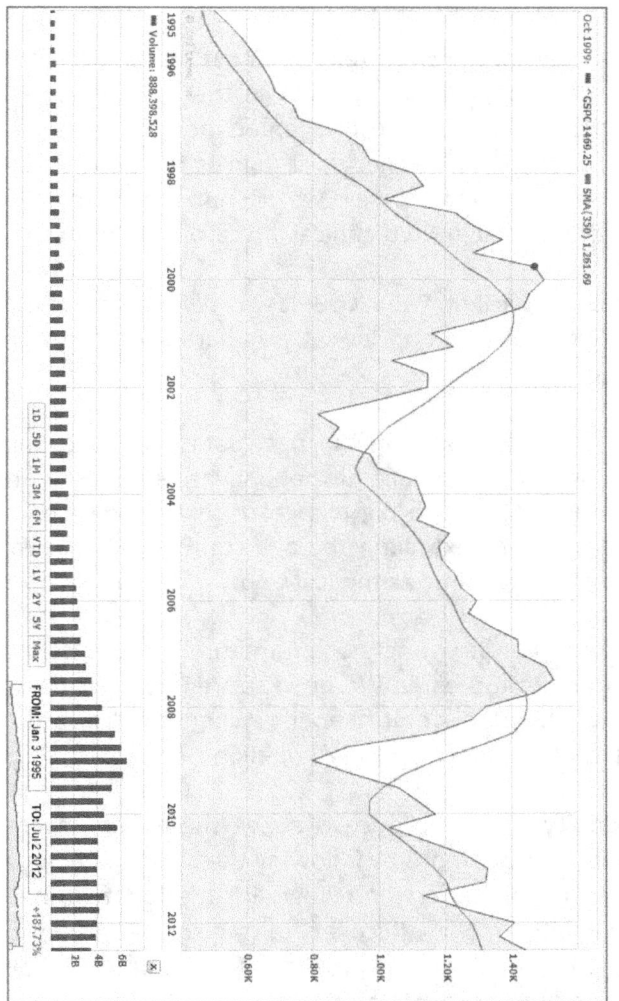

350 days simple moving average (SMA). Yahoo!Finance

The red line is the 350-day SMA, Simple Moving Average. If the stock price is below the moving average, it has detected a market plunge by this chart. Return to the market when the price is above the moving average line described as Early Recovery later. "350 days" are trading sessions. I have tried different "days" and 350 is the best fit for the last two market plunges, but it does not mean it would be the best fit the next market plunge.

We have two cycles described in the chart. From the above, we should leave the market in the first quarter of 2000 and return to the market on the first quarter of 2003.

On the second cycle, the chart tells us to get out in Dec. 2008 and come back in July 2009 approximately. Enlarge the chart by selecting 5 years instead of the maximum or use a larger monitor for a more detailed chart. The chart sometimes gives false signals to tell us to exit but tell us to reenter briefly. In most cases, we do not lose much except the tax consequences for selling. No technical indicators are perfect.

I started to come back on Feb. 2009. It was perfect timing but most likely or partly it was due to good luck. I was partially influenced by several articles I read.

Technical Analysis is based on the past data, so you cannot avoid the initial losses but it could reduce further and larger losses. From the above, the chart detected the two big plunges nicely allowing enough time to take actions. Will the next plunge be detected? It will I guess. However, it may not allow enough time as the last two.

Sometimes, we time it wrongly or prematurely and miss some gains by leaving the market too early. We need to treat it as buying insurance; it only pays big when the worst happens. When the "reward / risk" is too low, it is better to stay in cash. One's opinion.

Return to equity when the price is above the moving average (the red line). You should profit more by following the chart than 'Buy and Hold' or keeping your money under the pillow. For the last two market cycles, I returned to equities in Early Recovery (a stage of the market cycle defined by me) and profited. Can I be 100% sure for the next market plunge and come back in a timely order? Certainly not.

If most of your stocks are in tech, use QQQ instead of SPY. In addition QQQ is more volatile than SPY and the tech sector usually leads the market.

It can be created by following the steps; you need to create one yourself to detect the next plunge with current data.
- From Yahoo!Finance or any chart systems, enter SPY (or S&P 500 index) or an ETF that represents the total market.
- Select Interactive Chart.
- Click Technical Indicators.
- Select SMA (simple moving average).

- Enter 350 days (actually it is trade sessions). Many chart systems use 'month' as unit, enter 12 or 11.67 if decimals is allowed (=350/12) instead of 350.
- Enter 1-3-2000 on "FROM:" or any "from date" that fits your screen.
- Select Draw.

Note. I switch to Fidelity for charting now as I cannot produce the same info from Yahoo!Finance. It could be my fault or a bug that should be fixed.

2. Do the opposite of the flow of the dumb money.

When everyone is buying recklessly, making money and proclaiming that they are geniuses, sell. In 1999, my friend told me that he should quit his job and concentrate on investing as he was making many times in the stock market over his regular salary by spending half an hour a day. I would call myself a genius by making $1,000 an hour. When AAII's bullish sentiment (a contrary indicator to me) is over 70%, watch out.

On the same year, there were so many successful IPOs with '.com' names and these companies did not know how to make profits but blindly captured their market shares at all expenses.

They gave me $20 for just registering in their site. The poor quality of their ads showing their products during the Super Bowl reflected the quality of their management. The so-called 'MBA's business model' of capturing a potential market of one million potential sales by spending five millions is not Business 101 but Fool 101.

The inverse flow of money market funds is a good indicator too. The more money flowing into the equity funds by retail investors, the riskier is the market. Greed is a human nature. It is hard to resist buying stocks when your friends are all making good money in the market and you feel you do not want to miss the boat. I tried unsuccessfully to convince lottery winners not buying lottery and they showed me they had made another thousands yesterday.

3. Duration.

Cycles usually occur every four or five years. This is a very rough estimate as cycles often vary from 1 to 8 or even more years. The market plunge in 2007-2008 proceeded one of the longest market cycles. The longer it stays at the peak, the higher the chance the market will plunge and the further it will sink. I call it Newton's Law of Gravity or 'What goes up must come down'. When we follow the charts (technical indicators), we still stay in the market most of the time.

4. Valuation.

The average historical P/E of the S&P 500 is about 15. When it is over the average, be careful. Obtain the P/E of SPY (an ETF for the S&P 500) from Yahoo!Finance and confirm it in many other sources. When the average P/E of a sector is over 35, most likely there will be a fierce correction for that sector. When it is over 40, the market most likely has peaked. When you find fewer value stocks than before, it means the market is riskier now.

The P/E of S&P 500 was 28 in 2000. It was 18 in 2007 and 16 in 2015. Both are over 15, the average value for the last five years.

The value of the average P/E has to be adjusted as the market conditions are not the same 10 or so years ago. Today (2016) part of the earning (the E in P/E) is due to the low cost in borrowing and less wage cost due to hiring overseas. Most global corporations can offshore jobs to reduce expenses. The global economies are inter-connected far better than before. When the global economies fall, we will fall too.

5. Triggers to burst a bubble.

In 2000, the trigger was the tech bubble. In 2007 it was the housing (or financing) bubble. It was easy to spot a massive tech bubble in 2000. I moved most of my tech sector funds to traditional sectors (cash for 20-20 hindsight) in the beginning of April, 2000, which was too close for comfort to this market plunge.

Most investors including myself did not understand the workings of the derivatives of the mortgage loans and could not recognize the bubble. I made good money in the oil sector in 2007. However, in 2008 most of my investments were losers including the investment in the oil sector. If I followed the hints described in this chapter, I would have avoided heavy losses.

6. Rising interest rate.

It is more expensive for investors using margin to buy stocks, for companies to borrow money and for consumers to buy high ticket items and houses.

A related hint is rising margin debt (the debt used to buy stocks backed up by the current stock holdings). When we have a record margin debt as in 2016, the chance of a market plunge is high when the Fed hikes the interest rate.

When the Fed discount rate is 5% or above, be careful. This is also the time to buy long-term bonds. When it is 1% or less, most likely the market starts to recover. This is also the time NOT to buy long-term bonds. This strategy was proven in market cycles in 2000 and 2008.

7. Yield Curve.

When the short-term (say 3 month) interest rate is higher than the long term (say 30 years), it is abnormal and a bearish signal. Click here to check the yield curve.

http://www.treasury.gov/resource-center/data-chart-center/interest-rates/Pages/TextView.aspx?data=yield
http://blogs.marketwatch.com/thetell/2014/05/13/bear-market-wont-come-until-the-yield-curve-says-so-kleintop/

8. Rising oil price.

It is the same as the above as rising oil price will cause everything more expensive. However, today (2015-2016) is an exception. The falling oil price correlates with the market. It is due to falling too much and the oil-producing countries have to dump the stocks to rescue their economies.

9. Market experts.
There are always two camps predicting the market trend. Check out those that make sense and ignore those who try to sell you books or their services. The media try to scare you to improve the circulation. The reason I exited the market in April, 2000 is the result of reading an article that said the entire company of an internet company could fit into a conference room of a company with the same market cap. Good seeds fall in fertile soil will prosper. The opposite is true when bad seeds fall in any kind of soil.

10. Politics.

The long market rise from 2009 to 2016 is due to the low interest rate even the economy is not doing well. The interest rate is controlled by the Federal Reserve Bank, which is an agent of the government.

After WW2, the market has never been down in a year right before election.

Be conservative

As in any new strategy, test it out and try it out gradually with real money. Most of you paid less than $25 for this book and most likely you do not want to risk all your money based on a $25 advice, so consult your financial advisors.

You should not lose money by exiting the market too early, but miss the opportunity to make more money. If the market does not crash, treat it as insurance.

The chart worked fine for the last two crashes, but as in life there is no guarantee to detect the next market crash for the following reasons:

- It may not give us ample of time to react as the last two. The current market is high and is caused by excessive money supply. When the money supply is reduced (or no more QEn), the market will react negatively.

- When too many folks buy my books and use the same chart, it will lose its effectiveness. It is most likely not, but there is always a chance.

- Past performances do not guarantee future performance.

- The market is not always rational.

- There are more noises (crossing the red line and backing again briefly) since 2011. The chart is not the only indicator I follow. Adjust it according to your risk tolerance.

  However, if you follow the chart, you're doing quite well since 2000. From 2000 to 2010, we only have 3 exits/entries and one is very brief.

  Since 2011, there are several exits/entries as the market is not rational. However, if you follow it, you're still faring well as they tell you reentry very quickly. You do not lose or gain a lot by doing so. Even if you lose a little, it could be the best insurance you bought.

The noises would be increased if we use 200 days in SMA in the chart instead of 350. For the same reason, they will be decreased if I use 400 days but the signal will be later delayed.

As in life, there is nothing guaranteed, the chart is far better than market timing without charts and/or no market timing at all since 2000. As of 6/2015, I started looking at my charts more frequently months as we've been living dangerously on borrowed time for a long while.

Conclusion

This article provides my basic tools and my views on market timing. Market is not always rational otherwise there are no poor folks as stated before. When the market is about to plunge, run the chart more frequently and read more articles written by market experts.

Market timing is not an exact science but it is based on educated guesses. The better guesses should have more rights than wrongs in the long term. Your actions depend on your risk tolerance. Initially you should be careful on using any strategy that you do not have full understanding and enough proven record.

The following sub topics are separated in order to simplify a complicated topic.

Using VIX as a timing model

When I overlapped VIX and S&P500, I found a consistent pattern. However, it has not been conclusive to me. Try to enter VIX in any chart system such as Yahoo!Finance with S&P500 overlapped. In the summer of 2008, VIX jumped about 500% from about 15 to 89.

Links for more info

VIX
http://en.wikipedia.org/wiki/VIX
VIX from Yahoo!Finance.
http://finance.yahoo.com/echarts?s=^VIX+Interactive#

There are several articles on the topic.
http://seekingalpha.com/instablog/434935-south-gent/3373095-vix-asset-allocation-model.
Ted Talk: 1
http://www.ted.com/talks/didier_sornette_how_we_can_predict_the_next_financial_crisis

Other technical indicators

- Header and Shoulder would predict a market plunge as evidenced in 2007. The reverse pattern would predict a market surge as indicated in 2009.
- Double Top is a bearish signal and double bottom is a bullish signal.
- Death Cross is used to detect marge plunges and it does not require charting via finviz.com. Golden Cross detects when to return.
- MACD (Moving Average Convergence Divergence). When the indicator is below the zero line, it is bearish and vice versa. Use it as a secondary indicator to detect the market direction.
- When RSI (14) is over 65%, the market is most likely overbought (i.e. over-valued).
- Use the following SMA-20 as a secondary indicator as an alternative to the SMA-350. When the stock price is below SMA-20 (Single Moving Average for the last 20 sessions) for the consecutive 3 days, it indicates a possible market plunge. In theory, the institution investors dump the stock on the first day and then the retail investors follow on the second day. If it continues on the third day, most likely it is not the trick of the institution investors to take advantage of the retail investors.

Fear and Greed

This index from cnnFn.com is a similar contrary index. Leave the market when Greed is high and vice versa.

Many high-flying internet stocks lost more than 95% of their peak values. As in any bubble, the last ones to get into the bubble suffer most. The investors make out pretty nicely if they use the strategies below:

- Use stop loss to protect the profits. Adjust the order when the stock appreciates.
- Use SMA-20% (from Finviz.com). When the stock falls below Simple Moving Average for the last 20 sessions, sell it. Use SMA-50 instead if you have higher risk tolerance.

Other related hints on value

The oil and industrial commodities (copper, steel...) are within 20% of their record highs. From my memory, it is the first time that oil is in sync with the market due to the dumping of stocks by the oil-producing countries today.

The total market cap is higher than the GDP. As of Nov., 2013, "Market Cap / GDP" is about 110% (fair at 85%) and hence it is over-valued. Daily ratios can be obtained from GuruFocus.com, a paid subscription service. It does not work in the current cycle from 2008. It may be today due to most large companies are multi-national. However, today most large companies are global companies, so it loses some luster in using this ratio.

From my observation, the higher the interest rate is, the higher the chance for a market plunge will be. The companies will have less earnings due to the higher borrowing costs especially in businesses that require a lot of borrowing and/or most of their customers' purchases are via financing. The stocks are more expensive to buy using margin accounts. Hence, the market will not fare well when the Fed hikes the interest rate.

Q including intangible assets is with P/E in evaluating the value of the market. It is harder to calculate.

Shiller P/E (same as CAPE or PE10)
It can be used to detect the valuation of the market. The P is the S&P500 (or use SPY) and E is the average earnings of last 10 years. It can also be used on sector ETFs and stocks. Use it as one of the hints. The major flaw is 10 years is too long a time.

To simplify, most likely the market valuation is low (good to buy) when the P/E is below 15. The market valuation is high when it is above 20. As of 2014, it is far above 20 (17 in 2/2016). CAPE (cyclically adjusted price/earnings ratio) is available from the web by searching "CAPE P/E" to get the current reading.
Shiller's P/E   http://www.gurufocus.com/shiller-PE.php

From the above links, CAPE has been pretty decent. The reason why it does not work in 2014 is the excessive money printing that makes the market not rational. Treat it as a secondary yardstick at best.

18 Actions for different stages of a market cycle

There are different strategies for the different stages of the market cycle.

Strategies during market plunges

The market plunge is defined as the period between the market peak and the market bottom. It usually lasts for one year or two.

When you spot the potential plunge, consider the following actions. It depends on your risk tolerance and your investment style.

1. Contrary to popular belief, parking cash is a strategy too. Cash is needed later to move back to equities.
2. Be conservative: Buy stocks based on value and not based on momentum. Reduce your new purchases and take profits especially on momentum stocks. I buy one stock for every two or three stocks I sold during this stage.
3. Protect your portfolio with stop orders. It is one of the few times I recommend stop orders. If you watch the market every day, just place market orders when your stock falls to a specific price.
4. Buy contra ETFs for aggressive investors.
5. Sell cover calls. I prefer to sell the stocks I own.
6. Older folks may not want to sell the stocks with huge gains (due to tax consideration) or stocks that give them income stream of dividends. They can use options to protect potential losses for the stocks they own.

What to do after the plunge
In the first year after the start of the plunge, do not start to buy unless they are very good values. Aggressive investors should start closing their short positions/put options and selling contra ETFs.

When the market plunges, it usually takes at least one year to recover as investors believe they have to sell to protect their remaining nest eggs. Those sectors that cause the bubble will take even longer to recover.

After the plunge, watch out for the interest rate. If it is still high, it is the best time to buy high-yield bonds (i.e. junk bonds). Ensure that the corporation issuing the bonds would not bankrupt; the bonds from the old GM in 2007 lost most of their values. They will appreciate when the interest rate drops that the government would routinely do to stimulate the economy. 2008 is not a good year to invest in stocks and bonds except the contra ETFs and selling shorts, but 2009 definitely is (it is my Early Recovery phase of the market cycle).

Personally I prefer not to buy any stocks until the chart tells us to reenter the market. It is the fear that investors do not want to reenter the market. The market will always recover as in the past history.

Even before the recovery, some sectors (called consumer staple) are doing better such as health care, foodstuffs, utilities and pharmaceuticals that are always in demand. Interest-sensitive sectors such as housing and auto will suffer disproportionately. They are also called cyclical stocks. Consumer Discretionary are sectors that suffer a lot in a recession such as high-tech products.

What to do in early recovery and after
When the market is starting to recovery (2003 and 2009 in the last two market cycles), the potential profit is the highest. Buy deeply-valued stocks on companies that have been beaten. They will recover with the highest appreciation potential. I call it the bottom fishing strategy.

Larger companies are fishing too to acquire smaller companies that fit into their corporate synergy or small companies with the technology and/or the customer base they need.

Valued stocks could be defined a little differently in this phase. Many times P/E is not a good metric as most companies are losing money. 2003 is such a year. If you expect the recession will end in 2 years and the company has enough cash to survive in two years based on its annual burn rate, then it would be a buy candidate.

In both 2003 and 2009, I spotted at least one company that was acquired by larger company. From my memory, one company in 2003 was acquired by IBM giving me more than 2 times return. In 2009, at least three companies were acquired giving me an average annualized return of over 200%.

Momentum strategy rewards us best from the end of the early recovery phase to the peak phase. The up phase started in 2004 for 2000 market cycle and 2010 in the 2007 market cycle.

Metric performances & market cycle

From my limited testing on the last two market cycles (2000 and 2008), some metrics perform better than the other. This is for reference only. I select the following metrics. Grades are estimates from a hypothetical vendor.

- EY, Expected Earning Yield (Expected Earnings/Price).
- TG, Timing Grade. It is based on price momentum, increases in sales and profits...
- VG, Value Grade. It is based on fundamentals such as P/E, Debt/Equity...

Cycle stages	Performers	Bad Performers
Year before plunge	TG, EY	VG
Plunge to bottom	TG	EY
Early Recovery	EY, VG	
Up and Peak	EY, TG	
All stages	EY, TG, VG	

- They are in descending order. For example in All Stages, EY has better performance than TG.
- EY and TG are good in almost all phases. The exception for EP is poor performance during market plunges. For aggressive users, short the stocks that have high EY at this stage.
- EY turns out to be best performer during Early Recovery, a phase in the market cycle defined by me. In this phase buy stocks with high EY and VG. It has been proven in 2003 and 2009.
- I expect EY is part of the VG. However, my tests tell me otherwise.
- EY, TG and VG are metrics close to 'evergreen'.
- I also have other metrics that may not be relevant to the general discussion. They are growth of earnings, growth of E/P, growth of dividends...
- The performances of many AAII strategic screens are provided. Separate them in the phases of a market cycle and make the conclusions accordingly.

VII Market timing by calendar

Some periods are more favorable than others statistically. They do not always work as predicted, so do not commit more than 25%.

19   Market timing by calendar

The following predictions are based on historical data. You may have slightly different findings depending on when you start and when you end the test.

You can load the historical data of SPY via Yahoo!Finance and check out how close or different from my predictions. They are my predictions based on historical data. Use it as a reference only.

- Presidential cycle.
  Usually the market performs worse in the first two years after the election than the next two. During the 3rd year the president has to make the economy look rosy in order to buy votes. Statistically it is the best year for the market and is followed by a good year (the election year). The government may stimulate the economy, the stock market and employment by printing more money, lowering interest rate and lowering taxes.

  Democratic presidents have better market performance statistically than Republican presidents. It is not too logical as Republicans are more pro-business traditionally.

- Olympics.
  It has been proven that the host country has a better chance that its stock market appreciates the year after. It could be due to the exposure from the Olympics and / or the huge expenses in preparing the Olympics.

  The last two Olympics follow this pattern as of 12/23/2013:

Olympics Country / Year	ETF	Period	Return
United Kingdom / 2012	EWU	Jan. 3, 2013 - Dec. 23,2013	11%
China / 2008	FXI	Jan. 3, 2009 - Dec. 31, 2009	43%

  Greece could be an exception. It is too small a country to host this world-class event and it has wasted too many resources by building too many white elephants that the country can never justify. Brazil depends on its export of natural resources to China, so I do not count on its Olympics effect.

Winning a lot of Olympic medals has no indication for the stock markets. Both the Russian Empire and E. German were winners but disappeared in their original forms afterwards.

- Seasonal.
  Best profitable period is: Nov. 1 to April 30 next year. It is similar to the saying 'Sell in May and Go away'. It did not work since 2009 as it was Early Recovery in the market cycle.

  The market does not always happen as predicted. However, when more folks follow, it becomes a self-fulfilling prophecy. I prefer "Sell on April 15 and come back on Oct. 15" to act before the herd. The more practical strategy is to start selling in April 1 and become more aggressive (selling at closer to the market prices) when it is close to May 1. For the last five years, I do not find this prediction reliable.

  The explanation of the 'summer doldrums' could be the investors cash their stocks for vacations and college tuitions in the fall. Buying quality companies at the dips could be profitable.

- The worst month: September.
  The next worst month is October. However, if there is no serious market crash during October (and this month has more than its shares of crashes), it could be the best month to buy stocks.

- The best month for the bull: November.
  However, several market bottoms occurred in October and November. The next strong month is December.

- Best 30 days: Dec. 15 to Jan. 15, next year.
  It was correct for the period of 2012-2013.

- Window dressing.
  Institution investors sell their losers and buy winners around Nov. 1. From my rough estimate and on the average, the winners have a 2% percentage point better than the market and the losers have 1% worse than the market.

Recommend to evaluate the top 10 winners from last 10 months or YTD in Oct. 15 and sell them at 3% gain or two months later.

Recommend to buy in Dec. and sell them 3 months later. Include the stocks with more than 30% loss for the last 11 months or YTD, sort them by Earning Yield in descending order and evaluate the top 10 stocks.

In both cases, do not buy foreign stocks and stocks with return of capital. Ignore stocks not in the three major exchanges, with low volumes and stock prices less than $2. Do not buy in losing years such as 2007 and 2008. I have my tests with my own assumptions and I use tools not available to all.

It is a guideline only. Do not buy any stocks during market plunges. Current events should be considered first such as a potential war and the hiking of interest rate.

Afterthoughts

- I predict it will be a sideways market in the later part of 2013. I am following the sideway strategy: Buy at dips and sell at ups. One's prediction.

- Why September has a bad reputation?
  http://www.marketwatch.com/story/betting-on-septembers-terrible-odds-2013-08-27?dist=beforebell

The September of 2013 (2 days away at the time of writing) will have more problems. Check it out how many the following are correct on Oc. 1, 2013. Use it as a future guideline to predict the next September using the current market conditions then:

1. The market is not excessively expensive, but it is not cheap. It is due for a 5% correction.
2. Unrest in Syria (check any unrest in your next prediction on September).
3. High oil price due to Syria.
4. September is a statistically bad month for the stock market. However, it could be an opportunity to invest after the correction if any.
5. Interest rate is rising.

6. All the above indicate the market will dip. However, the rosier outlook is the global economies are improving even slowly.

- January effect.
  The performance of January may determine how the entire year performs. I cannot find any rationale but it has been proven right statistically.

- Earnings period announced in Jan., April, July and Oct. would cause big swings in stocks when they have surprises. Earning revisions could be a good predictor.
  http://www.investopedia.com/terms/e/earningsseason.asp

Links
Presidential Cycle:
http://www.investopedia.com/articles/financial-theory/08/presidential-election-cycle.asp

Calendar-based market timing:
http://stock-chartist.com/2010/10/calendar-based-market-timing/

Calendar market timing for 2013:
http://www.investorecho.com/archives/8047

20 Summary

I made the following charts so it is easier to time the market by calendar.

All dates are inclusive.

No.	Metric		Score
1	Seasonal	Nov. - April, Score = 1	
2	Best Month	Nov., Score = 1	
		Sep., Score = -1	
3	Best Days	Dec. 15 – Jan. 15 Score = 1	
4	Presidential Cycle	Election Year, Score = 1	
		1st Year in Office, Score = -1	
		2nd year, Score = -1	
		3rd year, Score = 2	
5	Presidential[3]	Democratic = 1 Republican = -1	
6	Market Cycle	Early Recovery, Score = 3	
		Up, Score = 2	
		Peak, Score = 1	
7	SPY (Finviz.com)	SMA200% > 8%[2] Score = -1	
		SMA200% < 0 Score = -1	
		RSI(14) > 65% Score = -1	
		Grand Score	

Footnote.
[1] Refer to Market Cycle chapter on how I define phases of a cycle.
[2] For simplicity, use Finviz.com. Enter SPY and you will find SMA200% and RSI(14) to predict whether the market is peaking and overbought.
[3] I'm political neutral. The selection is based on historical statistics.

Add up all the scores. The passing grade is 0. According to my table which is based on my personal selections/preferences, the market is favorable when the grand score is 1 or higher. I bet it is the first time you see such a scoring system for market timing.

Sectors for market cycle

Market Phase[1]	Favorable	Unfavorable
Early Recovery	Financial, Technology, Industrial	Energy, Telecom, Utilities
Up	Technology, Industrial	
Peak	Mineral, Health Care, Energy	
Bottom	Consumer Staples, Utilities	Consumer Discretionary, Technology, Industrial

Seasonal	Favorable	Unfavorable
Winter	Energy, Utilities	
End of year	QQQ, EWG	
Olympics	ETF for host country[2]	

Footnote.
[1] Refer to Market Cycle chapter on how I define phases of a cycle.
[2] Buy it next year after Olympics. It could be due to higher GDP or the publicity. However, be selective. Greece is too small a country to host an Olympics.

VIII Evaluating Stocks

21 Fundamental metrics

ROE

Return of equity (ROE = Net Income / Equity) could be the most important financial indicator to determine how well the management is doing their job. However, in recent years, this metric has been overused and loses its prediction reliability.

The company's return on equity for at least the last five years would indicate how the stock price endures major financial downturns as well as upturns.

Comparing the ROE to the average ROE for the sector is a good indicator on how well the company is managed compared to its peers. Some sectors including utilities have low average ROEs.

Market Cap (Capitalization)
Market Cap = Total no. of outstanding shares * share price

I recommend the beginners buy U.S. stocks with a market cap greater than 800 M (million). Here are the current conventions (everyone's convention is different) and they should be adjusted to inflation.

Class	Market Cap (million)
Nano Cap	< $50M
Micro Cap	$50M to $250M
Small Cap	$250M to $1B (billion)
Mid Cap	$1B to $10B
Large Cap (Blue Chip)	$10B to $50B
Mega Cap	>50B

The higher the cap is, usually the less risky the stock would be. Nano Cap and Micro Cap are reserved for speculators or owners of the companies. Small Cap and Mid Cap are for knowledgeable investors as most institutional investors would skip these stocks in these caps especially Small Cap. Large Cap, Mega Cap and some Mid Cap are the stocks traded by institutional investors. They are thoroughly researched continuously.

My metrics

My current favorites are Forward P/E, PEG, Fidelity's Equity Summary Score, Short % of outstanding shares, Free Cash Flow, ROE and Debt Load / Equity.

In addition, I use many summarized metrics from different sources. For example, one of my subscription services gives me a composite rank for fundamentals and another one for momentum. To illustrate, click here for Blue Chip Growth which is no longer free for stock analysis. Enter IBM as the stock symbol. As of 2/2013, it gives C for a Total Grade, D for Quantity Grade and B for Fundamental Grade. The Total Grade is usually a composite grade of other grades.

Use the metrics to screen through the stocks to reduce the number of stocks for further consideration.

Mid, high and low values of common metrics

Metric	Mid Range	Low Range	High Range
P/E (last 12 months)	< 10	>40	< 4
Price / Cash Flow	< 12	>30	< 4
Price / Sales	< 2.5	>3	< .2
Price / Book	< 2.0	>4	< .2
PEG	< 1.5	>2	< .2

High Range means good values (although in this table it means low numbers), but sometimes it is too good to be true. Low Range means bad values. To illustrate, many internet stocks in 2000 had P/E over 40 (bad) while a neglected bargain stock has a P/E of 3 (supposed to be good). A bargain could also mean they could have some hidden problems. In reality, I prefer the Mid Range. Using P/E to illustrate, it should be between 4 and 10. Adjust the range according to your personal tolerance and the current market conditions. If the market trend is up, you may want to relax the range to 5 to 12 for example otherwise you cannot find too many stocks for further evaluation.

These values are my selections based on data for about 10 years. They are used for predicting the performance of a stock in a year; review the ranges every 6 months in the current market.

The metrics with the high-range and mid-range values offer better predictions for the stock price appreciation. From the above table, the stocks with the low-range values have a better chance than other stocks to lose money in a year or so. Some favorable numbers could be high values instead of low values such as ROE.

However, the range values could change. When the market favors momentum or you do not keep stocks for less than a month or so, the momentum metrics including PEG and price growth could be better predictors. We need to check to see whether the current market favors which metrics: Value or Growth – some websites and subscription services identify the current favorite. In addition, the performance of each metric should be evaluated every 3 to 6 months. In addition, new range values need to be adjusted with the above table.

Fundamental metrics take a longer time (about 6-12 months vs. 1 month for momentum metrics) for the performance to materialize. The metrics in the above table besides PEG are all fundamental metrics. Except for financial stocks, P/B is always worthless.

Examples of searching with high range values

Stocks with low-range values for most metrics (such as 40 in P/E in the above table) could be risky. Hence, select the stocks with the mid-range value (e.g., 10 for P/E). Avoid the low-range values indicated by the metrics.

Here is one example of selecting stocks with high range values of P/E and P/B. Most likely, you will not find too many stocks with these criteria.

$E > 0$ and
$P/E < 4$ and
$P/B < .2$

E is earning per share and we need the company to be profitable.

High range values could indicate something is wrong with the company, e.g., a lawsuit pending. I would consider a P/E of less than 4 is suspicious. However, very small companies are often neglected by the market, so they could be solid companies. Don't forget to do your due diligence and spend more time in thoroughly evaluating the stock and its industry.

The stocks with the low-range values have a greater chance of losing money in the next year or so. That is proven statistically as a group despite some exceptions. AMZN[2] is not a valued stock by its high P/E or its high P/B. However, if the company is investing for the future by building infrastructure and capturing the market share, you may ignore these unfavorable metrics. Personally, I prefer fundamentally sound companies today.

Note. P/B is not a good metric for established companies and / or companies with a lot of research such as IBM. Many metric formulae are outdated due to ignoring intellectual properties, patents and market appeals such as brand names.

Example of a search for mid-range values
E > 0 and
P/E < 10 and
P/E > 4

In this case, you only include companies with positive earnings and P/Es within the range from 4 to 10 exclusively. You should find many companies with the mid-range values of P/Es.

Add other filters such as minimum price, market cap and average volume. If you do not find too many stocks, relax your criteria (start with mid-range values in the table), and vice versa to limit the number of stocks. If you usually find stocks with a screen but not today, it usually means that the market is overvalued and that you cannot find many bargain stocks.

Again, it is the first step to narrow down the number of stocks to be analyzed. Your metrics will not cover stocks with special situations. For example, IBM always has had a high Price/Book value for as long as I can remember and therefore it does not mean it should be excluded.

The searches based on fundamental metrics help us to narrow stocks for further evaluation. Occasionally I abandon the scoring system for some stocks under special conditions.

Compare a company's metrics to its sector's averages
This could be the most powerful comparison: Compare Apples to Apples.

You may want to compare the metrics of a company to the averages of that sector. The average of supermarket's P/S is extremely low and hence it has no meaning to compare a supermarket's P/S to most other sectors. Some sectors like utilities need high debt to run a utility company.

However, when the average P/E or other metric of a sector is suddenly lower than its historical average, it could mean that sector is out-of-favor and/or the sector is having a better value.

This following table compares Apple to its sector and a retail sector on a specific date for illustration. All the metrics will change.

Metric	Apple	Computer	Retail
P/E	11	19	24
(5-year average)	16	17	15
PEG	.6	N/A	1.4
Price /Cash Flow	9.4	8.1	9.2
Price /Book	3.3	3.0	3.6
EPS Growth	-6%	-42%	2.6%
(last 5 years)	62%	45%	11%
Operating Margin	20%	15%	8%
ROE	30%	14%	19%
Debt / Equity	2%	7%	88%
Inventory Turnover	76%	53%	4.55x

From the above table, some metrics only make sense for an industrial sector (Computer for Apple). In this case, you may want to compare AAPL to Computer, and not to Retail.

"Debt / Equity" indicates that the retail sector needs to borrow more than the computer sector for example. Of course, retail stores have high Inventory Turnover.

Top-down approach

First, compare whether the market is risky. Second, select the best sector; there are many sites including Finviz.com to select the best sector. Then compare the fundamental metrics of the major stocks within that sector.

Some metrics do not apply

Using financial institutions as an example, usually P/B is more useful than P/CF. However, the quality of a loan (not a metric here) is more important than all metrics as we found out in 2007. P/S is more important for retails. However, the expected P/E is most important for most other sectors.

When you believe a sector is the currently best (a criterion available in many screeners), select the best stocks in this sector.

Compare metrics to its five-year average

If the company's five-year average of P/E (available from Fidelity and many other sites) is 20 and today it is 10. It is 100% under-valued by this standard. Also, you may want to try other metrics such as debt/equity and compare it to the five-year average.

Growth Metrics

The growth metrics are growth rates of the stock price, sales, earnings, etc. They are useful for growth investors.

Even for value investors, the earnings growth rate is very important, as most stocks with substantial gains have increased their earnings growth first. If the earnings has grown but the price remains the same (i.e., PEG), then the potential for price appreciation will be higher and most likely it will return to the historical average P/E.

Momentum Metrics

Momentum metrics is part of growth. The rates of increase of the stock price, the volume... are the major metrics. Earnings revision is another one especially in earnings announcement seasons (usually 4 times a year).

Fidelity and many subscription services provide a composite rank with name Timely or similar name. The following could be part of this Timely score: SMA-50, Q-Q sales increase and recent price appreciation. In my momentum portfolio, I use these metrics and ignore all the other metrics as my average holding period is less than 30 days for momentum strategies.

Insiders' buying

Insiders sell their stocks for many reasons. When insiders buy a lot of their companies' stocks at market prices, take notice. Insiders know better than anyone about the health of their companies and their industries.

Select Insiders' purchases from one of the available sites such as Finviz.com. Ignore the option exercises. I prefer the high ratios of Net Total Purchase Value / Market Cap and the purchases by more than one insider. Be careful that the insiders purchase the stocks after selling a similar amount of stock in a brief time span.

OpenInsider is a good site for this info.
InsiderSights is a good one too with more capable tools that would take more time to learn.

Where to get the metrics
You can get this information from the website with no or low cost such as Finviz.com, your broker's site, AAII (very low cost) and Fidelity.

The following subscriptions are at a little higher cost but they are still less than $1,000 per year: Value Line, IBD, Zacks, VectorVest and Stock Screen 123. Many data from different vendors are duplicated such as P/E. You will save time by concentrating on one or two sources.

Many vendors provide a composite metric such as a value metric to cover P/E, debt... and a timing metric to cover Technical Analysis indicators, PEG, price appreciation rate...

Short % is a useful metric available in Finviz.com. For Fidelity customers, you can click on Research and then Stock. Enter the stock name, and then click on Detailed. I find Fidelity's Analysts' Opinions quite useful.

Finviz.com provides a lot of useful information free of charge. It also provides a screen function. The 'Help' button describes Finviz's functions and all the metrics monitored.

Other sources are: Insider Cow, NASDAQ Guru Analysis ...

Monitor the recent performance of the metrics
The predictability of most metrics has proven not to perform consistently as many investors and fund managers found out. My theory is that the specific metric works better in some market conditions than others. To test which ones work better currently, check their performance in the last three months and use those that perform well. This is what my scoring system in the book Scoring Stocks is based on.

Why some metrics fail sometimes

Most investors are using metrics to screen stocks, but few are successful consistently. Some investment companies have top analysts dedicated to projects looking for the right strategy. My guesses why they fail are:

1. Metrics need to be monitored to see its effectiveness on current market conditions.

2. Besides fundamental metrics, there are many intangibles.

3. When they have too many followers on the same metrics, they will not work such as ROE in the last several years.

4. Fundamentals need time (at least 6 months) to reflect the value of the stock. You're swimming against the tide as a fundamentalist. Trading momentum stocks using basic fundamentals will not work.

5. Watch out 'Garbage in and garbage out'. Some emerging countries do not have an organization similar to SEC to ensure the integrity of the financial statements of a company and some audit firms are being paid to cover their eyes. Even though there are frauds in some U.S. companies and with their auditors.

6. The metrics may be derived from obsolete financial statements. Check out the date. The most updated one could be available from the company's website.

7. Some companies borrow a lot of money to dress up the metrics such as P/E and ROE. They will look good short-term but not long-term. Ensure the debt/equity has not been increased recently for this purpose. I recall one utility spin-off had incredible fundamentals except the debt load. It is so high that all these fundamentals will deteriorate in the future due to servicing its high debts.

Footnote

[1] The stocks are classified into sector and then sectors are divided into industries (same as sub sectors). For example, oil is a sector and oil exploration and oil services are industries under the oil sector. For simplicity, I intermix the terms here as many sectors do not need further sub classifications for this discussion.

[2] AMZN is not a value stock by any standard. As of 1/1/2013, its P/E (from last 12 months) is 157 and P/B is 15. Both fall far into my low-range values. Its price rises from 256 from 1/1/13 to 270 today (1/22/13). Today its P/E is ridiculously over 3,000. The investors are betting AMZN's internet sales will take over the concrete stores and its investors do not care about profit but rather for market share. Does it sound familiar in the internet era? Its price momentum is indicated positively by any chart. It may be a good stock for traders, but it is too risky for a swing trader and a long-term investor like me (yes, I wear two hats). I do not short stocks in a rising market, but this could be an exception.

Afterthoughts

- The only recommendation from a very popular investment book I read is to select stocks by the return of equity (ROE). I will save you the time and money to read that book. I read the entire book in an hour at Barnes and Noble's and it saved me some money / time, not to mention cutting down trees for that book. Basically, it does not work today.
- DAL has an interesting Debt / Equity of over -1000% due to the negative equity. For a comparison, you may want to use Debt / ABS(Equity).
- Once in a while, I found the financial data was not consistent from different sources. Try to check out any discrepancy in the dates of the financial data of your sources. The financial statements from the company websites usually have the most updated data.
- Current Ratio = Current Asset / Current Liability. If it is below 1, then the company is having a tough time in meeting its current cash obligations.
- Dividend Yield is a valid metric for matured companies. I do not use it to evaluate growth companies or companies that need to plow back cash for research and development.
- If you use Finviz.com, you find three margins: profit, gross and operating. I prefer to use profit margin that is more useful for most companies. The other two may be relevant in some sectors.

  http://www.investopedia.com/terms/p/profitmargin.asp
  http://www.investopedia.com/terms/g/grossmargin.asp
  http://www.investopedia.com/terms/o/operatingmargin.asp

Use Wikipedia for more description.
- Enron had millions in profits but negative cash flows. Earnings can be manipulated but not the cash flows.

Insiders' selling usually does not cause any alarm unless excessively. Most insiders sell most of the stocks they have before these companies go bankrupt. Just common sense!
- Why fundamentals are important.
(http://seekingalpha.com/article/1612442-its-shorting-season)

On the same day when this article was published, RVLT was up 10% due to increasing sales in the earnings conference. However, the company is still not profitable. It shows how tough shorting is even with good arguments. That's why do not expect every purchase is profitable. However, with the educated guesses, you should beat the market in the long run.
- Due to my ignorance, limited time or my short period of holding stocks, I have not used intrinsic value that often.

Book value is different from intrinsic value. Book value is calculated by summing up the values of all pieces of a company such as a building and all equipment. Intrinsic value is the real value of a company. When two companies have the same book value and market cap, the company that generates more profit than the other one usually has a higher intrinsic value. When the intrinsic value is higher than the stock price, it is underpriced in theory.

Links:
Income statement: https://www.youtube.com/watch?v=ht-tzwyLPU
The following link provides more info on intrinsic value.
http://en.wikipedia.org/wiki/Intrinsic_value_%28finance%29
https://www.youtube.com/watch?v=I-T-Vyk2txc&authuser=0

22   Mysteries of P/E

If you believe you can make good money by selecting stocks with low P/Es solely, dream on. If it were that easy, there would be no poor folks. However, buying fundamentally sound companies would reduce the risk and improve the chance of its appreciation.

P/E is the most misunderstood indicator. To me, it is the most useful one among all metrics if it is properly used. Earnings are the key to stock appreciation and P/E measures its value. To illustrate on P/E, you pay a million for a hot-dog cart in NYC. Even if its earnings increase year after year, you will never recoup your investment as you have paid too much even for a good business.

"Buy stocks with P/E below 15 and earnings positive" is not true in many cases. P/E growth (PEG) should be considered at least as a prospect of the company. Many retailers were destroyed by Amazon and many newspapers were destroyed by Facebook and Google. Which sector do you want to buy: the sector in up trending or the dying sector even with a better P/E?

Most old books on value are based on old industries that are no longer applicable in today's market. Read these books but ask the above question.

Better definition
P/E should be inverted as E/P, which is termed as Earnings Yield. Earnings Yield is easy to be compared and understood. It takes care of negative earnings for screening stocks and ranking (comparing stocks with the better P/E first). If you sort P/E in ascending order, your order will be wrong with the negative earnings but right with E/P.

It is usually compared to a 10-year Treasury bill yield (or 30 years) or a CD rate. If the stock has 5% earnings yield and your one-year CD is 1%, then it beats the CD by 4% in absolute numbers and four times better. However, the CD is virtually risk free (with deposit amount limits in most banks). Earning yield is an estimated guess and it may not materialize.

Many ways to predict E/P
- Based on the last 12 months. Project it to the Forward E/P. It is also called the last twelve-month E/P.

- Based on analysts' educated guesses. Guesses may not materialize. Based on my experience, the expected usually predicts better than the one based on the last 12 months. This is the one I use most and many investing subscriptions provide this Forward P/E (same as the Expected P/E) or expected E/P.

Usually, I do not trust the analyst's opinions due to their conflict of interest. However, the earnings estimate is my exception.

- Based on the last month or the last quarter. Latest information could be better for predictions. However, they are not good for seasonal businesses such as the retail where most sales are done during the Christmas season.
- Besides the Pow PE described later; I take the average of the earnings yield EY as:

The Avg. EY = (EY from the last twelve month + Expected EY + EY from the current month of prior year) / 3

It averages out using figures from the past, the present and the future. If no one has used it, I claim shamelessly it is my original idea.

Best E/P could not be the best
Very high E/P could be signs of troubles ahead such as a lawsuit pending, fraud, etc. If you find companies E/P over 50%, it means two years' profits could be equal to the entire cost of the company! I can tell you right away that they probably smell fishy unless you believe that there is a free lunch in life.

However, from time to time, some bargains do exist due to certain conditions, or the Wall Street is just wrong about the company. I found one in my year-end screen and that gave me huge return. You need to find out whether they are bargains or traps. When the E/P is low (sometimes even negative) but is improving fast, it could mean big profits for you. Fundamentalists may miss this opportunity in the early stages due to the unfavorable E/P, but it could be the most profitable time to buy. Sometimes, it could be a turnaround.

During a recession, most good companies have a hard time in promoting new products as the consumers are thrifty. At the same time, it usually is the best time to develop products if they have enough cash to finance them. In this case, there will be no alarm even with negative earnings. The only alarm is when a company cannot meet the debt obligations.

Some companies can manipulate earnings via dirty tricks in accounting. It could make this year look really good, but it is harder or even impossible to continue the same trick for many years. Check out the footnotes in the financial statement.

E/P and PEG

For value investing, E/P is usually used and the higher the better. Watch out when it is extraordinarily high.

PEG (P/E growth) measures the rate of improving P/E. '1' is supposed to be neutral to most investors. When it is below 1, it is undervalued, and vice versa.

PEG = (P/E) / Earnings Growth Rate

They have a similar problem with P/E with negative earnings.

Which of the following two stocks do you want to buy based on their historical earning yields and earnings growth?

1. A stock that has a 10% earnings yield with no earnings growth.
2. A stock that has an 8% earnings yield with 50% earnings growth.

If the earnings growth continues, in next year the second stock should pay 12%, substantially better than the first stock. This is another reason we should use forward earnings rather than historical earnings.

PEG may give a low value for companies that pay high dividends. To correct it,

PEG = (P/E)/ (Earning Growth Rate + Dividend Yield)

When the general market favors growth stocks, weigh more on growth metrics including PEG. I claim no credit on the adjusted PEG.

Fundamental metrics

E/P is one of the metrics you should use but not exclusively. If the earning yield is high but the % of debt is high too, then a good bargain may not be as good as it appears to be.

Some other metrics may not be easily found in the financial statements such as the intangibles, insider buying, pension obligations, trade secrets, losing market share, brand name, customers' loyalty, etc. It is interesting that most metrics change its ability to predict from time to time.

P/E variations

There are other P/E variations like Shiller P/E (same as CAPE and PE10). Shiller P/E can also be used to track the current market valuation. It is controversial and its value is easily misinterpreted. Hence, use it as a reference only unless you understand all its issues. I prefer to use a two-year average of the P/E instead of 10 as I believe the market changes too much over a ten-year span. Currently Shill P/E does not work that well as before. It is due to the excessive printing of money.

Compare a company's current P/E to its average P/E in the last 5 years. Also compare it to the average value of the companies in the same industry. The average P/E for high-tech companies is different from supermarkets for example. They are available from Fidelity.

P/E is more reliable for a group of stocks (SPY for example) instead of individual stocks which have too many other metrics and intangibles to deal with. When you compare the total return of an ETF to a corresponding index, you need to add the respective dividends to the index to ensure a fair comparison of total returns. As of this writing, the S&P 500 is paying about a 2% dividend.

EV/EBITDA is another way to measure the value of a company. This metric has its advantages and disadvantages over P/E. It includes other important data such as cash and debt. EBITDA/EV is equivalent to E/P including other mentioned metrics. I prefer to use it over E/P. Some sites do not provide it if the earnings is negative. The disadvantage to me is it does not use expected earnings. This ratio can be found under Yahoo!Finance.

Garbage in, garbage out
I do not trust most financial statements from emerging countries, especially the smaller companies. Watch out for fraudulent data. Most metrics can be manipulated. Recently I have a US stock that lost 18% in one day due to the SEC's investigation of its financial data.

The announced earnings may not be reflected in the financial statements that you use from the web. Ensure your data is up-to-date by checking the date of the financial statements. Seeking Alpha has transcripts for the earnings announcements that would save you a trip to attend the companies' quarterly meetings.

Sector and entire market
You can find the value of a sector using the P/E of an ETF for that sector. It is similar for the market. For example, use SPY (an ETF simulating the S&P 500 index). If it is lower than the average (15 to me), then most likely the market is good value and a buy signal. It is one of the many hints for market timing.

Where to use P/E
Each highlight of the following corresponds to one of my books. Click it for the description of the strategy.

My book on top-down approach starts with a safe market, then sector analysis, fundamental analysis, intangible analysis and optionally technical analysis. P/E is one of the many metrics in fundamental analysis.

There are many styles of investing. In general, fundamental analysis is important when you hold the stock longer.

- P/E is important in Long-Term Swing, Dividend Investing, Retirees and Conservative Strategies.
- My max value is 20 and 25 for tech companies. I ignore it if they have high potential for appreciation that could be indicated by insider purchases. However, many unknown companies then had a P/E over 50. Tesla had a P/E over 1,000 at one time.
- P/E is moderately important in Short-Term Swing and Sector Rotation.
- P/E is the least important in Momentum Strategy and Day Trading.

Summary
Again, one metric should not dictate the reason to trade a stock. Compare the company P/E to its industry average and its own five-year average. In addition, many industries have cycles. If you buy it at the peak of the industry, the P/E may mislead you. Besides fundamental analysis, you need to consider intangible analysis and time the entry / exit point by using technical analysis. Intangible analysis evaluates information that cannot be summarized into numeric metrics such as a lawsuit pending.

True P/E
"EV/EBITDA" is available from Yahoo!Finance and other sources. The true EY is "1/Ture PE". I call it "True" for the lack of a better term as it

represents the financial situation of the company better. This could be the most important metric for many.
EBITDA: https://www.youtube.com/watch?v=C2eoh3X4efM

Earnings can be manipulated. For example, the company management can lower the P/E ratio by buying back its stocks. In this case the earnings per share is boosted but in reality, there is no change in the company's financial fundamentals. The true P/E takes into consideration the reduced cash. EBITBA stands for "Earnings Before Interest, Taxes, Depreciation, and Amortization".

Be careful when EV or "EBITDA" is negative. Most likely you should avoid the stocks with a negative EV.

Yahoo!Finance usually leaves EV/EVITDA blank for financial institutions such banks, loan companies and REITS. In this case, use forward earnings yield (= 1 / Forward P/E or Pow Earnings Yield described next.

I prefer True Yield based on Forward P/E instead of P/E as it has better predictable power to me. To illustrate, Apple has a P/E of 21.61, Forward P/E of 19.46 (both from Finviz), and Enterprise Value / EBIT of 16.72 (from Yahoo!Finance). The True Yield is 6% (1/16.72). The True Yield based on Forward P/E is 7% (6% * 21.61/19.48).

Pow P/E

You should use the described "EV/EBITDA" and hence "Pow P/E" can be ignored. There are some cases that Pow P/E is better: 1. "EV/EBITDA" may not be available for reasons such as negative asset and 2. Use of Forward Earnings instead of Earnings based on the last twelve months. The following is an exercise on how I simulate it from Finviz.com with metrics that are readily available.

I modified P/E to take care of cash and debts. I use my last name due to being easier to distinguish from P/E and it has nothing to do with my ego.

Pow P/E = (P - Cash per Share + Debt per Share) / (Earning - Interest gained per share - Interest paid per share)

Pow Earnings Yield = 1 / Pow P/E

Here is a comparison of E/P (Earnings Yield), Expected Earnings Yield (Forward E /P), True Yield (EBITD/EV) and Pow Earning Yields, which is based one Forward (Expected) Earnings as of 10/14/2021.

	CARS	MPAA
Earnings Yield	1%	7%
Expected Earnings Yield	12%	12%
True Yield	13%	11%
Pow Earnings Yield	5%	9%

P/E is not always important

The following is my test from 1/2/2020 to 10/14/2020. RSP is similar to SPY except that the stocks in the S&P 500 index are equally weighted. EY (= E/P) is Expected Earnings Yield and there are no stocks with EY less than 0. DY is Dividend Yield. GPE is the growth of P/E. As in my book, I use annualized returns and dividends are not included. This test does not mean a lot, but it tells us what these metrics behave during this period, or it indicates **Value is not a good metric in this period**, and it may indicate momentum is better in this period. Most big winners start as small companies with **high P/E** (from 30 to 100). Many of them have important technologies or special systems that would change the world such as Microsoft, Facebook, Amazon and Walmart to name a few. Their sales have increased substantially year after year.

Examples of not depending on low P/Es. Before the financial crisis in 2008, P/Es of most bank stocks had 10-year low. After they announced the earnings, P/Es of many of them surged to over 100 and the stock prices suffered losses of more than 80% within 12 months. The stock price of Bethlehem Steel with P/E of 2 at one time went to zero. Need to find out why the stock is so cheap via intangible analysis and qualitative analysis.

The following is very rough testing and there are many limitations in the database. However, the conclusion is quite convincing to me and some are opposite to the contrary beliefs. For example, I expected the higher EY the better, but not in this test.

	Ann. Return	Indicator	Comment
RSP 500 All	-2%		
EY (top 10)	-54%	Bad	Contrary
GPE (top 10)	-20%	Bad	Contrary
Select All or top 100.			
DY = 0	16%	Good	
DY (top 100)	-19%	Bad	
DY / 1 and 2	2%		

EY 3 to 4	15%	Good	Second best
EY 2 to 3	6%	Good	Third best
EY 1 to 2	31%	Good	Best
EY 0 to 1	-39%	Bad`	

I use some metrics from a service I subscribe to that are not included here. Two major metrics of this subscription have a return of around 20%. Most subscriptions including the free Fidelity (to some extent) give you three composite scores: Total, Fundamental and Timing. I wish to check out the recent predictability of Fidelity's Equity Summary Score if they have a historical database. Most of them take out the delisted and /or bankrupt companies in their databases.

Link: P/E: https://www.youtube.com/watch?v=4KkTGx2bK_4

23   Score your stocks

Enter the fundamental metric information such as P/E on any 100 stocks into a scoring system. If the top 25% of the stocks perform a lot better than the rest in 6 months consistently, then it is a good scoring system.

I have been using my own scoring system for years. It sums up the individual scores for selected fundamental metrics. When the total passes a certain number, evaluate the stock further for potential purchase. This scoring system has been updated many times for refinements and adapting to the changing market conditions. All metric information can be obtained from web sites.

Many companies and academic projects must have worked on this kind of stock scoring systems. However, few if any can prove their systems work consistently.

I may have found the reason why it does not work consistently. The fundamental metrics change from different market conditions. To illustrate, the current market conditions may favor value while some other conditions favor growth. I monitor the performances of all the fundamental metrics periodically and make changes accordingly. Hence, I call my scoring system Adaptive Stock Scoring System (do not use the acronym).

24 Adaptive Stock Scoring System

No.	Metric	Good	Bad	Score
1	P/E (use expected P/E if	Between 2.5 and	> 50 or < 0, Score = -1	

		available)[6]	12.5, Score = 2		
2		Price / Free Cash Flow	< 12, Score = 1	>30 or < 0, Score = -1	
3		Price / Sales[1]	< 0.8, Score = 1	< 0, Score = -1	
4		Price / Book[1]	< 1, Score = 1	< 0, Score = -1	
5		Analyst's Opinion[2]	> 7, Score = 1	< 4, Score = -1	
6		Short % (check reason for high %)	Between 30% & 40%, Score = 1[4]	Between 10% & 20%, Score = -1	
7		Insider Purchase[3]	Score = 1		
8		Profit Margin annualized[3]	> 25%, Score = 1	< 5%, Score = -1	
		Compare Q to Q last year for #9 and # 10			
9		Revenue Growth[3]	> 15%, Score = 1	< 0, Score = -1	
10		Earning Growth[3]	> 20%, Score = 1	< 0, Score = -1	
11		Intangibles	Positive, Score = 1	Negative, Score = -1	
				Grand Score	
		Stock Symbol Date[5]	Current Price	SPY	

Footnote.

1. Negative values for Sales (due to accounting adjustments), Equity and Book are possible but not likely.
2. It is from Fidelity web site. If you have no access to it, adjust it according to consensus rating.
3. This metric can be found from many sources. They may use different terms for the same data.
4. A short squeeze could be coming when a stock is over-sold. If the critical problem of the company cannot be recovered easily, change the Score from 1 to -1.
5. The last row is for your information only. SPY is used to measure whether it will beat the market by comparing the return of this stock to the return of SPY.
6. Earnings yield E/P (the reversal of P/E) is between 8% and 40%.

Score. Score each metric and sum up all the scores giving the Grand Score. If the Grand Score is 3, the stock passes this scoring system. Even if it is a 2, it still deserves further analysis if you have time.

For some reason I do not know why and how to explain, the top 10% (15% for long term and 5% for short term) of the stocks we score do not perform better than the passing grade. It happens in two of my scoring system. Be suspicious on them and it has happened for more than one time. The stocks scored in the bottom 10% are consistently poor performers and that's good. To simplify the usage, ignore stocks that are scored greater than 7.

The metrics from #1 to #6 are yearly metrics based on last twelve months except the 'expected P/E'. They are popular value ratios.

Metric 9 and 10 are quarterly comparisons to the same quarter last year.

Some metrics such as the Analyst's Opinion can be obtained directly from Fidelity.

Metric
The fundamental metrics are also described in Chapter 12-14. For even further information, search the metric in Wikipedia or any financial site.

- P/E.
  Price to Earning is a primary value ratio (Chapter 14). The Expected Earning has better predictive power than the one from last two months.

- Price / Cash Flow (same as Price / Free Cash Flow).
  Cash Flow is one of the few metrics that cannot be manipulated. It is a red flag when it is increasing fast. Statistically for long term, it is not a good indicator but it adds safety to the stock.

- Price / Sales.
  Different industries have different averages for this metric. A supermarket business should have a very low ratio. Adjust it to the industry accordingly.

- Price / Book.
  Usually it is not a good indicator for matured companies such as IBM.

- Analyst's Opinion.
  Fidelity has a good handle on this metric. It is based on the past predictive accuracy of the analysts.

- Short Percent (= Shares being shorted / shares outstanding).
  The stock buyers who short the stocks frequently are right more times than wrong. The percent between 10% and 20% is high to me.

However, when it is too high, a short squeeze may be coming. When there are too few shares to sell, the stock price could boost up due to supply and demand. Need to find out the reason why it is so high. If the reason is valid to short the stock, stay away from this stock no matter how high the stock scores. Any scoring system is not sacred and it can be ignored for many situations such as a pending serious lawsuit.

- Insider's Purchase.
  When the insiders purchase their company's stock at the market price, most likely the company is doing well. No one knows the company and its sector better than the officials of the company. Ignore options. Ignore the purchases after the selling. Insider's purchase explains why some lowly-scored stocks appreciate fast. Hence, ignore the low scores for stocks with heavy insider purchases and include it to further analysis.

- Profit Margin.
  Ignore or relax this metric in a recession. For those industries that do not have gross margin, use operating margin instead.

- Revenue growth.
  Ignore or relax this metric in a recession.

- Earning growth.
  Ignore or relax this metric in a recession.

- Intangibles.
  The outlook of the company, its industry and the stock market are described in Chapter 10.

  For simplicity, each outlook scores -1 for poor and 1 for good. Add up the three scores. For 1 or higher, it is positive (Score = 1) and vice versa. There are more to it such as serious lawsuits pending, new products, sector rotation, changing market conditions....

  This metric has not been included before as it is part of my further analysis. You may want to do the same. Further analyze the high-scored stocks. If a red flag surfaces, skip the stock. Red flags can be detected from or not from the financial sheet. When you use a financial sheet, ensure it is the most updated that usually can be found in the company's web site.

If you feel the intangible is important to this stock, use the range of -2 to 2.

Holding Period

The performance monitor uses the holding period of 6 months. After six months, it should start to lose the predictive accuracy as the stock fundamentals most likely change. Hence, evaluate the bought stocks again at that time using the same scoring system. In my last monitor, it did not lose the predictive accuracy, but in the long run it should.

Check out your tax rates for long-term and short-term capital gains. For non-retirement accounts, you need to make more adjustments such as selling the losers/winners before/after the required holding period for long-term capital loss/gain (as of 2013, it is 12 months).

Fundamentalists are swimming against the tide. It takes time for the market to realize their values. Hence, selling too early (3 months or less) without good reasons is not recommended. When a stock passes the profit target, consider selling even if it has been bought just over several days.

Variations
Enter your changes to this scoring system to suit your investing style and/or different market conditions. The current system uses fundamental metrics. For growth style of investing, add the appropriate metrics such as PEG, price momentum, etc.

This current scoring system will not work on momentum strategies (holding stocks less than 2 months) and day trading.

My recent performance monitor on metrics

This article serves as an illustration on how to do your own monitor. By the time you read this article, the findings could be outdated. In addition, it is based on my stocks actually screened and the number of stocks is too limited to draw a general conclusion.

I monitored the performance into two: one for short term and one for long term. Score 3 is my passing score for both short term and long term.

How score scores

	Avg.	<3	3	4	5	6	7	>=8
Short	7%	2%	8%	11%	7%	14%	11%	-10%
Long	8%	4%	13%	14%	7%	21%	4%	-10%

Explanation
- The score system works if it is sequentially proportional to the return percentages. It is to some extent.
- From the table, we should use 3 as the passing grade for both short term and long term.
- Do not buy stocks when the score is 8 or higher. It is consistent from my previous monitors. Do not know why. I assume that when the stock is too good to be true, most likely it is not.
- When the stock scores between 3 and 7 inclusively, it is a buy. It is quite similar to the previous monitors. It also destroys the price efficiency theory.

How reliable is the score?

As stated, it only applies to me for the time being. The reliability also depends on the size of the sample. The following shows the number of stocks.

	Total	<3	3	4	5	6	7	>8
Short	747	397	113	97	69	41	27	3
Long	555	299	75	70	53	30	25	3

How fundamental metrics score

The following table shows us the predictability of the metrics.
Short Term: (7% return for the average)

Metric	Parm. 1	No.	%	Parm. 2	No.	%	Predict.
EY	>14	203	4%	<5	94	0%	Good
Blue Chip BC	A	150	7%	F	63	-4%	Good
BC Fundamentals	A	191	14%	F	66	-11%	Good
Fidelity Analyst	Buy	150	10%	Sell	279	3%	Good
P/B	<1	162	1%	>2	333	9%	Bad
ROE	>25	180	9%	<2	110	4%	Good
GRT	<20	71	-4%	>25	685	6%	Good
P/CF	<20	179	8%	>30	99	5%	Good

Earn Gr Q-Q	>50%	227	6%		<5%	68	0%	Good
Sales Gr Q-Q	>25%	153	7%		<5%	154	0%	Good
Debt/E	<.1	172	15%		>1.5	69	2%	Good
RSI(14)	>60	85	9%		<40	33	-2%	Good
SMA 200%	>5	94	1%		<-5	19	-4%	Good

Long Term: (8% return for the average)

Metric	Parm. 1	No.	%		Parm. 2	No.	%	Predict.
EY	>20	28	3%		<5	77	-1%	Good
Blue Chip	A	99	8%		F	62	-4%	Good
Blue Chip Fund.	A	178	15%		F	65	-11%	Good
Fidelity Analyst	Buy	90	17%		Sell	208	4%	Good
P/B	<1	15	2%		>2	227	9%	Bad
ROE	>25	135	11%		<2	93	4%	Good
GRT	<20	67	-3%		>25	488	9%	Good
P/CF	<20	133	11%		>30	54	9%	Good
Earn Gro Q-Q	>50%	141	11%		<5%	68	0%	Good
Sales Gro Q-Q	>25%	97	8%		<5%	110	2%	Good
Debt/E	<.1	168	15%		>1.5	61	4%	Good
RSI(14)	>60	27	22%		<40	7	0%	Bad

Explanation

- I skip the metrics from various subscription services.
- The returns are used for comparison ignoring many yardsticks such as comparing to the market index and excluding dividends.
- P/B is not a good metric from my samples. RSI(14) is fine short term but not long term. However, due to the limited data on RSI(14), they are not conclusive. SMA-200% is not available for the long term as it is a new one for me.
- Short term is usually about 4 months and long term is about 12 months on the average; it is just a general guideline.
- Some data are both long term and short term by playing trick by not updating the stock prices of some data; some data could be eligible for both short term and long term as they are close in the specified ranges.
- The prediction of the metric is good if they're as expected.

- Your score i derived from the above metrics. Weigh more on the metrics with better predictability. Modify ('adapt') your scoring system based on your monitor.
- EY (E/P) is expected earning yield. GRT is earning growth rate.
- The stock has higher chance of appreciation if it is rated A in both the Blue-Chip composite score and its fundamental score, Buy in Fidelity Analysts' Opinion, ROE> 25%, GRT > 25%, Debt/Equity < 10% and Earning Growth > 50% for the long term. It is quite similar to the short term.

When you cannot find these stocks, relax the selection. I would start with Earning Growth > 30% as my primary metric.

IX   Technical Analysis

25   More on technical analysis

This chapter describes some TA indicators that can help us. Click on the links for better description.

- Finviz.com.
  It has SMA20, SMA50 and SMA200 to represent the short-term, intermediate-term and the long-term indicator. SMA stands for Simple Moving Average and n for days for the duration of the average (for example, 20 days for SMA20).

  If you are a long-term investor, use SMA-200 (or SMA-350). Using SMA-20 would cause a lot of sells / reentries.

  Buy when the price is above the moving average line and sell when the price is below it. Finviz.com provides the percent of moving above the moving average to indicate how much the price deviates from the average.

  If you hold the stock for an average of 50 days, use SMA50, and so on. If you hold stocks for an average of 90 days, you have to create your own SMA using one of the many web sites including Yahoo!Finance and specify 90 for the period.

Try other similar technical indicators such as EMA, which is supposed to weigh more on the more recent data. A weather man can predict tomorrow's weather better than the weather a week away.

- RSI(14) indicates whether the stock is overbought or oversold. RSI oscillates between zero and 100. Traditionally, and according to Wilder, RSI is considered overbought with a value above 70 and oversold with a value below 30 as described in the article.

    When it is oversold, most likely the stock will fall, and vice versa.

(http://stockcharts.com/school/doku.php?id=chart_school:technical_indicators:relative_strength_index_rsi)

Click here for another article.
(http://financial-dictionary.thefreedictionary.com/Relative+Strength+Index)

- Cup and handle is a popular indicator that the stock price would surge.
(http://www.investopedia.com/terms/c/cupandhandle.asp)

- Double bottom indicates that the stock will move up.
(http://stockcharts.com/school/doku.php?id=chart_school:chart_analysis:chart_patterns:double_bottom_revers)

    It shows a double bottom for Apple in 2013.

    The reverse is double top.

- Most indicators can be used on a market ETF to predict the market direction. It can use a sector ETF to predict a sector such as housing.

- Fidelity has a software system named Wealth Lab available free to qualified customers to test technical indicators with a historical database for back testing. Check the current availability.

- TA usually does not spot the bottoms/peaks predictably, but the trend. To me, it is more profitable to understand 4 technical indicators fully than more than 4. The four indicators to me are SMA (EMA), RSI(14), MACD and candlestick. You can also detect market change by using [RSI and MACD](#).

http://www.youtube.com/watch?v=adSGUkNX5LA

26   Examples on using technical analysis

I have outlined how we can spot market plunge using TA and I use it to monitor the market every three months or so (recommend to do it every month and even more often when the market is risky). Here is an example on how to use it to trade individual stocks.

I have to admit I do not use TA that much on individual stocks and clearly I am not an expert in TA. If this article stirs up your interest, read more books or attend seminars / classes on TA. However, this book describes the basic and most useful technical indicators. There are many good and free articles from Investopedia on this topic. Personally I prefer to seek fundamentally sound companies at bargain prices and wait for their full appreciation. It has been proven to me.

TA is very useful for momentum and day traders. With the rising volumes, you can detect that the stocks are traded by managers of mutual funds, hedge funds, insurance companies and pension funds, and profit by riding on their wagons.

Some stocks are good for TA. Usually they are larger companies with above-average volumes and are fundamentally sound. Avoid the stocks that are trending downwards unless you're bottom fishing. Let me pick CSCO (a cyclical stock) for illustration. I bought it several times in 2012. I sold some in 2013 and 2014 making good profits. This is quite different from what short-term traders would use the following information for.

The green line is 50-day simple moving average (SMA) for the following chart using one year data.

If it does not display clearly on a small screen, type the following on the browser on your PC.

http://ebmyth.blogspot.com/2013/05/chart-for-ta-example.html

Buy the stock when it is above its SMA and sell when it is below. Following the chart would make good money based on this simple rule. Also, practice the strategy "Sell on May 1, Buy back on Nov. 1".

Not all stocks follow this profitable pattern. Fundamentalists may try to pick the bottom in late July while chartists enter positions on its upward trend. The chartists have an advantage to stay away from stocks in their downward trend.

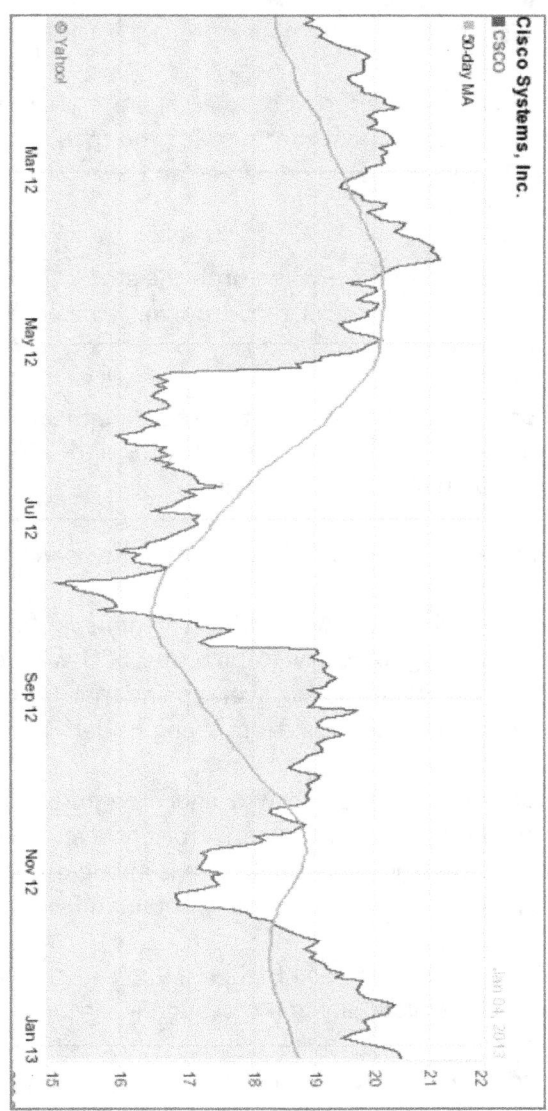

Table: CSCO   50-day SMA   Source: Yahoo!Finance

We can improve the trades by:
- Use different moving average in number of days (50 in this example) and other indicators such as EMA (a moving average that weighs higher on more recent data). It may improve prediction accuracy and/or cut down the number of trades. RSI(14) suggests overbought / oversold conditions.

- Instead of selling the stock for cash, consider selling the stock short. Selling short is not for beginners for sure.

- The accuracy is usually improved by a separate chart for the sector the stock belongs to and another one for the market. For CSCO, you can use an ETF for network companies and SPY (or a similar ETF) to represent the market.

  In theory and in theory only, when both the stock, the sector that the stock is in and the market all move down, it has a high chance to move down, and vice versa.

  We use 50 days (in SMA) for short-term holding of stocks (90 days for longer holding), 90 days for the sector ETF and 350 days for SPY. Again, 'days' is actually 'trade sessions'.

TA is not for most fundamentalists but it should be used

For a bargain hunter like me, TA would not benefit me a lot for picking stocks at the bottoms. I would try to pick up CSCO with prices ranging from 15-17 and all below the moving average line that TA would not show me a Buy signal. However, for short-term swing traders TA is a Godsend.

To me, TA is good indicator for growth and momentum for short-term trading. Some fundamentalists may use TA for entry and exit point. Some recommend buying the stock when the price is above the SMA-200 (same as SMA-200% is positive that can be readily obtained from finviz.com).

It is profitable for 'Buy High and Sell Higher' if you can protect your profits effectively. This is also called 'Buy at a reasonable cost'. One's opinion.

In selecting a tool, you have to understand how, why to use it and whether it fits your investing style. I use TA for market timing for the entire market more than on individual stocks. When I have more time, I would use TA more frequently. My portfolio has too many stocks that I should cut down.

Most of us cannot spot the bottom of a stock; I had some successes but most likely they were due to luck. When a stock is moving up from the bottom, there is a good chance it will move further up. TA shows it and its volume confirms it.

Conclusion

Even a fundamentalist like me can benefit a lot by using TA. This book touches the very basics of TA but the most useful TA indicators.

Besides monitoring the fundamentals of the stocks you bought once every 6 months, you should analyze their technical more often (1 month to 3 months depending on your available time). When the market is risky (close to the SMA average), run the SMA chart more frequently (say once a week).

Filler:

On Wells Fargo, the bank

My three cents.

1. Need to be patient as we're swimming against the tide. It takes at least half a year for the market to realize its value.

2. Need to time the market. When market plunges, most if not all stocks plunge with the low tide.

3. Consider the debt and the net current asset. This bank stock is fine but it is hard to check the quality of the loan. My Pow EY = (Expected Earning) / (Price - (Net Current Asset / Share) + Debt / Share.

How can the bank not making money? I pay them 4% or so to borrow and receive virtually 0 for interest.

X Tools

27 Covered calls

For basic description of a covered call from Wikipedia, click here (http://en.wikipedia.org/wiki/Covered_call).

It is like collecting rents from your apartment you bought. The difference is that the renter has an option to buy the apartment at a preset time and price.

The rents are quite substantial if you have good planning. To start with, you want to buy stocks that have a market to sell. Usually they are large companies with high trading volumes.

Since one contract is for 100 shares of a stock, you cannot sell a covered call on 50 shares of a stock. On the other hand, when you have 1,000 stocks, the commission of 10 contracts would be more than the cost of 1 contract depending on your broker's schedule.

It is time consuming to keep track of the covered call but it is well worth your time and effort. If the stock price exceeds the strike price of your covered call, you may want to buy the same shares back, so you would not miss further appreciation of this stock.

However, if it is in a taxable account and you have a loss in the forced sell, do not buy it back otherwise the tax loss is not allowed (i.e. a wash sale) for the year as of 2016. When the contract expires, you may want to start another contract on the same stock if the stock has not been sold.

Covered calls do have its disadvantages such as higher commission rate and sometimes forcing you to sell at a higher tax rate for short-term capital gain in taxable accounts. It is avoidable by using covered calls on stocks that are qualified for long-term capital gain. In addition, you need to buy them back when they increase in price beyond your strike price or lose its potential to appreciate further. Using another put could allow you not to lose any gain beyond the strike price. However I prefer to use my time for something more productive and this insurance is not cheap. One's opinion.

One company advertises their techniques using covered calls could give their users 3 to 6% monthly returns. If you believe in this fantasy, you do not need this book. There is no free lunch.

My recent experience

I sold Netflix covered call with the strike price about 2% higher and 3% premium (from my memory) but the price shot up 12% higher in one day, so I'm potentially losing 7% profit. However, it turned out to be a good experience as Netflix went downhill later (8/2012).

Normally I prefer to sell covered options for stocks with quantity from 100 to 600 shares (i.e. 1 to 6 contracts) for the longest time (about 2-3 months). Some non-volatile and small stocks are not candidates to write covered calls. Some stocks are not optionable. Typically high-tech stocks have higher premiums to be collected as their stock prices fluctuate more. The right stocks can generate 10% or even more in a year in addition to the fluctuations of the stock prices.

In general, if I feel the market will be down for the period, I use covered calls especially for stocks holding over one year (unless I have short-term loss to offset any short-term gain) in taxable accounts. Watch out for any tax change that may affect your total return.

Recently I attended a sales pitch on a 3-day training course on a strategy for making 24% per year and it is quite possible especially the S&P 500 returns about the same. I hope it was available to me 15 years ago. It seems to be too good to be true.

How to sell covered call

First you need to open an account with your broker and apply to trade options including covered calls to start.

Check how your broker charges commission. Say, how much they charge for one contract and 10 contracts of a stock.

The covered call is an agreement to sell the right to the buyer the option to buy the stock at the strike price for a specific date range (a.k.a. expiration date). Typically options are expired on Friday other week of the month.

You need to write covered calls on the stocks you already own. One contract is 100 shares of stocks. Check out the option chain to select the price, expiration period and the strike price. Normally, the strike price should be higher than the current market price. You may want to have an expiration date 2 weeks or longer. When the contract is expiring in a few days, the contract has little value and most likely the small 'rent' is not worth the risk and the commission.

When the covered call is sold, you receive the 'rent' immediately and any dividend during the 'rental' period.

When the option is 'called' due to the price rises above the strike price, your stock will be sold and you have to pay the regular commission.

At this point, evaluate the stock whether you want to buy it back. If the stock surges, you may have to pay a higher price – thus losing the extra appreciation. In addition, you may have to pay higher capital gain tax if it is held less than the required period for long term capital gain in a taxable account.

Note. Notice that some stocks are not optionable and/or not practical to write options. Most brokers charge a flat rate for the first contract (such as $7) and an incremental fee for each additional contract. Shop around as the fees vary if you write a lot of covered calls.

The better stocks for covered calls are large US companies with large average volume. The option (a.k.a. the 'rent') pays better for volatile companies such as high-tech companies. From my rough estimates for illustration, the annualized return on covered calls for AAPL is 25% and C is 12% after commission.

Buyback, Diluting and Spinoff

Buyback will not change the fundamentals of a stock.

The following are all theories. When a company buys back its own stocks to reduce the number of outstanding shares, the remaining shares should appreciate in value in this aspect. However, the company uses its own cash, and hence the stock value should remain the same. It is a no-win and no-loss situation and the Supply and Demand should not affect the stock price in buyback.

However, the management understands the value of its company and its sector it is in better than anyone. The buyback could be the best way to use the company's cash compared to giving dividends, plowing back to research / development, or taking advantage of the easy money available. They also in theory consider the total return for their average stock investor such as taxes.

In practice, most officers take care of themselves first (a human nature): How to boost the value of their stock options. In the last several years, boosting dividends has proven to be a good way to do so.

If the number of the outstanding shares has been reduced, many metrics with earning per share will be improved such as P/E (unless P is decreased accordingly). If the company borrows money to buy its stock, the metrics on debts will head to the other direction.

Watch out that the management buyback may be used to grant options to them. Buyback improves the EPS as E is a constant and the number of shares is decreased. Hence, EPS is not a good metric to me.

Stock dilution means increases outstanding shares. In most cases, it is not good for the stock price. The company has no better way to secure finance.

Spinoff depends on the situation. If one part of the company has a lot of liability such as a major pending lawsuit, it is better to spin it off.

Links
Fidelity Video: covered calls.
https://www.fidelity.com/learning-center/options/selling-covered-calls-video
Investopedia articles: Basics and Definition
http://www.investopedia.com/articles/optioninvestor/08/covered-call.asp
http://www.investopedia.com/terms/c/coveredcall.asp

28 Diversification

LTCM, a hedge fund run by smart people, and Isaac Newton both made one serious mistake in investing. They both bet all in one bet and they lost it big. They were the smartest folks on earth but they violated one basic principle in investing: diversification.

Another example is the potato. Irish made good living in their primary crop: potato. When a virus came, they lost all the potatoes and caused the potato famine.

Diversification improves a portfolio's performance in the long run and it reduces risk. Diversification includes other asset class besides stocks such as oil, gold, cash (yes even cash as a safety net to grasp better opportunities ahead), real estate, etc. However, stocks historically produce the best return. In addition, most stocks are quite liquid as it takes a minute to sell them compared to selling a house for example. You can buy other assets such as gold (GLD), money market funds and real estate (via REITs) via the low-cost ETFs.

When an asset is over-valued, it will return to the average historical value with one or two exceptions. Gold is one exception, but it is partly due to the depreciation of USD and the previous prolonged downfall of gold adjusted to inflation.

Simply put, owning 10 to 15 good stocks with less than three stocks in the same sector (which have to be good sectors to start with) achieves diversification goal for most. When one sector crashes, you still have two more good sectors.

Every one's situation is different:

- Depends on your wealth and your age.
  For younger folks with limited wealth (less than $50,000 to invest), a portfolio of 3 stocks (preferably most in ETFs) in different sectors or one diversified ETF could be enough. Your objective in investing is saving money for a down payment for a house, paying your loans including college loans and/or improving your earning power by taking classes.

  Retirees may want to maintain a larger percentage of your holdings in cash and/or invested in bonds (long-term bonds could be very risky when the interest rate is going up). Those wealthy enough can fully invest in stocks as losing 50% of their portfolio doesn't alter their lifestyle. Most business owners should invest in stocks and other vehicles instead of plowing back to their businesses in order to diversify their investments.

Portfolios with more than a billion dollars such as in most mutual funds owning 10 stocks with 100 million each are just too risky to me.

Holding cash is safe but it loses its value due to inflation. To illustrate this point, consider these three scenarios in 1950:

1. An apartment bought in for $10,000 in NYC or in your home town.

2. An investment in the Dow Jones 30 Industrials for $10,000.

3. A 3.5% certificate of deposit or one of the U.S. Treasuries for your $10,000.

By now, all real estate investments should have appreciated many, many times over and most stock shares value would have multiplied also. The $10,000 CD gain has lost real value due to inflation. Our capitalist system punishes us for not taking risk. In the long term, risk is smoothed out over time.

- Excessive frequency in re-balancing your portfolio for diversification takes up time from evaluating stocks. It may cost you in transaction fees but they are low in today's self-directed brokerage accounts. In addition, it may have some tax consequences in taxable accounts.

    The advantage of churning the portfolio (but not excessively) can improve the quality of your portfolio with most updated information about the companies you invest in.

    Many brokers display your current diversification in the monthly statement summaries. If not, use a simple spreadsheet to classify the sectors and the asset classes in your portfolio.

- Diversification can easily be achieved by buying indexed funds and/or ETFs. They are less volatile. I recommend it to all folks with less than $50,000 to invest.

- Diversification does not mean to pick simply a stock in other sector that has the opposite correlation of the stock you own. The stock quality comes first.

- Diversification takes a back seat to spotting market plunges. When most stocks plunge such as during 2007-2008, diversification does not save your portfolio, but spotting and reacting to market plunges will.

- Some of our stocks will lose values. If they were due to our mistakes, write them down and learn from them. If they were frauds (not avoidable in many cases), diversification would limit our losses.

- Over diversified is not good either. It takes out our resources to monitor the stocks we own. I usually have a lot of candidates of stocks to buy in a rising market. To compromise, stay focus on stocks that I have heavy bets. Focus investing could be very profitable.

My suggestions on diversification

Portfolio up to	Strategy
$ 50,000	ETF that simulates the market
$100,000	80% in ETF above + 20% in a sector ETF(s)
$500,000	10 stocks with less than 3 in the same sector
$1 Million	Same as above + 50% in ETFs if you do not have enough time to monitor your portfolio.

As described, everyone's situation is different. If you have more time for investing, you should be able to handle more than 10 stocks. Playing market timing (i.e. switching to cash) depends on one's risk tolerance. If you are good in stock picking, you should buy stocks instead of ETFs. On a personal note, I usually have more than 10 stocks.

29 Trade plan

You should have a trade plan. It should include the following basics:

1. Objective.
2. When, what stocks and how many to buy.
3. When and what stocks to sell.
4. When and how to monitor your trading strategies.

The follow is my suggestion. Adjust them according to your personal requirements.

Be disciplined

It would make your trading to be a discipline which will provide better results in the long run and save you time. Following the trade plan would not allow your emotion to take over.

To illustrate, you have a specific day (Monday or the first day of the month) to check the value of your portfolio. Checking it several times a day is a waste of energy and it could cause harm to your emotions.

Objective

Set up your objective and requirements first. Your objective could be seeking the highest profit, profit at the least risk, protecting principle, generating income or a combination. Beating the market should not be your primary objective.

For example, a better objective is making more than 5% per year in the next 10 years at the least risk. Why 5%? I estimate we have 3% inflation and 2% taxes.

You can be conservative and aggressive at the same time by setting up two accounts, one for each objective. In addition, you may want to define the maximum investment amount for each account.
I have three objectives and they usually fall into different accounts and different holding periods.

- Profit at the least risk. Buy value stocks. Review bought stocks every 6 months. Non-taxable account.

- Momentum. Buy momentum stocks for maximum short-term (1 month) profits. Roth account.
- Conservative. Define a larger safety net. Conserve cash. Move all to stocks only when the market is most favorable.

Contrary to the above, most investors' or traders' objective is beating the market by a specific percent. It is fine too to measure how you perform against the market. For ultra conservative investors, not losing money is the primary objective.

If you made 10% and the market was up by 20%, you did not do good performance wise. However, do not blame yourself if your primary objective is conserving wealth. Most likely you had a high percent of your portfolio in cash and/or safer investments which do not appreciate a lot but they conserve your wealth.

Be flexible

Every one's trade plan is different. You should start a simple one and add features that would be useful to you. Keep it simple as you will not follow a complicated one.

Other features are: how you screen stocks, your average holding period, tax consequences, performance monitor, etc. This chapter shows you the very basics of a trade plan and you should start one if you do not have one.

You can refer to any chapter of this book in your trade plan. To illustrate, refer to the chapters when to sell a stock and spotting market plunges.

You can change your objective. When the market is risky, you want to be more conservative for example.

Disciplined but adaptive

Stick with the plan consistently. When your strategy that has been proven before does not work now, you should still stick to it. It is a common mistake for traders switching different technical indicator when the current one does not work. It explains why most beginner traders lose money.

It should be adaptive. When the current market favors growth, stick with a growth strategy.

A sample trade plan

You can review what stocks to buy and sell once a week or once a month depending on how active you are in the market. List the criteria you want to buy. Define your average holding period for a specific objective. Also define when and why you want to sell a stock.

Personally I prefer to have two sections: Common Tasks and Specific Tasks. Common Tasks includes 4 categories: Weekly Tasks, Monthly Tasks, Quarterly Tasks and Yearly Tasks. Evaluate stocks to buy on Tuesday every week for example. Update the portfolio and check out the chart on marketing timing on the first week of every month. Review performance of the portfolio quarterly (or half a year). Perform year-end tasks.

Specific Tasks include tasks I have to do on specific dates such as filing tax return, transferring stocks to my children and renewing investing subscriptions.

Weekly Tasks:

Mon	Covered calls
	IBD-50 review
Tue	Momentum strategy
Wed	Sell Momentum stocks over 2 weeks.

Monthly Tasks:

Mon	Performance monitor.
	Market timing: Market & Correction.
Tue	Find stocks using selected strategies.
	Find stocks using screens.
Wed	Evaluate stocks
Thur.	Buy stocks
	Sector rotation.
Fri	Evaluate any stocks to sell.
Any	Monitor momentum performance.

Quarterly Tasks:

1	Monthly tasks.
2	Performance monitor.

Year-end Tasks:

1	Tax adjustments for taxable accounts.
2	EOY purchases.
3	Spreadsheet for taxable accounts.
4	Fully invested in Dec. 15-Jan. 15
5	Screen performance monitor.
6	Dogs of DOW.

Review your performance and the trade plan

If you do not know what you did, how can you know what you're going? Review every trade transaction and monitor their performances.

Learn from your losses. Did you stick to the trade plan? If you lose too many times and/or take too much risk (evidenced by many losses and/or big losses), you may have to modify your trade plan. However, the trade plan may not be good to the current market (for example trading growth stocks in the bottom of the market cycle).

If you have to let the winners get away too often, review what's wrong. Sometimes, a lesson is not a lesson but just bad luck.

Learn about yourself

Learn about your risk tolerance, how mentally prepared are you on big losses and big wins. If you have more money than you can use for the rest of your life, conserving wealth should be your primary objective.

To illustrate with a portfolio of one million, your average stock position is $100,000 if you only have time to follow 10 stocks.
To many, the portfolio with 10 stocks is quite risky. You may consider having 10 stocks of $50,000 each and invest the rest ($500,000) in ETFs, mutual funds and/or bonds. Ensure no three or more stocks (some prefer 2) are in the same sector.

Prepare for some losses. Reduce the average loss to small amounts. I prefer 25% maximum loss for volatile stocks and 20% for other stocks. Some prefer using stop loss orders of 10% to 15% loss. Today's market is too volatile to stop losses less than 15%. One's opinion. You should have some big winners but let them getting away by selling them too early. One way is to use stop orders (10% less than the market price) and adjust the stops periodically (say a month) for the appreciating stocks.

A Quickie

Write down your objective and what tasks you do every week, month and year in the inside back cover in this book (hard copy only). If you do not do it now, you will never do it.

Trade journal

Keep a journal of your trades and ideas. Review it from time to time why you bought a specific stock. It is far better than recalling the experiences from memory.

Everyone should have a book such as this one to record their experiences. I do not recommend publishing one. You should spend your time in investing. Unless you're famous, most likely publishing is not profitable.

It should be part of a trade plan. You use it to monitor your performance of your trade. When you use a screen that is for short term, you want to exit the trade accordingly. When the screen does not perform, it may mean the market is not favorable to this screen and you should skip using it with actual money. Here is a screen shot of mine. I group the trades under different screens.

A	B	C	D	E	F	G	H	I	J	K	L	M	N	O	P
Performance			Price		$					Date			Return		Status
Stock	QTY	Account	B.P.	S.P.	Buy $	Sell $	Profit	Curr P.	% better	Buy Date	Sell Date	Days		Ann. Ret	
LAKE	2,000	401K	10.93	13.99	21,860	27,975	6,115	9.45	48%	07/15/15	11/24/15	132	28%	77%	S
ABTL	1,500	ROTH	16.60	18.50	24,900	27,750	2,850			07/16/15	09/10/16	422	11%	10%	B
ELMD	5,000	401K	4.01	4.22	20,054	21,095	1,041	4.81	-12%	03/17/16	04/07/16	21	5%	90%	S

The formulae are:
B.P. (Buy Price) =IF(B3="","",IF(D3="","",D3*B3))
% better =IF(I3="","",(E3-I3)/I3)
Days =IF(K3="","",L3-K3)
Return =IF(D3="","",(E3-D3)/D3)
Ann. Ret =IF(N3="","",N3*365/M3)

Add any columns you want such as Account.

30 Tax avoidance

Tax avoidance is a good way to save some money legally. Tax laws change all the time. Check Wikipedia on current investment taxes. Consult your tax lawyer and my knowledge in taxes is limited.

Some even went to the length by using life support to prolong the lives for several weeks so to qualify better estate tax exemption in the following year. Do not implement what I did as tax laws change frequently and every one's situation is different. Here are what I did and hope they will be applicable to you.

- Sold most profitable stocks that I owned more than 12 months in taxable accounts in 2011. I bought some back. I maintained a 15% tax bracket, so the tax bill from Uncle Sam is virtually 0 (not exactly due to more tax on social security and Medicare as a result of the trades). I still had to pay state tax. As a retiree, I can control my income.

   I bet this is the same trick Romney and Buffett used to pay their taxes at low rates.

- Converted part of my Rollover IRA to Roth in 2012 and 2013. I paid taxes today. However, the Roth conversion gives me tax-free appreciation for the trades in this account and it will lower tax and my minimum withdrawal requirement in the future.

- The taxes from dividends in the retirement accounts are deferred but eventually they will be treated as regular income when they are withdrawn. Very few have higher incomes during their retirement. If you are the lucky few due to the successful investing in your retirement accounts, you may end up with higher tax bracket during your retirement, particularly when you are forced to withdraw at age 70 ½.

- Gifted some appreciated stocks to my children. Good for them and not good for Uncle Sam. You can gift up to $14,000 (in 2015) for each spouse to each child without paying any Federal tax. For a family of four, you and your spouse can gift up to $56,000 (= 14,000 * 4) a year in 2015.

   The cost basis of the transferred stock is quite complicated. Check out the current tax law. The cost basis of the appreciated stocks are carried to the receiver, so it would lower your capital taxes as most of us are in higher tax bracket than our children.

From my experience, the cost basis of the depreciated stocks after the transfer is the market price on the transfer day as of 2016. I do not understand it enough to comment but just tell what I have experienced. I tried to offset my son's unexpected short-term capital gain by transferring a losing stock and that does not work.

- My lawyer set up trusts for me including my house. They will avoid probate hopefully. From the current tax law (as of 2016), the cost basis of your stocks will be stepped up or down to the stock prices of that day you pass away. Ask your heirs to keep a business paper for the stock prices or tell your brokers to adjust the cost basis on the day you pass away (send him an e-mail from hell or heaven depending on your new residence ☺). Of course, you have to tell your heirs now to take care of these tasks without using the described email. Again, ask your tax lawyer for details.

  Make sure you specify the beneficiaries in your and your spouse's accounts to avoid probate. Check your local state laws. Some states take more than a year to finish the probate process for a house. As of 2014, my state (Mass.) has an exemption of 1 million, not portable to your spouse, and they calculate the entire estate when it exceeds the exemption. There is no estate tax if my estate is a million dollar. I have to pay a rate on 1,000,001 if it just exceeds it by one dollar. That's why we should move 30 miles north to New Hampshire.

  I estimate that it takes about three years for the average estate to be distributed. You want to cut down the duration by having a will to start, so you do not want to pay extra to your lawyer.

- At age 70 ½ (as of 2016), you are required to withdraw them in a schedule and it could put you in higher tax bracket. Roth withdrawal is not counted in the mandatory withdrawal for a person's lifetime as of 2016.

- Roth IRA if qualified could be the best deal.

- I simulate my next year via my tax preparation software and adjust my income accordingly.

- To avoid the extra tax filing such as some oil partnerships, buy them in your non-taxable accounts.

Afterthoughts

- Tax audit signs.
  http://money.cnn.com/gallery/pf/taxes/2014/03/14/tax-audit/index.html?iid=HP_LN
  To summarize, you're supposed to fill a form (8283) when the donation exceeds $500. Your business would be treated as a hobby if you do not have a profit in three out of the last five years. Check the current tax laws.

- Joke on Romney.
  http://www.tonyp4idea.blogspot.com/2012/11/from-air-force-one-to-prison-one.html

- As of 2013, the dividend tax is 20% max. Do not believe it is no tax in tax-deferred accounts. When you withdraw, it will be treated as a regular income and it can be as high as almost 40% (as of 2013). Your dividend tax rate depends on your income.

- When you trade 5 times or more a week, investigate whether you're eligible to trade as a business by the current tax rule. A business allows its owner to deduct business expenses.

- Fidelity: Investment tax.
  https://www.fidelity.com/learning-center/mutual-funds/tax-implications-bond-funds

  ETF Taxes on Foreign Stocks:
  http://seekingalpha.com/article/2491465-foreign-withholding-taxes-in-international-equity-etfs

- Avoid wash sales in your taxable accounts
  http://en.wikipedia.org/wiki/Wash_sale
  .
  I placed one order to sell a loser at a higher price and another one to buy it back at a lower price. When there is a big swing in price for that stock, both orders were executed within 30 days. I cannot claim the

loss of the sold stock for that year. However, the loss can be adjusted to the cost basis of the newly-acquired stock as of 2013.

There are many ways to avoid it. Try not to buy it back within 30 days (check the current regulation) and this is the best way. Buy a similar stock in the same sector. Buy it in your children's account – check the tax law.

Links
Tax Avoidance:
http://en.wikipedia.org/wiki/Tax_avoidance

Tax Law:
http://en.wikipedia.org/wiki/Income_tax_%28U.S.%29

Without paying (gift tax) :
http://en.wikipedia.org/wiki/Gift_tax_in_the_United_States#Gift_tax_exemptions
http://www.irs.gov/Businesses/Small-Businesses-&-Self-Employed/What%27s-New---Estate-and-Gift-Tax
AMT: http://en.wikipedia.org/wiki/Alternative_minimum_tax
Estate planning fun. http://tonyp4idea.blogspot.com/2014/08/estate-planning-101-for-me.html

XI Strategies

A strategy is the whole process in trading stocks:

1. Buy stocks when the market is safe.
2. Find stocks.
3. Evaluate stocks: fundamentals, objective, qualitative and technical.
4. Buy stocks.
5. Sell stocks.

In addition, we use a theme. You select the one that fits your objective and risk tolerance. As in the chapter on finviz.com screener, we have strategy for fundamental stocks and growth stocks. Here are five themes:

1. Long-term swing.
2. Top down.
3. Sector rotation.
4. Tom's conservative strategy.
5. Dividend stocks.

To illustrate, Long-term swing strategy looks for stocks that are fundamentally sound. Evaluate them after half a year of holding to sell or continue to hold.

31 When to sell a stock

There are many reasons to sell a stock as follows.

Personal

1. Has met my targets/objectives.
   It could be a 10% gain in a very short-term swing, x% return in 4 months for a short-term swing or y% gain after a year for long-term trades. Define x and y depending on your risk tolerance and how often you trade.

   I bought 4 stocks in one day during the August, 2015 correction and placed sell orders with 10% more than my purchase prices. I sold one in a day and another one within a month. This is my strategy for correction – sometimes it works and sometimes it does not.

   Never look back. Do not blame yourself when the prices are better than your trade prices. When the market is volatile, use a higher percent of the current prices. Be disciplined. Stay on the same strategy and detach yourself from emotions.

2. Realize that we have made a mistake. Do not let your ego block your eyes. It could be due to bad analysis, bad data, unexpected fraud, lawsuits, and/or unforeseeable events that you have no control of. It is better to get out with a small loss. I prefer a 25% loss as a threshold for long-term strategies and a 10% (or less for some strategies) loss for short-term strategies.

   We have to determine whether it is a mistake or not. If the 'mistake' is just bad luck or due to conditions we cannot possibly predict or control, then it is not a mistake. If it is a mistake, learn from it. When we diversify, one bad loss should not cause a big dent in our portfolios. The stop loss is a good tool most of the time except when there is a flash crash.

   If the criteria have been faithfully followed and it does not work well, check out whether your criteria are wrong, or it does not work on the current market conditions.

3. When we have too many stocks in the same sector, we will want to replace some stocks to better diversify our portfolios.

When the sector is rising, we want to weigh more on that sector at the expense of diversification, and vice versa. Set a limit of how many sectors you should hold.
4. Need cash for living expenses.
5. To reduce a tax burden by selling some losers. Tax consideration should not be the primary reason for selling. Take advantage of the favorable tax treatment for long-term capital gains. In short, sell losers within the short-term limit (currently a year), and sell winners after 365 days; check the current tax laws.

   Harvest tax losses. Sell losers and buy back similar stocks (or same stock after 31 days to avoid wash sale). It is not too clear in which you can buy back the same loser in your children's account under the current tax law.
6. To take advantage of a lower tax. In 2013, we can pay virtually zero (except the increase of tax on social security payment) Federal income taxes on long-term capital gains when our income is below a specific tax bracket (15% as of 2015). Check out the current tax laws. Evaluate the sold winners for a possible buy back.

Market Timing

7. When the market or the sector plunges, sell stocks or stocks within the sector.
   For temporary peaks, evaluate which stocks in your portfolio to sell based on fundamentals. The objective is to raise cash for buying opportunities.

Deteriorating appreciation potential

8. There may be some stocks that have a better appreciation potential than the ones you currently own. Churning the portfolio by replacing better stocks may cost some brokerage commissions (some are free today) and taxes for taxable accounts, but it improves the quality and the appreciation potential for the entire portfolio.
9. The company's fundamentals have changed for the worse. If you use a scoring system, compare the current score with the score you actually bought the stock for. Apple is a good example from 2013 to 2015. Buy when the fundamentals are good and sell when they are not.

   The basic fundamentals are expected P/E, the quarter-to-quarter earnings growth rate / the sales growth rate, and Debt /Equity.

When your stocks have passed the peak and started to decline, sell them. When they are heading to bankruptcy, sell them fast.

Hints that the fundamentals are degrading

Evaluate the stocks you own at least every 6 months and check their daily news at least once a week that can be easily done using Seeking Alpha's portfolio function.

- The cash flow is decreasing fast. Cash flow is not a particularly good predictive indicator for appreciation, but a good indicator on whether the company will survive. This metric is very hard to manipulate.
- A new or pending lawsuit. Check out how serious the lawsuit is and be aware that a minor lawsuit can be ignored. Companies always sue against each other.
- A big drop in sales. Do not be alarmed when a new product, or a new drug is going to replace a major product. Compare sales to the same quarter of prior year to avoid seasonal fluctuations (Q-to-Q info I available from Finviz.com).
- Management deteriorates- One hint is the deteriorating ROE from the last quarter.
- The extravagant lifestyle of the CEO and the many easy loans to officers.
- Poor operations. They include recalls of products such as the GM recall on ignition switches, product secrets being stolen and customers' credit card info being stolen. Boeing's 747-Max is a warning call.
- A successful product from the competitor, or the current product is losing its market share, or becoming a low-profit commodity.
- Insiders and/or institutional investors are dumping the companies' stocks far more than the averages (2% for me) especially in heavy volumes and by more than one insider. Info is available from Finviz.
  - Have more than one insider dumping a lot of the stock within a month and no insider purchase in that month.
  - Have more than one insider decrease their holdings by more than 10%.
- When the SEC or any government agency pays attention to a company, it usually means bad news.
- Deceptive accounting practices have been discovered.

- Increasing receivable and/or inventory at an alarming rate.
- Earnings have been restated too many times.
- Short percentage is increasing fast – someone found something wrong with the company.
- The invalidity of 'one-time charges'.
- Abnormal return rate of the company's pension fund comparing to the average of the companies in the same sector.
- Too many and too costly reconstructing charges.
- The entire stock market is plunging as indicated by our chart in detecting market crashes.
- The stock price does not move up with good news. It shows the price has peaked.
- The accumulation amount is far less than the sold amount. When the stock price is up, the accumulation is less than the sold stocks when the stock price was down the last time. It indicates that no more accumulation is ahead and hence the stock will be down most likely.
- Death Cross. Many times the stock price falls for unknown reasons. Technical tells us something is wrong. "A death cross **appears when the 50-day moving average crosses below the 200-day moving average**, an event that many chart watchers view as marking the spot a shorter-term correction morphs into a longer-term downtrend." The opposite is the Golden Cross.
  https://www.youtube.com/watch?v=BaZxE12cZP4

Afterthoughts

- Another article on this topic.
  http://buzz.money.cnn.com/2013/04/05/stocks-sell/
  An article from Investopedia. Nothing new but it is worth having the same second opinion.
  http://www.investopedia.com/financial-edge/0412/5-tips-on-when-to-sell-your-stock.aspx

- It also depends on your strategies. I sell most of my stocks in my momentum portfolio within a month. At least one strategy I know of does not keep any stock during the peak stage of the market cycle – the easiest time to make money but also the riskiest time.

  If you use charts for trading, sell the stocks that are below your moving averages or other technical analysis indicators. Personally, I do not use charts for making sell decisions due to my limited time.

- Sell when the company is heading into bankruptcy as described before. The red flags are: 1. Negative cash flow. 2. Heavy insiders dumping the stocks. 3. Pending major lawsuit. 4. Fraud from the management.
- Risky periods for a stock.
Earnings announcement (4 times a year), settling a major lawsuit and/or during an FDA event in approving a drug are risky periods for a stock. A fluctuation more than 5% in either direction is normal. Some use options to buy insurance. Most ignore it. For the majority of the time, heavy insider purchase is a good indicator. There are rumors (or educated guesses) on earnings before their announcements. Zacks is supposed to be a good subscription for earnings estimates.

Selling a winner

Let the profit rise and at the same time protect your profit. Tesla quadrupled its value in 6 months. Examples abound such as Amazon and Yelp.

If you do not know what to do, here are my suggestions:
- Sell half of the stocks.
- Sell the dollar amount equal to what you paid for.
- Use trailing stops. I did not do this when my Game Stop stock appreciated by 300% and it turned out for far more appreciation. Guilty as charged.

You do not want to sell these rocket stocks even if their fundamentals do not make sense. Buffett does not touch these rocket stocks and he usually misses these big gains. However, many of these rocket stocks such as BRRY (Blackberry) will eventually fall losing most of their value. I bet the institutional investors move the market in either direction and usually they read the same analysts' reports. You profit as a contrarian if you have a good reason to act against the herd.

The following example uses a 10% trailing stop – mine is a little different from the official trailing stop described in the link section. Set the stop at 10% of the current price (i.e., 10% less than the current price), not the purchase price. You need to change the stop when the price rises but do not change it when the price falls. Review your stops every month or more frequently if time allows.

To illustrate, when the stock price rises to 100, set the stop at 90. When the stock price falls to 90, sell the stock at the market price. When the stock price rises to 200, change the stop price at 180.

The stop should also be set according to how volatile the stock is. Some stocks are more volatile than others. Most charts show the resistance line. This line assumes the stock price should not fall below this line in normal fluctuations. Set the stop at 2% below this line so your stock will not be stopped out in theory.

Do not stop orders on stocks with low volumes as they can be manipulated, especially after hours. In this case, you just place market orders to sell them.

To avoid flash crashes, do not place stop orders. Instead, do it mentally (mental stop is my term). When you see that the stock falls below your stop with no sign of a flash crash, sell the stock using a market order.

Of course, there is no bullet-proof scheme. This one should work in the long run. This is my suggestion only, so examine whether it works for you. Small cap and/or stocks with small average volumes fluctuate more.

Examples

I have too many bad examples of selling the stocks too early and sometimes holding them too long.

I made over 40% in a few weeks on ALU, but it went up more than 300% in the next two years. It was acquired in early 2016 by Nokia paying a good premium. I was right that ALU had a lot of valuable patents and I was wrong to dump it when I found out Cisco did not have any intention to acquire it – a big mistake by Cisco and the U.S.

FOSL is another example to teach us to use mental stop loss. FOSL was priced at $33.70 on 1/4/2010. Its fundamentals were just fine with an expected E/P (expected earnings yield) at 6% but decreasing earnings. It gained 115% later in 2010 - not expected.

On 1/3/2011, the expected E/P was still at around 6% and improving earnings. It gained 9% for the year – a little disappointing.

On 1/3/2012, the expected E/P was 7% and a huge earnings growth. Now, we expected a better performance for the year and it did by gaining 20%.

On 1/3/2013, the expected E/P was about 6% and the earnings gain was respectable. It gained 28% to $121. So far, so good.

On 1/2/2014, the E/P and the earnings growth were about the same as in 1/3/2013. However, it lost 7% for the year while SPY (an ETF simulating the market) gained 12%. There was no warning. Did the institutional investors lose the interest of this stock?

On 1/2/2015, the E/P was 7% and the earnings growth was about the same as the previous year. It lost 69% (vs. SPY's 0% return with dividends)!

From 1/4/2010 to 1/3/2016, the annualized return of FOSL is 0% (vs. SPY's 13%). Actually, after dividends, SPY should have an annualized return of about 15%. The lessons gained here are:

- Fundamentals (using EP and earnings growth in this example) may not always work. Otherwise, 2015 should have the same gain as 2014.
- The rosy outlook of the stock may be priced in already. When the outlook fails to materialize, the stock tanks.

Links: Fidelity Video: Trailing Stop Loss. 2 3
https://www.fidelity.com/learning-center/trading/trailing-stops-video
https://www.youtube.com/watch?v=l7EHWyOrfu4

https://www.investopedia.com/terms/t/trailingstop.asp

Examples of overpriced stocks

In 2011, there were discussions on the high valuation of Netflix in several articles in Seeking Alpha, an investment website. LinkedIn and Facebook shares were believed to be overvalued even before their IPOs. Here are some of my thoughts on Netflix and the same concept can be applied to other stocks.
- Reward / Risk ratio.
  If the stock has the same probability to move up by 30% and move down by 50%, it is overvalued by 20% (50% - 30%). As of 2011, Netflix shares may rise, but it is too risky for me.
- Compare the P/E to its five-year average.
  The current P/E is 60 and the average for the last 5 years is 30. From this metric it is overvalued by 100%.

The 'E' in P/E can be either expected (same as forward) earnings or based on the last 12 months (same as trailing or historical). It has been proven that the 'expected' is a better indicator than the 'historical'. AAII demonstrated this by comparing the performances of the expected PEG screen and the historical PEG screens over a long period of time.

- Fools who invested in the high P/E stocks and did not do their due diligence in 2000 had parted with their money fast. I could not convince my friends to take money off their internet stocks. It is similar to asking the lottery winners not to buy lottery tickets.
- Buying an expensive stock is like over paying for a hot dog cart in NYC for $100,000. The buyer will sell many hot dogs, but the rate of return of the investment will be minimal, and it will never recover the initial investment. "Buy high and sell higher" is a momentum play. It works if it is played with stops, but I prefer to "Buy low and sell high".
- Following a decent and proven investing strategy consistently should lead to success through persistence and adjustments. In the long term, a bad strategy always loses money.
- When the market favors growth / momentum (vs. value), it is OK to buy stocks with prices higher than the intrinsic values by a small percentage. The tide is on your side. However, be attentive to any indication that the market is changing direction. For example, NFLX has an average annual return rate of 177% vs. SPY's 14% from 1/3/2011 to 1/3/2020 without considering dividends. Hence, a trailing stop would do the job for the rocket stock.

32   Define Swing trading

The definition varies from different folks. I define it as several styles in investing. Basically it is not "buy and hold". Most well-known companies have great returns in the first ten years, but not the second ten years. If you follow this strategy, use "Buy and Not Forget". Holding index ETFs is better as they replace better stocks once or so a year.

We exit the market when the market is plunging and reenter afterwards as indicated by my simple technique. To me, "Buy and Hold" is dead since 2000 as illustrated by the few articles praising it after 2000. The average loss of the last two major market crashes is 45%.

Evaluate your requirements, your available time for investing and the size of your portfolio, and then decide which style would fit your requirements.

I further subdivide swing trading into long-term (6-12 months), short-term according to your average holding period. This book describes both strategies. Many tools can common to all the strategies. However, long-term swing stresses more on fundamental metrics than momentum metrics. P/E (Price / Earnings) is a fundamental metric and SMA-20 (Simple Moving Average for the last 20 sessions) is a momentum metric.

To summary, this book categories swing trading into short term (holding for 3 months) and long term (6 months). The following belong to even shorter terms: Momentum (less than 1 month), Rotation (1 – 2 month), Insider (3 months), Headlines (1 – 3 months), Day trading (1 day and not discussed in this book). The holding periods are for guidelines only.

First do not buy any stocks if the market is risky. Value stocks are for important for long-term swing.

1. **Long-term swing (about 6 to 12 months)**

I also call it long-term swing. Most of my money was made using this strategy. It is simple and effective.

Buy a stock with favorable fundamental metrics. When you buy a stock based on values, you're swimming against the tide. Hence, it will take at least 6 months for the market to realize its value.

After 6 months from the initial purchase or sometimes even earlier, evaluate the bought stock again based on the same fundamental metrics used. If the company's outlook and/or the fundamentals changes for the worse, sell it. If not, keep on holding the stock for another 6 months and repeat the same evaluation. We would like to keep the stocks over a year for better tax treatment on long-term capital gain; check the current tax laws.

We have to be flexible in the holding period. If there is any major event such as a major lawsuit or a new fierce competitor or a new competing product, evaluate the situation and decide whether you should sell the stock. To keep you informed, enter the bought stocks into the portfolio in SeekingAlpha and check the articles under the Portfolio tab. In addition, use finviz.com to check articles on the stocks you own.

This is the primary investing style for me. Most of the wealthiest investors use this or a similar method. Buffett holds his stocks longer. Soros and Jim Rogers bet on longer-term development of the economy.

2. **Short-Term (3 months) Swing.**

Most associate it with swing trading and it may be the reason you bought this book. Contrary to the popular belief, it is the hardest way to make money while #1 is the easiest and requires less work. If you believe you can learn it by studying several books, most likely you will lose your shirt. Most beginners cannot compete with the experienced, disciplined professional traders.

Books are no substitute for the experience in actual trading with real money. The following is my recommendation to pursue using technical analysis for swing investing:

Study one or two indicators (SMA is a good one) thoroughly. The most common mistake for beginners is using several technical indicators that they do not understand completely. Try out finviz.com to use screen to select stocks based on technical parameters.

Beside this book, read a book on the experiences of actual, expert traders. Take a class. One charges several thousands of dollars but it lets you trade with real money provided by the company.

Using SMA (Simple Moving Average) as an example, the experienced can find a buy signal when the stock price or a sector ETF moves above its moving average and sell when it moves below the moving average. It is quite simple, but it works for most stocks and probably it is better than most other technical indicators.

The common number of days (actually sessions) affects how you want to keep the stock. For example, use SMA-20 (20 sessions) if you keep stocks for average 20 sessions. SMA-50 and SMA-200 are common parameters. For starters, you do not need to learn charting by entering the stock symbol in finviz.com and it will display the three common parameters. To illustrate, if SMA-50% is positive, it is normally a buy signal.

The stocks that are usually better fitted for technical analysis are large cap stocks with high volume. I prefer stocks that are fundamentally sound and do not short them at least initially. For volatile stocks, I prefer higher percent such as SMA-50% > 10% instead of > 0%.

Try the stock in its historical chart and decide the best parameters for charting this stock. Past behavior does not guarantee future behavior, but it is better to have a guideline than with no guideline.

Be aware that this discipline requires you spending a lot of time on the screen. The shorter the duration (hence the faster the parameter such as 20 instead of 50 in SMA), the more time you need to check your stocks. That's the reason you do not want to keep more than 15 stocks for this style of investing.

I use technical analysis more frequently to detect market crashes and sectors that proves to be a better indicator than on stocks. Technical indicators usually work better in shorter durations than fundamental metrics.

When the market is safe, the sector the stock belongs to is favorable and the stock is favorable as measured by SMA, then the chance of its appreciation is high.

Besides charting and many sites providing technical indicators and patterns, use finviz.com to specify them in the screener. The following are quite useful besides Bollinger Bands, MACD and SMA: RSI(14), Double Bottom, Golden Cross (opposite to Death Cross) and Inverted Head & Shoulder. Use Wikipedia, Investopedia, StockCharts, Stockpedia or Google to find out their meanings and examples.

Again, it is better to start with one or two indicators/patterns and thoroughly test out their performances before committing real money. Day trading is not covered in this book. Basically it is riding on the wagon of the institution investors as detected by the huge volume.

- Buy at the support line and sell at the resistance line. It is important to have stops to reduce short-term losses and let the winners run higher. Even with a 40% win percent, you can make huge profits with the above strategy.

- There are many strategies for short-term swings. This book describes Simple Moving Average (SMA-50), Bollinger Bands, RSI(14) for over/under bought... Stick with one instead of jumping from one strategy to another.

- The size of the bet is important. Recommend to reduce the size of the bet when it the bet is risky and/or the potential appreciation is low.

3. Trade by headlines

Headlines usually drive the market briefly as indicated. Need to evaluate the headline news and trade fast. Depending on the news, I trade sector ETFs, market ETFs and sometimes stocks. Personally I have not practiced it enough to draw a conclusion due to my limited time, despite the potential return is very good.

4. Sector momentum / bottom / rotation

It is hard to detect the bottom of a sector, but it is easy to track the trend. I rotate ETFs and my annuity funds monthly based on momentum. In a nutshell, I buy the winner of last month.

5. Following insiders

Purchases by CEO and CFO at market prices in substantial quantities is a good sign. Do not forget to evaluate the fundamentals and avoid many traps. Charts usually can identify the trend after these purchases especially on the rising volumes. Check out the web site Open Insider. I check out insider purchases once a month.

6. Momentum

I also call it short-term swing (1 month for me).

Buy the momentum stocks and sell them within a month.

I use subscription services and select the momentum stocks before my own evaluation. Most of my subscription services assign a timely score. It only takes less than an hour a week.

Alternatively and for those who do not subscribe investment service, use momentum metrics and technical indicators to spot the trend. Use the technical screen of the free finviz.com to screen stocks.

The annualized return is about 100% from Dec. 2012 and the annualized return this year (as of 3/2014) is about 50%. They are inflated due to not considering the following:

- the cash between trading,

- the exception of the rising market during this period, and
- the contra ETFs to hedge the market.

When the market is risky, I skip using this strategy. The exception is buying contra ETFs that have favorable technical indicators such as SMA.

Summary table for Swing strategies

	Long Term	Short Term	Moment.	Headline	Sector Rotation	Insider
Avg. Duration	6 - 12	3	1	Vary	1 - 2	1 – 3
Fundamental	100%	50%	20%	10%	10%	50%
Technical	0%	50%	80%	90%	90%	50%

Explanation

The above are guidelines. It varies from stock to stock.

- For Long Term Swing. Evaluate the stock every 6 months and decide the hold and sell action.
- The average hold time for headline depends on the news. You have to react to it fast. It is similar to the insider strategy.
- In general fundamentals are important to stocks you intend to hold them long term. For other strategies I still prefer value stocks. However, when you only keep the stock for a month or so, I prefer momentum metrics such as SMA-20. The percentages indicate the balance between the two categories of the metrics.

33 Tom's conservative strategy

Tom's conservative strategy

The following is a summary of Tom's conservative strategy as described in his profile in Seeking Alpha web site. Use it as an example and modify it to fit your investing philosophy. You need to ignore your friends telling you how much money he is making when the market is up. You also need not to tell them how much money you're not losing otherwise you do not have any friend.

I believe the best performance is achieved matching a strategy to the current market conditions and there is no Holy Grail in investing.

Click here for Tom's strategy.
(http://tonyp4idea.blogspot.com/2012/05/tom-armisteads-investment-strategy.html)

A winning strategy for couch potatoes

My friend John has a very similar strategy similar to Tom's. My friend is making money with the least risk. He only buys stocks after the market crashes and sell stocks when the market rises. Ignore all market pundits. It is recommended to anyone who does not have time to monitor his/her investment.

He bought stocks in 2008-2010 and sold them after 2010. It was great profit for him in 2000-2008 using this simple strategy. However, he missed the gains from 2010 to 2014. It is unusual that we have such a long bull market. I beg he is still beating most mutual fund managers with this simple strategy that does not require much work.

Enhance a good strategy

Following the favorable stages to trade in the market cycle described in this book, buy in the Early Recovery phase (about 1 ½ year after the crash or use the entry point described in the chapters on Market Timing), sell in one or two years after and maintain cash for the rest of the time.

Here are some options if you have time to watch the market.

- Buy some good stocks in Nov. 1 and sell them in April 1.

- Buy some good stocks in Dec. 1 and sell in Feb. 1 to take advantage of the best (statistically) period of the year.
- Buy stocks in the year before election and sell them after a year.
- Add long-term bonds when the interest rate is high (say more than 5%).

Spend the rest of the time in the comfortable couch (i.e. enjoying life) or sip some fancy tropical drink served by some beautiful tropical lady in some nice tropical island. Not a bad strategy!

How to cure poverty

Contrary to the popular belief, the best cure for the poor is reducing our generous welfare and training the poor. If you have to cut down all the goodies to take a job, you will not take a job. Laziness is a human nature.

Giving them fish all their life is bad.

Teaching them how to fish is good.

Ms. Thatcher said or something similar from my memory: Socialism will die when we run out things to give. In another words, the parasites and the hosts both will die.

---

34 Top-Down investing in a nutshell

Only buy stocks when the market is favorable. Find the best industry (a subsector) and then find the best stock(s) within the selected industry. In doing so, our chance of successful investing is substantially increased.

It is so simple and it has been proven by many including myself. I just wonder why it has not been extensively practiced. I offer a simple trade plan as follows:

1. Do not invest when the market is plunging. I have a simple way to detect market plunges without any expensive subscriptions or tools.

2. Select the best industry. For example, Technology is a sector. Computer and Software are industries (subsector under Technology). From time to time I use sectors for simplicity and most free sites do not sub divide the sectors into industries.

    If you're a value investor, you may not want to choose the timeliest sector but the most under-valued sector. Value investors should hold the sectors/stocks longer (such as 6 months or even longer) for the market to recognize their values.

    In addition, you need to detect sector/stock rotation by the institution investors who control over 75% of all trades (i.e. smart money). They will rotate sector/stock when they find better profit potential in another sector/stock.

    If you do not have time to research on stocks, trade ETFs for sectors and skip the next step.

3. The final step is to select the best stock(s) within the sector via fundamental analysis (including intangible analysis), insider trading analysis, institution trading analysis and technical analysis.

Do not let these terms scare you. We will start with the simplest approach without any subscription and a lot of effort. Many free sites including finviz.com will tell you the best recent performers.

4. The next step is when to reevaluate and sell the stocks when conditions change or they meet your objectives. If the market is plunging, sell all stocks.

Stick and repeat the entire process.

The easiest retirement planning system

Have a budget and live within your means. Buy good stuff that last for a long time. After saving enough cash for emergency and planned expenses such as vacation, new car, college, etc., invest your extra money in a retirement account (Roth IRA if allowable) with 80% in a market ETF and 20% in a short-term bond ETF.

Run the chart described in the market cycle chapters once a month. If the chart tells you to exit the market, move all to cash. Reenter the market when the chart tells you so. It beats most if not all of your financial plans from the best experts money can buy.

Afterthoughts

My late friend had a 'buy and hold strategy' that worked pretty well. Most of his stocks were big companies. He died with a house worth more than a million and many millions in stocks. His only mistake was not to transfer more of his stocks to his heirs before his death. He died on the year when the estate exemption returned back to a million. Uncle Sam was the biggest winner and won big without any effort.

35   Sector Rotation

Sector rotation has been proven to make good profits at the least risk if it is properly implemented. This book improves your odds in making profits than traditional schemes in sector rotation by:

- Market Timing. When the market is plunging, do not buy any stock including sector ETFs and sector funds. This book provides a simple chart to detect market plunges. Basically it is a sector rotation between SPY (an ETF that simulates the market) and cash (or an ETF of short-term bonds).

- The next rotation strategy involves four ETFs in a rising market described in Chapter 4. Optionally, you can include a contra ETF to time the market. Buy the best performer of last month of the selected ETFs.

- Some sectors perform better in different stages of a market cycle.

- Many free sites describe the best sector performers such as Seeking Alpha and CNNfn.

- Evaluate sector using Technical Analysis and Fundamental Analysis. Use the same tools to evaluate individual stocks within a performing sector – top-down investing.

- You should spend one hour or two a month to determine which sector to rotate to or move your portfolio to cash when the market is risky. The "Buy and hold" strategy does not perform since 2000.

- Subscription services. There are many. Even if you subscribe these services, you should read this book to evaluate their services and use this book as a second opinion. When your portfolio is over $100,000, $100 for a yearly subscription should pay itself in the long run.

- Market timing by calendar and presidential cycle.

- My recent experiences in sector trading.

- Be careful on many books on this topic were written by professors who may never make a buck in the stock market.

- Some "best" sellers were written more than 10 years ago that do not have today's basic tools such as technical analysis and bear any resemblance to today's market, which can be manipulated by institution investors.

- Most large companies today are global companies. The importance in investing foreign companies to diversify is less important than before.

- When China expands, natural resource-rich countries would most likely benefit.

- Most similar books have one strategy and this book has 11 strategies. You can combine the strategies such as market timing with last month's best-performed sector.

Besides industrial sectors, I include bonds, contra ETFs, sector mutual funds, countries, commodities, etc. Today, most sectors are covered by ETFs. For example, you do not need to buy gold coins to invest in that sector but the ETF GLD.

Sectors

The primary sectors are: Basic Materials, Consumer Discretionary, Consumer Staples, Energy, Financial, Health Care, Industrial, Technology and Utilities. Click the links or search from Wikipedia for description of these sectors.

https://www.fidelity.com/sector-investing/overview

We can sub divide a sector into industries. For example, Technology can be divided into Computer and Software. Some industries such as banking software can cross more than one sector.

The above links describe sectors pretty good by Fidelity with the exception of Technology, which is divided into several sectors such as Software, Computer and Telecom by Fidelity. Here are my views on the major sectors.

Consumer Staples and Discretionary

Consumer Staples are food, beverages, household products and the products we buy as necessity. They are recession-proof. The US products have demonstrated high quality and safety. With the growing middle class in developing countries such as China and India, we expect they should grow outside the USA. Currently it is not due to tariffs.

Consumer Discretionary are just the opposite.

Sector Timing

During a recession some sectors such as Consumer Staples and Health Care work better than other sectors such as Technology. They will be opposite from above during the go-go era when consumers have more money to buy non-essential goods and companies have money to invest.

Some sectors are more volatile than others. Some sectors such as Health Care would benefit by the growing or aging global population.

Sectors	Major Industries	Favorable
Basic Materials	Metals, Mining, Chemicals	High inflation / Growing economy
Consumer	Auto, Building, High-	Low interest rate

Discretionary	end Retail	
Consumer Staples	Food	Recession
Energy	Oil, Gas, Exploration	Growing economy
Industrial	Machines	Economic recovery
Health Care	Delivery, Drugs, Biotech	Recession for Delivery
Financial	Bank, Insurance	High interest, Growing economy
Technology	Computer, software	Growing economy
Utilities	Electricity, Gas	Recession

A list of sectors.
http://www.investorguide.com/sector-list.php

36 Dividend investing

This is a popular strategy now and is expected to be so for the next 20 years. We have a lot of retirees who depend on incomes from investments. The low interest rates in CDs and bonds drive these folks to dividend stocks.

Here is a simple screen to find these stocks. First find the stocks that have dividend rate more than 2% (about half of the S&P 500 stocks). Take out those sectors that give dividends as a return of equity (REITs and many partnerships). Eliminate the stocks with bad fundamentals such as high expected P/E, high debt (compared to companies in the same sector), etc. Next ensure they should have a good history of maintaining or increasing dividends (i.e. dividend growth).

However, when a strategy is over-used, it may not work anymore (see related chapter). There may be a mild bubble on these dividend stocks (due to too many followers). We will discuss how to protect our dividend portfolio.

In addition, we should not buy (actually should sell) stocks during a market plunge. I will describe how to detect market plunges and corrections. Since 2000, we have two market plunges with an average loss of over 45%.

There are at least three major ways to receive dividends:

1. Dividends given to stock owners (registered on and before the ex-div date).

2. [DRIPs](http://en.wikipedia.org/wiki/Dividend_reinvestment_plan), Dividend Reinvest Plan.
   http://en.wikipedia.org/wiki/Dividend_reinvestment_plan

3. Covered Calls. You can receive 'rents' and dividends while 'renting' your stocks.

I will skip those stocks (REITs and partnerships) that return capitals as they would usually depreciate the stocks.

XII Investment advice

We need to distinguish useful information from garbage.

37   Newsletters and subscriptions

I've been using investment newsletters / subscriptions for years. Many are priced reasonably and some are even free. While a lot of them are garbage, some are very good.

When you have a lot of money to invest and you're not using a financial adviser and/or not subscribing to any investment service, it could be a big financial mistake. You do not want to be penny smart but pound foolish. However, you could be among the few exceptions if you have the knowledge and time to make use of the free financial data, guidance and articles from the web.

You need a computer, access to Internet and a spreadsheet in order to use most subscription services effectively.

I'm not going to compare specific systems / newsletters, but will include general pointers on how to select them. Yesterday's garbage could be a gold mine today if the subscription improves and/or the market conditions fit what they recommend.

First, you need to find what you need and how much time you can afford to use them. If you have $20,000 or less to invest, most likely you just buy an ETF such as SPY as your investment both in money and time will not pay off.

Here are some pointers.

- Newsletters giving you specific stocks to buy do not require much of your time. However, if they're successful, there will be too many followers buying the same stocks to drive up the prices of the recommended stocks at least temporarily. The owner and his insiders will buy the recommended stocks before you. I had several of this kind of newsletter, and so far I have not renewed any one of them.

- If I found the Holy Grail in investing, do you believe I'll share it with you for $100 or so? I only will after I invest my findings first. My subscribers would push up the prices for me and then I unload them before them.

- If the volumes of the recommended stocks are small, they can be manipulated easily either by the newsletter owners and/or by your peer subscribers. The first ones to sell the recommended stocks win and the last ones to sell lose.

- I prefer systems that can find a lot of stocks by providing many searches (same as screens). However, it will take a lot of time to learn and test their performances that would require a historical database. Most likely, you need to further research on each stock screened. The service would select a limited number of stocks for further analysis, so it will save time.

    From my experience, the best performance comes from the stocks that have been screened by more than one search especially for shorter term (less than 6 months). My theory is that they've been identified by more folks and the buyers jack up the prices. There will be more profits to buy them ahead of the herd and sell them before the herd.

- We all receive promotional mails that they could at least triple the return of your investment. Just ignore them. If it is that good, most likely they will keep them for themselves. Same for seminars to boost some penny stocks. Sometimes the recommended stocks will rise initially to lure you and other suckers to move it. Watch out!

- A 'guru' told me that he made a big fortune in silver a month ago. Guess what? He also recommended selling it two months ago and lost a lot of money in doing so. He is always right but he will not advertise the times he was wrong. We call it a double talk technique.

- There are free (or deeply discounted) subscription services. Take advantage of them. Some services require you to spend a lot of time, so ensure you have the time. Keep track of the performance yourself via paper trading.

- Subscribe the newsletter to fit your style of investing. If you're a day trader, newsletters on long-term investment are not good for you. Some subscriptions handle all kinds of investing styles and you need to find the strategies and recommendations to fit your style.

- Newsletters on penny stocks are most likely too risky for most of us. I define penny stocks as less than $2 and a market cap less than 100 M. However, I do buy stocks with prices around $2 in stock price or a capital cap less than 100 M. Actually I bought ALU at $1 but ALU's market cap then was about 2 billion. The stocks with prices between $1 and $10 represent the most volatile and some are real, ignored gems as most analysts do not do research on them.

- There are many sectors like drugs, mines and banks that we cannot evaluate effectively ourselves. It is better to seek expert advices.

- Remember there is no free lunch in life. The higher potential return of a stock is, the riskier the stock is.

- Some newsletters / subscriptions save us time by summarizing the financial data like a value rank and a growth rank. When the market favors growth, you use the growth rank (vs. a value rank), and vice versa.

- Be careful on the commercials particularly from radio in selling to peoples' fears and their greed by overstating without necessarily telling the whole story. There is no free lunch. It is not possible to make 25% in covered calls consistently or making another gold rush from $400 to $1,800.

- TV financial shows usually exaggerate in order to sell their staffs. Analyze before you act on the news.

- As a retail investor, most of us cannot afford to do extensive researches. Many researches and market opinions are available in the internet free. Start to search such information from your broker's site.

- Do not trust the performances of the newsletter providers. There are many ways to manipulate their performances as described in the next chapter.

- Most compare their performances with S&P 500. It is legal for investment newsletters to inflate their performance with dividends while comparing to an index without dividends.

  To illustrate, for the last 10 years, S&P 500 has an average annual return of 1% on appreciation and 1.5% on dividends for a total return of 2.5%. Hence, the performance should compare to 2.5% not 1%.

- The performance of last 10 years is more important than that of 25 years. Their method of stock evaluation / ranking hopefully has been improved. In addition, the last 10 years is a better prediction of the newsletter than the last 25 years.

- When the new major researcher takes over the subscription, s/he may not have the same expertise as the previous researcher.

- Ensure they change their strategies according to the current market conditions. For example, 5 years ago ADRs (U.S. listed stocks of foreign countries) perform better than the current 5 years.

- Few if any use real money for their portfolios, as they cannot cheat with real money. That's why you never achieve the compatible performance by following what the portfolio trades if they do not use real money. Do not trust any performance claims even from reputable monitor services unless the portfolios are in real money or can be verified.

  Some sample portfolios trade excessively and they may not fit your investment strategy not to mention the broker commissions

- When a subscription service has several strategies (say 10 for illustration), it will advertise the best returns of its top strategies (say 2 in our example) for a specific time period.

Contrary to not recommending investment services, here are very low priced or even free subscription services. By opening a small account with a broker, you can access their research. Check your current broker's website on evaluating stocks. AAII is a low-priced subscription with on-line stock research. Yahoo!Finance is very popular among investors. Seeking Alpha is a good web site.

Afterthoughts

- My friend told me he saw an ad that would show him how to make $500 a day for working a few minutes before the market opens. He is nice enough to share his 'discovery' with me. If it is for real, I would be the first one to sign up. If it really works, it will not work very soon. When a strategy is over-used, it will not work. Unfortunately, a fool is born every minute as the same ad has been there for a long time.

- Currently I spend about $1,500 for all subscription services. I believe $200-$600 should cover the basic. To start, you can use your broker's web site for tools. Some have a lot of research for evaluating stocks and some even include searches. Try the biggest broker's research as they spend more on this area. Even if you do not trade with them, use their research by opening an account with the minimum balance.

- If the offer is too good to be true (like making $500 every day with little effort and little investing money), it probably is not. If they give you a free 50" TV for spending $299, most likely it is a trap with bait. Remember there is no free lunch.

    However, some bait is good like the free 30-day trial offer for an investment service or the free dinners I attended seminars on estate planning. It is part of the business cost. If I do not attend more than two dinners, eventually I would end up paying two free dinners for someone I do not even know. This book could be the best deal for your entire investment life if you invest time to read it, digest it and use the ideas that are applicable to you and the current market.

- How to monitor the recent performance of a subscription service. Do not trust their claims and the past performance may not have anything to do with the current or future performance unless they are from reliable sources.

Most subscription services have a free 30-day trial offer. Take advantage of it. Before you sign up, ensure you have enough time to test it out. If you do not have time, you can sign up again using your brother-in-law's name.

To illustrate how to monitor their recent performance, if they give you 20 stocks every week, save the prices and check their performance in the same period you usually hold the stocks. It has busted many well-advertised and very popular subscription services. I prefer to compare the performance to S&P 500 index. It is better to compare it both in an up market and a down market as some strategies amplify their performance by selecting riskier stocks.

- There is one among hundreds of 'highly profitable' subscription I receive. Its rocket strategy can help you to move $500 to $500,000 in six months. I must be stupid not to subscribe their service. They told you how. Of course, they did not use real money in their portfolio. I could if I just selected the big winners (after the fact) and did not tell you my losers. Again, it is that great, they must be stupid to share it with me.

38 Retirees, take notice

When we retire or are being laid off, we have plenty of time. It is bad not to do anything financially and mentally. However, the worst could happen to us: We invested in some venture without due diligence and lost our entire savings. There are so many real-life examples.

Everyone enjoys eating out. Some believe they can make money in opening a new restaurant. Wrong. It is the human nature to be overly optimistic even on this toughest business. Their friends and family members do not want to dampen that enthusiasm. Most new ventures fail miserably.

Investing in stocks is another popular one. Many take a course in day trading. If their system works that well, why do they want to show it to you? When you want to invest in stocks, you should have many years of investing experience and do not gamble with the money you cannot afford to lose.

One retiree lost all his money in the stock market which has too much volatility, and died because of worries. After several years, the market revived but he did not.

One retired headmaster worked as a partner in a small brokerage firm. Despite having fame and fortune initially, never-the-less he eventually lost all his money. He executed an order without checking his client's maximum bet allowed. The bet was a total loss and this verbal order based on trust could not be legally bound.

The retired and famous baseball player from Boston lost all his money by owning a company that made video games. Even though he was an excellent baseball player, he was not a business man and his failure was almost a sure thing. For every successful story, there must be more failures that are not publicized. In most cases, no ambition is the best ambition during our retirement. Investing in something we do not understand will likely cost us money, effort, frustration, and even our health.

Withdrawing 401Ks and IRAs.
(http://tonyp4idea.blogspot.com/2012/09/withdrawing-iras.html)

39 The advantages of a retail investor

Why we, the retail investors, can beat the professional fund managers? It is not likely if you consider all those research resources they have. It is likely after you read this article. However, in reality, the average retail investor does not beat the market due to switching between stocks and cash at the wrong time. Via the greed, they invest in the peak of the market and via fears they divest in the bottom. They do not expect the market would return in the bottom but it always does.

Most fund managers are smarter than I, better educated in investing than I, have ten times more research tools than I and have ten times more computer power than I. However, most of them do not beat me, the average casual retail investor. In addition, I spend less time in stock research than an average fund manager (most working at least 60 hours a week) - I have a life too and they don't. ☺

It could be:

- They cannot beat the market all the time. When they do, money flows in and vice versa. It is very hard for them to perform with extraordinary cash. When everyone is cashing in their funds, they need to sell stocks even though they have good fundamentals and/or better potential to appreciate.

  The saying "When there is blood in the streets, most likely it is the best time to buy" is correct. 2009 is a recent example. Fund managers cannot take advantage of this opportunity as most clients had cashed out.

- Most cannot play market timing freely and they have to satisfy all the rules set up for the fund. Every time they want to buy a stock, they need to ensure no rules have been broken such as a restricted percent of a stock to the fund. Most funds prohibit their managers to short, buy contra ETFs and/or maintain high cash position. Basically, most are not allowed to react to a market going up or down.

- When they trade, their high volumes are tracked by day traders who can ride on their wagons. Hence they have to pay more to buy and get less to sell.

- By my rough estimate, they have about 1,000 stocks (about 600 for larger funds) to deal with. I as a retail investor have about 3,000 stocks even skipping most stocks with prices below $2 or not listed in the three major exchanges.

Their stocks have been fully evaluated by analysts and newsletters / subscriptions such as Value Line and /or some firms specializing in stock research for them. Hence, they do not gain any advantage by following their peers.

The small and mid-cap stocks are risky but are more rewarding statistically. Many fund managers cannot buy them due to the sizes of their funds.

- Their performance as a group is actually worse as the closed funds due to poor performances are not included. It is termed as survivor bias.

- Not nimble enough.
  By the time when they have done all the research and received the approval to buy a specific stock, I may have bought the stock already. Usually it takes at least a week for a large fund to complete trading a stock.

- The high expenses.
  The fee is about 1.5% for an average fund. The expenses are 2% plus 20% on the profit for an average hedge fund. When the fund also owns the broker, watch out how it can make its brokerage arm more profitable by jacking up the fees. The hedge fund's usual 20% on the profit and no penalty of losing your money encourage its fund managers to take bigger risks.

- Not spend enough time to do own research.
  Most do not spend enough time on basic research and figure why some strategies work and some do not at certain market conditions. They spend a lot of time in following the fund's and the company's objectives, rules and regulations. One fund manager with over 30-year career I know did not do more research than I in the last five years.

- Wrong objective.
  The objective of most funds is beating the common index after expenses. Most fund managers do not want to take too much risk and their personal objective is job security. One will not lose the job if his performance is similar to a target index.

My objective is to beat the index by a good margin at acceptable risk. However, I stay more in cash and I do not care about the performance when the market is risky.

- Most likely their good performance could be due to taking too much unnecessary risk and the high leverage. Their performances improve when the market is good, but degrade when the market is down. When I see the market is coming down, I would park more cash and I only use leverage when the market is going up.

- They buy the same stocks as their peers are buying. If they do not perform within a certain range of a benchmark, they get canned. Hence, they stay away from risky stocks that usually have better profit potentials. We pay them to research these risky stocks to separate the gems from the garbage, not to follow the herd of their peers.

* Retail investors have a lot of advantages over fund managers. However, I advise not to be traders especially day traders for beginners. Statistically most amateur traders lose money as they cannot compete with experienced, disciplined traders. My books do not teach you to be a trader. Even if you study several good books by great traders, you will still lose money initially. No books can replace the actual trading experience.

However, discipline, knowledge and due diligence will make you money in the long term.

XIII The economy

The economy usually follows the market in six months. However, there are many exceptions and 2013 is one of them.

40   The evils of printing money

I just explained to my grandchild that money does not fall from the sky or grow on trees.

Every time we print money, it does the following:

1. An invisible tax is added to the rich as their purchasing power will be decreased.

2. Your children and grandchildren will pay for it.

3. Selling a piece of our asset to foreigners.

4. Our products are less globally competitive as we have to add more taxes to pay for the loans. It is more competitive initially as our currency has been depreciated, but this will not last long.

5. Give more reasons for the rich to give up citizenship and move to another country. Most become rich for being smart.

6. The end of the USD being a reserve currency is closer.

The only winners are the lobbyists and politicians, who bought votes with the money from your pocket.

It will help the stock market in the short-term, but it is very damaging for the long-term economy. That's also the primary reason why the recovery of our economy is taking forever. Printing money to the maximum is not a solution but a problem.

Afterthoughts
- We have inflation (such as most products in the super market) and deflation (such as housing expenses) since 2008. Click here for detail. http://tonyp4idea.blogspot.com/2012/11/inflation-and-deflation-at-same-time.html

- As of 6/2012, we have 16 trillions of debt and it is substantially less depending on whether you include the entitlements. Besides the poor environment, unpromising economy, our children and grandchildren inherit our huge debts. It is about $54,000 debt for each baby born today. However, many foreigners want their babies born here!

- The U.S. is heading to the same path as Japan by jacking up the money printing press. The similarities are:

    1. Both try to flood the market with free cash. It gives the market a false boost (in nominal term and in after inflation term).

    2. The next generation(s) will have to pay for their citizens' debts.

    3. Both governments are running out of tools to stimulate the market. I guess you cannot have interest rate negative (that means I pay you interest to lend you my money).

    The differences are:

    1. The US has a lot of resources (ores, oil, gas, timber, land, farm land...) per capita and the shale energy could save us for the next 50 years.

    2. The U.S. welcomes immigrants (we need to do it selectively) to reduce some of the demographics problems such as social security, welfare, work force...

    3. Japan will continue another decade of the last two lost decades.

Filler:
Relatively speaking (as Einstein said), the US is in far better shape than Japan. Investors should stay away from Japan except the delicious sushi. EU and China and the commodity-rich countries (Russia, Brazil, Australia...) will be in between.

We are not economically better than our parents. Our children will be even worse with loans to pay from our governments. ###

41 Low interest rate

As of 2013, we have the lowest interest rates for a long while, which is normal in a recession. It is a great time to buy a house (especially with the depressed house prices) and / or borrow money.

Low interest rates have many impacts on our investment:

- Usually they're better for the stock market as corporations can borrow at cheaper rates and hence improve the bottom line. In theory but not today, it should be great for the housing market and retailers.

- Corporations can borrow money at favorable rates to buy back their own stocks or acquire other companies to boost their own stock prices.

  However, prolonged period of low interest rate will damage the economy. Japan is one example.

- Dividend stocks will prosper from investment on bonds moving to stocks until interest rate starts moving up.

- Folks including retirees, who depend on fix incomes, will suffer.

- Eventually long-term bonds will suffer big time when interest rate moves up.

The government has to lower the rate to stimulate business, but at the same time it cannot prolong the low rate too long.

Afterthoughts
- As of 8/2012, the yield of 10-year Treasury Bill is about 1.75%, the lowest in my recent memory. It is better to keep cash now than CDs, so we do not miss any opportunity to move back to equity.

- Today, we've the lowest interest rate in memory but we're still in a recession; the Fed is running out of tools to improve the economy.

42   Inflation and deflation

The historical annual average is about 3% inflation. CPI is not a good gauge any more after energy and food are not included.

Inflation is:

- An invisible tax to the rich.

- A strategy to lessen the loan burden. To illustrate, your loan of $1 can buy a loaf of bread now, and you will pay back the $1 plus negligible interest that can buy only half a loaf of bread due to inflation. China is the loser and the USA is the winner in this deal.

- An invisible salary cut.

- An invisible cut to your entitlements/welfare. Social security is supposed to be adjusted to CPI, which can be manipulated by the government by not using food and energy to reduce social security payment increases.

- An invisible cut to your investment incomes (dividends and appreciation).

Deflation is no angel:

However, deflation is far worse than inflation to the economy. When the company produces a product and finds out they have to sell it for less due to deflation, then their profit would be cut and they might need to lay off employees.

To illustrate, a manufacturer of making phones calculates the component costs and the expected sell price. If the cost is too high or the profit too low, he would skip the project.

Inflation and deflation at the same time

As of 6/2013, we have both inflation and deflation at the same time for several years now.

We have inflation in most of our basic necessities: food, gasoline and heat (especially important for the NE) with the exception of rent due to the depressed house prices. Electronic stuffs and PCs are deflated considering how much we can buy today vs. last year. Cars have been slightly deflated when figuring in the extra features.

Outlook

The government should ensure inflation and deflation within an acceptable range (3% to me). It has printed a lot of money and lower interest rate to stimulate the economy and at the same time it could have accelerated inflation. When the economy does not improve, it has run out of tools to improve our depressed economy.

However, the shale energy and time would cure all problems. When the economy is improved, it will accelerate inflation and will also increase the interest rate.

Afterthoughts

- The dollar has lost more than 90% since the FED was created due to inflation. However, it only affects you if you save your cash under the pillow. Our capitalism system punishes those who do not invest and take risk. If you invest in long-term CDs, you're doing barely OK. If you buy any stock such as Edison's new venture or a piece of real estate in your town in 1913, most likely it beats inflation by a good margin and Uncle Sam would glad to share your fortune.

- From my personal experiences.
  The Big Mac Value Meal cost about $1 in 1970 and now it costs $6 – 6 times in 40 years.

  An average house in my hometown in 1980 cost $45,000, and now it costs $450,000 - 10 times in about 30 years.

  Houses in most cases are better deals. Besides paying the tax-deductible property tax and interest, we can live in them.

  The $10,000 under my pillow in 1980 has no gain today, but it gives me a headache every time I sleep on it. ☺

- A bag of 10.5-ounce Lays potato ships is $4.29, and the next day it was downsized it to 9.5 ounces. All items in the grocery store are just like that. The millionaires have no complaint as their stocks (as of 6/2013) have been up and up.

- For those who have jobs, you have a deflation when your same income can buy you more of your basic supplies / services than last year with the exception of food and gasoline.

  Investors' investments are beating the inflation from last year. The wealth gap is widened between the middle class and the rich. Five years ago, the gas price is less than $2 and now it is over $3. We still have high unemployment and high under-employment. Most recent college graduates cannot find jobs or jobs in their choice. It happens all over the world.

- Inflation is controlled by the government via the rate of money being printed and / or easing credit. When we have more money chasing the same quantity of products / services, we have to pay more for them or we call it inflation. In shorter term, it may be distorted by other events such as the deteriorating housing prices.

  With excessive printing, I see hyperinflation in the coming years.

- Inflation is rising.

Labor

We have to divide it into two categories: labor that can't be outsourced and labor that can be.

Labor outsourced to China (your iPhone for example) and India is still relatively cheap.

Labor in the US like flipping burgers, fixing your plumbing problems, or your telephone services will be increased in cost. If they are not, they will be manipulated by the government via welfare (we pay for them eventually via taxes) or the unions. A worker at Burger King cannot survive without government subsidy or family largesse.

Commodities

All commodities including farm land will increase in value due to:

1. Supply and demand - the net growth of population is rising.

2. Excessive printing of money. You will be able to buy half a loaf of bread with the dollar that used to buy you the full loaf.

- My official definition of Fed in my joke book.
  Fed is an agency to the government, or more like a (selected) mistress to the president. The two are not officially related. But, they're on the same bed most of the day. That's why the president always looks so tired.

  I worked there. Unfortunately I did not climb the corporate ladder all the way otherwise we do not have this economic mess. Same reason the Celtics lose as they did not recruit me.

Greatest salesman I ever met

First he makes good jokes and then he tries to be your best friend. All are done in minutes. He tells you he is an artist ignoring all the material stuffs in life. His partner is the business brain who will not sell you these fancy stuffs cheap, so you're lucky today.

I nodded on all his life philosophy and his generous donations to the poor made me cry. After I bought one expensive item from him, I felt I took advantage of the 'poor guy'. It is my real experience, expensive but worth to learn the salesmanship of a great one.

---

43   The states of the United States

Contrary to popular belief, we DO make and build something especially per capita wise. We're still the largest economy on earth and are number one in most disciplines in science and technology. We have a stable government with an enviable constitution, workable regulations, highly-educated citizens and the strongest defense (or offense to me).

Our government and the private citizens (Gates and Buffett for example) donate funds and assistance to poor countries more than the other five richest countries combined. We provide food to the world. We export our culture via movies and music. We accept foreign students to enrich our culture, fund our colleges, and provide us with skilled workers when they graduate.

We have a lot of innovations such as Facebook. Most of our products have high profit margins such as airplanes, heavy equipment, high tech products including Apple's consumer products and medical equipment. Nobody can deny that.

Our success leads to higher living standard. Naturally the higher labor cost and more regulations to protect us and our environment follow. Too many regulations would restrict businesses in taking risks (such as developing new drugs and nuclear reactor technologies) and add costs to product developments.

We have to leave the low-end products to low-wage countries such as China. It is called free trade and globalization, which would benefit all participants if they play the game fairly. China's 1.35 billion citizens would not be able to buy our expensive products if they do not have the cash from selling their products to the world.

We have to protect those products that we have an edge. It is not an easy job just by comparing the quality of our high school education to the rest of the world. Japan and S. Korea have passed us in auto and consumer electronic industries. China is at the gate with bigger impact in the future. China is catching up with us. In addition, it has a large internal market, plenty of qualified engineers / scientists, low-wage workers and incentives / guidance from the government. The most important is their desire and spirit to succeed after three centuries of humiliation.

God still blesses us with the new discoveries of shale energy that could extend our prosperity to another 50 years. It gives us more time to fix our problems, but time is running out. The benefits of the shale energy will be clearer by 2015. It could turn out to be a pure fantasy or even a sham. We are still a net natural gas importer (most from Canada) and our gas industry is currently sitting on heavy losses.

Compared to China, we have far, far more farm land and natural resources especially per capita wise.

Our welfare system is too generous due to our previous economic booms. If the able welfare recipients lose the free medical care for taking a job, do they work? They're lazy but not stupid. With the long dependence on this welfare system, they cannot break the viscous cycle of poverty. Multi generation of teenage mothers is one among many examples.

The new immigration bill could be a disaster. If it is passed, how many new legal residents will collect welfare (they can't today as they're illegal) and how many illegals are encouraged to cross the defenseless border. I hope the new immigrants will contribute more than burden our society. Only time can tell. However, protecting the border is easy by severely punishing the employers. When there are no jobs, they will not come. The USA is still the best country for immigrates.

There are many frauds and fats that the government can trim. The government employees are assigned to tiny work load and they are overly compensated. Should we assign them to chase after the frauds in Medicare, food stamp and cheatings in disability entitlements that are so common?

The two wars are bankrupting this country and we need to prevent starting future wars and end the current wars. As of 2013, our military budget is larger than the total of the next top five countries combined.

From this article, you know the government can fix a lot of our problems. Printing money is not the solution, but the problem by itself.

We need to encourage productivity and discourage consumption. Buying a car is consumption and building a bridge is improving productivity. Welfare to the able poor is consumption and teaching work skills to the poor is improving productivity that leads to production increase.

What worries me most is: We're declining while many developing countries (China in particular) are surging up.

The future will be decided by our high school system which is falling apart. Our society is too permissive from gun controls to legalizing drugs, which may bring infant defects. Our lawyers sue every one for profit no matter how ridiculous the cases are.

Solutions are quite simple

To summarize, we should cut most expenses and balance the budget. It is hard to implement as most do not want to bit the bullet. We're a nation of free loaders with over 40% not working.

1. No illegals to legal. When they become legal, they will collect welfare legally and bring their families in for the same reason.

2. Train and encourage the able welfare recipients to work. Cutting their benefits in taking a job will not encourage them to work. Clinton's Initiative has more holes than Swiss cheese.

3. Cut down our generous welfare. That's why we have three generations of teen-age mothers. Laziness is a human nature.

4. End the endless wars. If they do not want to fight for their own freedom, why should we (suckers in their eyes)?

5. We cannot borrow forever and pass our debts to next generations. USD will not be a reserve currency in 10 years. Printing money excessively is a short-term solution but a problem long-term problem.

6. Invest in our infrastructure.

7. Cut down foreign aids. A big brother is only in the mind of our leaders.

8. We need a small and efficient government. Guard changing when another party takes over is expensive.

Afterthoughts

- Will the new immigrants strengthen our society?
  http://www.americanprogress.org/issues/immigration/news/2012/12/10/47406/progressive-immigration-policies-will-strengthen-the-american-economy/

- Immigration reform will likely depress the average wage over the next 10 years, according to the Congressional Budget Office and also will likely increase our burden in our welfare and entitlement systems.

- Paul said:
  This WAS a country where government did not buy votes. When my grandparents came to the U.S., there were no Federal social programs, no Social Security, no Medicare, no welfare and no income taxes. Millions poured into this country looking for opportunity -- not a safety net...

- From ZeroHedge: (http://www.zerohedge.com/)
  The only recovery you'll see this summer is after a night of heavy drinking...

  Nothing has changed since 2008, nobody was arrested, no laws put in place, nobody held accountable. We all know that companies like JP Morgan and Goldman Sachs bundled toxic sub-prime mortgages into securities and paid off the ratings agencies to rate them AAA then bet against them using CDS with companies like AIG. So what does the government do? Reward their criminal and fraudulent behavior by completely bailing them out and then giving them oodles of cheap credit.

  Have to hand it to them...credit.....credit does not exist. There is only debt, masquerading as credit, which we have been taught because it sounds better. It is a debt crisis and the other side of debt is not credit, but a counter-party/underlying asset. The whole world awash in debt with no solutions offered, most money is created through debt but what they don't tell you is that the interest is never created.

- The USA citizens can be divided into 3 groups according to taxes they're paying:

  1. About 40% not paying Federal tax. When this group grows, we will bankrupt. Representation without taxation is worse than taxation without representation.

  2. Middle class. We're being squeezed by the other two groups.

  3. The rich 5%. They pay most of the taxes. However, in the last two

years, they're fleeing to other places that have low tax treatments. The geese that lay the golden eggs are flying away. Without them, we're squeezed even harder until we're forced to move to the first group and bankrupt the country.

The government needs to encourage folks and/or train them to work. Raising minimum wage is making the problem worse. The government should encourage businesses to stay in the USA and not to tax the very rich excessively.

Links:
Military budgets:
http://247wallst.com/2013/06/27/countries-spending-the-most-on-the-military/?link=mktw

Filler:

Reality

No stock picking contest for me. In order to win this beauty contest, you have to find the riskiest stock (penny stocks, unlisted,...). If it is down to zero, you do not lose anything. You never get killed in crashing a video car. The winner of one popular site wrote an apology post for recommending a stock that lost most of its value.

XIV Two industries

They are used for illustration on sectors.

44 Airlines

How to become a millionaire according to Buffett: "First, become a billionaire and then invest all in airline stocks!"

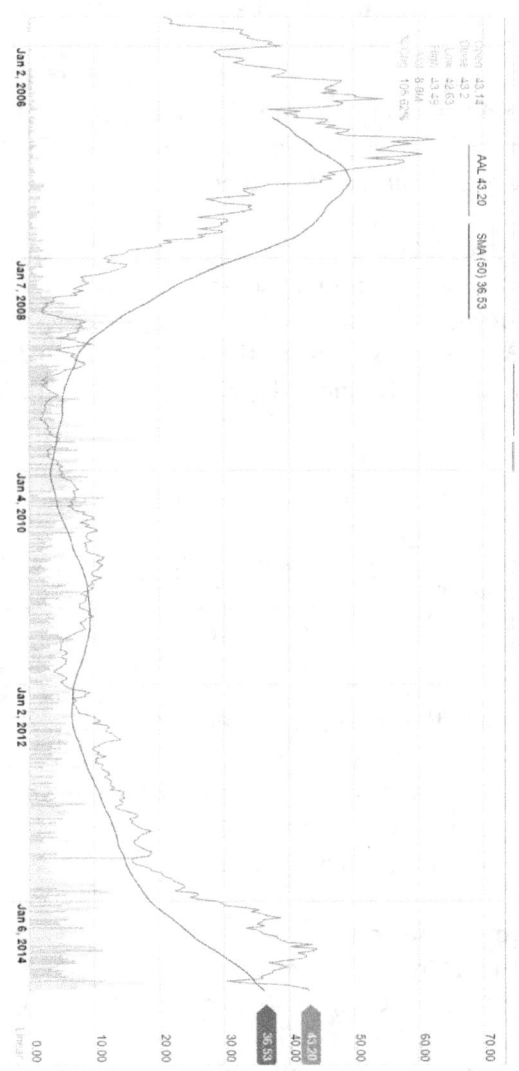

Source: Yahoo! Finance   AAL

He may be right in his time when he made the statement. But, it is not true lately as evidenced by the following chart. You can buy American

Airlines (AAL) for less than $10 from 2008 to 2012 and today in 2014 it is 4 times as much. The pattern has been repeated by other airline stocks.

I cannot find a decent ETF for airlines, so I use AAL (the stock I still own). From Yahoo!Finance, it is the maximum period allowed to draw the above chart. AAL used to be AMR.

It has a peak in Nov. 2006 and it has been down until 2012.

SMA-50 is the Simple Moving Average for the last 50 sessions. It did not help you to avoid the plunge from its peak in 2006, but it reduced your loss and recommended good reentry points. Personally I prefer 200 sessions to reduce the number of trading.

Why I bought US Air (LCC)
It had appeared in my performing screens (the better performers in the previous six months) several times from 12/2012 to 4/2013. I bought them in 6/2013 two times. Due to the merger with AAL, officially they were bought on 8/12/2013 and 8/13/2013. As of 11/2014, I have a 163% gain.

The following is a summary of my evaluation.

LCC	Passing Grade	12/15/2012	4/24/2013
Score System #1	15	38	31
Score System #2	2	3	6
Price		12.78	16.30

It scored very high in the two dates I evaluated LCC.

The first score system includes grades from many investment services I subscribed. The second one has been described in my book Scoring Stocks using fundamental metrics available free.

Opportunities come and gone
If I have a time machine, I should have sold it at $45 in June, 2014 and bought it back it at $31 in Oct., 2014. As of Nov. 12, 2014, it is $43.

I used Turbo Tax to simulate how much tax I have to pay in 2014 tax return without considering any change of the tax laws. In June, 2014, I had over my limit in the long-term capital gain. That was the reason I did not sell my AAL. Taxes should not be considered in making an investment decision.

The threat of Ebola caused the stock to plunge to $32 from $45. I did not take advantage by buying more shares due to my (expensive!) vacation in October. I should have left some buy orders at 10% less than the current price. The Ebola threat was only temporary and shortly it went back to $43.

Analysis of airlines

Pros are:
1. Many airline stocks look like bargains if you look at its low expected P/E only. My Pow P/E taking consideration of cash and debt could be a better metric.

2. The outlook on the economy should be improving.

3. The falling oil price makes the airlines more profitable. It may not be immediate as many airlines hedge the fuel and many long-distance carriers have to buy from foreign countries with set prices.

4. Air lines merger means fewer airlines and less competition.

5. Find ways to make profits such as charging for luggage. The next frontier charge could be the use of the lavatory and that is why they call themselves Frontier Airline. ☺

Cons are:

1. High debt (planes are expensive), a common and traditional problem in this industry. If AAL cannot service its debts, it will bankrupt. Its debts are more than three times its capital cap. Alarming!

2. High pension obligation, the same cause to bring down the old GM. Most especially the newer ones switch to employee-funded pensions as in most other industries.

3. High wages demanded by the unions.

4. Unable to raise the prices of the air ticket; they have not kept up with inflation over the years until recently.

5. Deregulation has its problems. The government should regulate some industries and airline is one of them. The government should do a

better job on what and how much to regulate this industry. I hope to regulate the ticket prices as thy do on utilities.

6. Besides competition from other airlines, trains, high speed trains (little impact in the US), buses and cars offer a lot of competition especially for short-distance trips. Airports are usually located a long way from downtown.

   The major airlines also face competition from new, smaller with leaner operation, direct flights and newer planes with better fuel mileage, not to mention the incentives to the foreign airlines from their governments. Many attractive ones will be acquired.

7. Merger will have fewer airlines and reduce competition. However, when two losers merge together, they become a bigger loser. The Virgin Air could provide long-term synergy to the US airline, but it is too high a price to the acquirer to me. Currently, most mergers of large airlines have been done except Alaska, JetBlue and several smaller ones.

8. The hub concept is getting more impractical with rising fuel prices (now falling) and the inconveniences to their customers. The future will be less stop overs with larger and newer jets that are more fuel efficient. It could be an efficient way for some routes such as filling international flights for smaller cities.

9. High cost of terrorism.
   Most foreign airlines are subsidized by the government. Our government has bailed out other industries but not the airlines here. The only bright point is the airlines profit by jacking up the ticket prices, but you can't do it excessively in this poor economy. Besides terrorism, events such as wars and Ebola could cause the airline stocks to fall.

10. Future shortage of pilots.
    Many retire and many find new jobs in Asia. It is not an exciting profession as in the previous generation. It is also due to the military reductions in the 1990s and the raise of minimum training hours coupled with the maximum hours for pilots. However, the larger planes would reduce the number of pilots. It has not been materialized yet except in smaller airlines. Union protests could bring the company to a halt.

In my original article written several years ago, I recommended to evaluate the impact of a bankrupted airline. The above con conditions could be reduced for a bankrupted airline. In 2011, American Airline was under the bankruptcy protection. Following this advice, you could have bought it for $10 and make a good profit by now. Will the readers who took my advice please stand up?

China's impact

China has impact on almost all industries and airline is no exception. The growth of the airline industry depends on Asia and China in particular. The increase of Chinese travel is due to:

- The fast growth of the middle class. China becomes #1 in tourist spending. It is due to the high tariffs of foreign goods
- China's growing business requires a lot of traveling to and from foreign countries.

Be more careful to invest in China's smaller airlines in China. Their short-distance travels are facing competition from high-speed rail.

Analysis of Airline Stocks (11/12/2014)

	Passing grade	AAL	DAL	LUV
Score System #1	>=15	20	15	22
Score System #2	>=2	7	4	3
Expected Earning Yield	>5 & <35	17%	9%	6%
Debt / Equity	<1.5	3.5	.82	.31
Analyst Rating	>7	8.0	9.6	9.6
EB/EBIT	>5	3	11	13
F-Score	>7	6	5	7
ROE	>=15%	15%	83%	6%
SMA-200%	>0%	16%	20%	43%
RSI(14)	<60	71	71	75
Price		43.43	43.40	39.37

I selected three major airlines to represent the industry. I also selected the metrics and scores that are meaningful to this industry. It seems to be a good buy even after a good gain in 2014.

All three airlines pass both my score systems.

AAL and DAL are similar except that DAL has its own refinery and AAL has a huge Debt/Equity. LUV dominates in numbers of passengers within the USA and it is expanding to foreign countries close to the US.

All three airlines are overbought. The trend (SMA-200) looks good for all of them. However, the trend could be reversed very fast as we experienced it in mid Oct.

Explanation
- Scoring systems have been explained.
- Expected EY, Debt/Equity, ROE, SMA-200% and RSI(14) are obtained from Finviz.com.
- Analyst Rating is from Fidelity. If Fidelity is not your broker, use Recommendation from Finviz.com.
- EB/EBIT and F-Score are from GurruFocus.com.

The above is the Fundamental Analysis. It should be followed by the following:

Intangible Analysis includes the percentage of union employees, how much they hedge fuel price and the median age of the fleet from the following link
http://www.airsafe.com/events/airlines/fleetage.htm

Qualitative Analysis includes articles for the company you're interested. First, start looking for articles in Seeking Alpha.

Technical Analysis times the trend and overbought condition. Many investors do not buy a stock that is in its downward trend (i.e. he price is below its SMA-200).

Conclusion

As of 11/2014, I can see airlines are bargains judging from the high earning yields. I am cautious on the high debts (AAL in particular). I predict the stock prices will still rise at least to Feb., 2015. Now, it is the window dressing time for fund managers and they will buy winners like most of the airlines. However, their stock prices could change very fast. I recommend buying them and protect your investment using stops. It belongs to the strategy "Buy high and sell higher". In addition, follow how the institution investors and insiders trade.

45   Apple

Contrarian

I have been contrarian several times and most times I made good money. We need to have good arguments to be contrary. Otherwise, we're committing financial suicide.

Many investors commit the same error: Invest in a company because they love the company's products. We need to check in the fundamentals of the company and its prospect. I have nothing against Apple. Actually I recommended Apple before based on its great fundamentals while everyone was dumping it. Where were today's enthusiastic analysts?

Scoring Apple

When I was writing the book Scoring Stocks, first I used IBM but its low score would not be a good example. Then I switched to Apple (AAPL). It scored almost the highest. I recommended AAPL at $55.72 (split adjusted) on April 19, 2013, the date the book was published. It is another example that fundamentals work. However, when we're swimming against the tide, we need to be patient. At that time, the media and institution investors ignored fundamentals. The best argument of not buying Apple was "Apple has turned from a growth stock to a value stock". They think they cannot get fired by thinking the same as the herd. Just garbage talk from the smartest folks!

Fundamental analysis as of 02/23/2015

	Passing grade	AAPL	Industry
Score System #1	>=15	16	
Score System #2	>=2	2	
Pow EY	>=5	6%	
Expected Earning Yield	>5 & <35 span="">	7%	5%
Debt / Equity	<.5	.30	.29
Analyst Rating	>7	9	
EB/EBIT	>5	13	
F-Score	>7	6	
ROE	>=15%	37%	27%
SMA-200%	>0%	29%	
RSI(14)	<60 span="">	78	
Price		$132.06	

Explanation:

The first scoring system incorporates many vendors' grades. The second scoring system is from my book Scoring Stocks using metrics available free from many web sites.

Pow EY – Earning Yield (E/P) takes cash and debt into consideration.

Expected EY, Debt/Equity, ROE, SMA-200% and RSI(14) are obtained from finviz.com.

Analyst Rating is from Fidelity. If Fidelity is not your broker, use Recommendation from finviz.com.

EB/EBIT and F-Score are from GuruFocus.com.

How Apple scores

It scores fine but not spectacular. The score from my book in April, 2013 is 5 and now it is 2. Fundamentally it is not as good as before.

P/B and P/S are usually not useful for high tech companies. However, Apple's P/B at 6 is exceedingly expensive as compared to Google's 3. When most analysts like the stock, usually it will rise in the short-term. RSI(14) shows it is overbought. To conclude, its fundamental score passes but not in flying colors.

The brief Fundamental Analysis should be followed by the following:

Intangible Analysis (described next).

Qualitative Analysis includes articles for Apple. First, start looking for articles in Seeking Alpha. Large companies like Apple are hard to manipulate, so most articles are not 'pump and dump'.

Technical Analysis detects the trend and overbought condition. Many investors do not buy a stock that is in its downward trend. SMA-200 is a good trend indicator. Its price should be above the SMA-200 (same as SMA-200% is positive).

Intangible Analysis

Apple has lost a visionary leader Steve Jobs. I hope he was not replaced by similar managers at Microsoft, who are responsible for Microsoft's lost decade with few innovative products. Apple has a lot of cash to finance new projects. High tech business is tough as they need to build a better mouse trap continuously. When the mouse trap becomes a commodity, it will not have a good profit margin. That's one reason that Buffett does not invest in Apple.

There are bright spots and bad spots for Apple:

1. Apple Text Book. Imagine all students carry iPads instead of text books. Several educational apps have been created for iPads.

2. Apple TV.
   It is a loser so far with a lot of risk and potential competitors. However, the potential is great. It could give all cable companies a run for the money. Wider internet channels would make it more feasible. Will the cable companies provide these speeds to allow Apple TV and similar products to step into their turfs?

3. While the iPad and iPhone are peaking in the hardware, iTune, software and contents for these devices to access have no limit. We have witnessed how iPad helps the folks with autism and iPhones for the blind. I can envision many other similar applications.

4. Apple moves to Kindle's market. The standard iPad is too big to be used to read books during commute. You need to hold an iPad with both hands. The mini iPad, even making fewer profit margins, will be Apple's answer to Kindle and a good addition to cover the lower end of its product lines.

5. All the mobile phone technology is originated by the first generation (if not counting Motorola) that Apple has a lot of patents. Its lawyers will milk money from Samsung and prevent cheap mobile phones from coming to the USA.

6. Apple Pay.
   I saw a similar ad from a credit card company a while ago and not recently. Apple has a proven history of picking up some failed products and turning them into gold. It is a big test for Tim Cook. Hong Kong had a similar application many years ago but its card does not need battery. The advantage of that application is you do not have to carry changes. In the current form, Apple Pay will not make a big splash in Apple's bottom line.

7. Apple iWear/Apple Watch.
   There will be cheap Chinese products flooded in our market. However, the selling point is the prestige of Apple. For a similar

reason, my $50 Casino has no respect even it is more accurate and more functional than an Omega costing many times more. The major problem of Apple Watch is the short battery life. If you have to charge it one or even two times a day, it will not be too useful. Only social climbers would buy the $4,000 that does not function as a $10 watch. The other problem is how secured the data.

8. Apple has a lot of cash. Dividends usually boost the stock price and the option values granted to the management. However, it is important to plow back to development and acquiring technologies. They may have paid too much for Beats.

9. The major worry is whether they can maintain the urge of upgrade. If the new enhancements would not give me reason to upgrade, I would not be the one waiting in long line in bitter cold weather to upgrade my iPhone just for my dumb ego. It accounts the majority of Apple's profit.

The other risks are the competition from Samsung and a little-known company Xiaomi.

> Xiaomi, a Chinese phone maker, will most likely come to the USA in 2016 after conquering several emerging markets. Its phone is almost as good as the latest model of iPhone at about half the price. It also has a low-end version priced at about $100 that would set up a standard for entry smart phones.
>
> Xiaomi prices the latest phone model barely above the manufacturing price and makes money in the decreasing component prices. It gains more profit by stretching the model to a longer life.
>
> Apple's lawyer will prevent its entry that Samsung found out the hard way. For starters, Xiaomi needs to modify the user interface to avoid some of the obvious lawsuits in the USA.
>
> When the phone becomes a commodity, both companies have to make money in the content. Today Apple depends on iPhone for over 50% of its sales. After 2016, Apple may face some challenges. Eventually the smart phones may become a commodity product. Xiaomi have to fix a lot of problems before they can sell their products in the USA. This is similar to what Lee

Iacocca said about Hyundai: When they fix their problems, we'll be in big trouble.

While the fundamentals are still great, I predict the stock will not increase at this pace. In 2016 or Apple problems surface, I predict Apple's stock will face real challenges. Will there be another miracle? I do not bet on it as Tim Cook is no Steve Jobs.

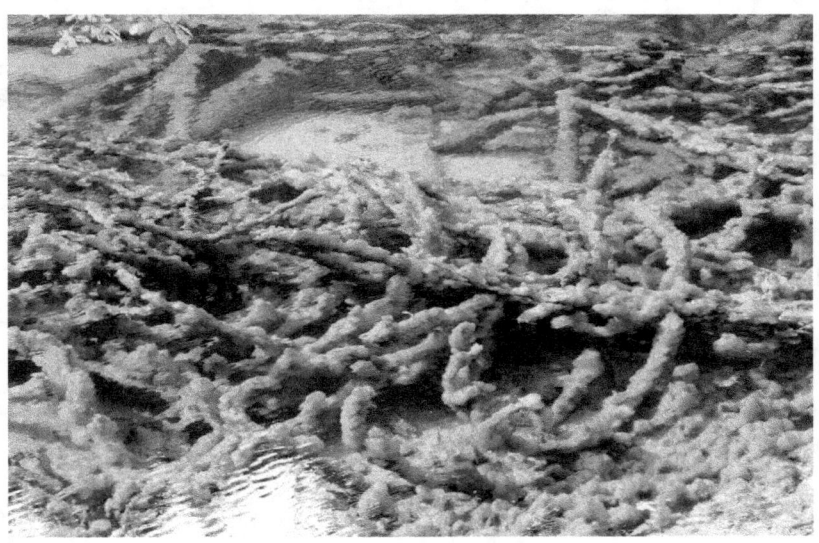

XV Bonus

46 *Monitor my big gainers*

This chapter checks the characteristics of my big winners and the next chapter is on my big losers. The purpose of these two chapters is to demonstrate how to check out the common characteristics of the winners and losers in addition to what strategies work and what do not work in the recent market.

Once the common characteristics of our big winners have been identified, search stocks with the same characteristics. It does not always guarantee the same result. However, it would increase your trading profits more often than not.

In my system in evaluating stocks, it consists of two major parts:

1. Screen for stocks (same as search).
2. Analyze the screened stocks (scoring them to start).

The database

The following data accounts for all the portfolio holdings and the stocks I sold this year in my largest taxable account as of 6/1/2013. My trading strategy keeps track of a lot of stocks, about 50 in this account. This monitor includes 21 stocks (CSCO bought two times), which had a greater than 25% return. The result is too small to draw a concrete conclusion. However, the result of this monitor is quite compatible with the results of the previous monitors.

To increase your database, consider the following:

- Include the stocks that you have evaluated even if they have not been bought. Highly recommended.
- Include the entire year of sold stocks not only YTD.
- Relax your threshold of the big gainers (use 20% instead of 25%).
- Include all accounts. I skip some accounts as they serve different purposes such as one for momentum strategy.

The results

The results are summarized by the following four tables:

Performance

It is a rising market. I should have compared my performance to a market index.

Table 1: Performance Summary.

No.	Avg. Return	Avg. Annualized	Avg. Holding Period
21	50%	111%	211 days

Source

Table 2: Source of the stocks:

Sources	Web & media	Deeply valued	Acquire candidate	Misc. screens	Short squeeze
No.	4	3	3	10	1
Annual. Return	75%	53%	204%	115%	164%
Stocks	ADM, BSX, C, EMN	CSCO, CSCO, MSFT	CAMP, FFCH, ADES	ACAT,BIIB CUZ,DGI,NSIT, STRZA,USNA, OMX,DLTR	DECK

The returns are annualized for better comparison.

Web and Publication.
There are four (from a total of 21) stocks are selected from articles off from the web, magazines and newspaper. When I was convinced that there was great appreciation potential, I bought that stock without further evaluation (not recommended). I was lazy but you should do some evaluation. Need to distinguish whether the authors are pumping-and-dumping the stocks they recommended.

Deeply-valued stocks.
Three of the stocks were quite deeply valued. I placed an order with prices about 5% lower than the market prices betting they are still on its way down a little. About three out of six orders were successfully executed. If I have the time machine, I should place market orders on all six as the market is rising. Try to buy all the deeply-valued stocks in the future.

I doubled my normal bet on most of these stocks (CSCO about 4 times). As of 5/2013, these deeply-valued stocks have not realized its potential values and they're the under-performers in the group. However, the average 53% annualized return is nothing to sneeze at!

Update 3/2016. Both CSCO and MSFT have been doing great. From 5/1/2013 to 3/1/2016, their average annualized return is 16% vs SPY's 9%.

Candidates to be acquired.
There are quite a few candidates that would be acquired by other (usually larger) companies in the early recovery of the market cycle (a phase defined by me). However, with plenty of easy money around due to low interest rates and the high corporate cash reserves, it extends the acquisition craze to 2013. This phase will end when the Fed begins to tighten the money supply. These stocks represent the better return from the group and I should have doubled bet on all of them even they normally are smaller and unknown companies.

The potential candidates to be acquired are usually smaller companies with a technological edge and/or having a valuable customer base. Sell them when they're no longer candidates.

Miscellaneous screens.
A screen consists of criteria in searching stocks such as P/E < 20. There are 10 stocks from miscellaneous screens (same as searches). The performance of each screen is further analyzed. It is better to use the screens that had better performances most recently. My screens are different from yours and some require subscription services, so they will not be disclosed here.

Short squeeze.
The short squeeze happens when the stocks that have been over-sold by the shorters. When the stock is over-sold, those seeking a short position cannot find the extra shares lent to be shorted and sometimes the shorters are forced to cover their shorts due to the high expenses of shorting that stock (interests and dividends).

If the company is not heading towards bankruptcy, any good news would also boost the stock price. This is the typical situation, but it does not work all of the time with TSLA as recent example as of 5/2013. However, I bet TSLA will fall again from its unjustified high price of over $170 per share. Only time can tell.

Increase bets on stocks that have better appreciation potential

The confidence in my predictions for CSCO's future is so secure that I have bought it four times, and then 2 times for BSX and STRZA. All scored high in my scoring system.

Table 3: Score (using the score system in my book Scoring Stocks:

Avg. Score	Foreign Country	Insider Purchase
3.00	0	1

The average score of 9 stocks is 3 and it is the passing grade in my score system. The stocks that have not been scored usually have good appreciation potential, deeply-valued from first impression, and / or recommended by convincing articles. The scoring system is a guide line and we do not have to follow it religiously.

There is not a single foreign stock in this group. I usually do not trust the financial statements of the smaller, foreign countries. The next chapter may convince you to skip most of them at least for now or until it is proven otherwise.

Only one stock has meaningful insiders' purchases out of 21. The data base is too small for any conclusion. From my past data, Insiders' Purchases with purchase prices close to the market prices is a good predictor.

By Sectors
Table 4: Sectors:

Sector	Tech	Health Care, equip & drug	Consumer goods	Finance	Retail	Misc.
No.	6	4	3	3	2	3
Ann.	77%	230%	102%	60%	57%	78%
Stock	CAMP CSCO, CSCO, DGI, MSFT NSIT	BIIB, BSX, USNA, ADES	ACAT, ADM DECK	C,FFCH, BANR	OMX, DLTR	CUZ, STRZA, EMN

Tech.
Technology companies are doing fine but they are also included in the worst performers described in the next chapter. I rate it a neutral. Just buy the tech companies with high scores and good outlooks of the company and its sector. In general, tech is doing good in a rising market as consumers have more money on high tech toys and companies have money to invest such as upgrading accounting software.

Miners.
Miners are not doing well in this period as described in the next chapter. Monitor this sector as they may be rotated back in when the economy improves with higher demands for industrial ores. There is no miner in the winners' circle.

Health care, medical equipment and drugs.
With the aging population, the companies in health care, drugs (generic preferred), and medical equipment should be doing great. It is the best performing sector. The last 90-day performances of ETFs specified in sectors are better predictors for sectors.

Conclusion
The data base of 50 stocks is too small to make any conclusion. However, this result is pretty compatible to the previous monitor about 6 months ago and a large database (with about 200 stocks) that includes stocks that have been evaluated but not bought for a year.

Personal performance monitor

I have more sophisticated ways and better tools to monitor performance. Most of them require subscriptions (though most of them are low cost), so it will not do the average reader any good to describe them here. They are briefly described as follows.

1. Searches. I have the name of the screens with their average returns. Currently I have about 20 screens I use to search for stocks.

2. Evaluate stocks. Each screened stock should be scored and the performance after 3 months should be compared to S&P500 or its corresponding index such as tech stocks to QQQ. The prediction accuracy of each fundamental metric should be checked periodically.

In addition, I divide the data base into short term (about 6 months) and long term (about 12 months). For taxable accounts, You may want to buy stocks in taxable accounts to take advantage of the lower capital tax on long-term gains – check current tax law.

Afterthoughts
- Health care sector. Click here for a SA article. (http://seekingalpha.com/article/1503232-bull-of-the-day-biogen)
- We need to check how the portfolio performs when the market goes down. The best performance is it beats the market in both market directions. However, there is no evergreen strategy. You should use a strategy that is supposed to be favorable in specific market conditions.

Links

Selling short:
http://en.wikipedia.org/wiki/Sell_short
Short squeeze:
http://en.wikipedia.org/wiki/Short_squeeze
Over-sold:
http://www.investopedia.com/terms/o/oversold.asp

47 Monitor my big losses

This chapter is a repeat of the last chapter except with my big losers. It is more important to learn from big losers so we will not buy the potential losers if they fit into a certain pattern. You may benefit more from my mistakes or what are identified to be not working in the current market conditions.

The database

The database is smaller due to the current rising market. Partly, it is due to my avoiding the potential losers from previous monitors.

I delete the stocks which have less than 25% loss. It only has 11 stocks from a total of about 50. A database of 11 stocks is too small to draw any conclusion. However, the results are compatible with previous results. In another words, they follow similar patterns.

The results

As in the last chapter, the results are summarized by the following four tables:

Table 1: Performance Summary.

No.	Avg. Return	Avg. Annualized	Avg. Holding period
11	-43%	-163%	223 days

From here on, annualized returns will be used.

Table 2: Source of the stocks:

Sources	Deeply valued	Acquire candidates	Misc. screens	Short squeezed
No.	0	0	11	0
Annualized Return			-163%	
Stocks			BPI,NTE, SIGA,SIM, VELT,STEC, IAG, END,DEER, CRUS,HXM	

All the stocks here were from my screens. I still find the screens with better recent performances still perform better than the average.

There is not a single stock from the categories of web & publication, deeply-valued list, being acquired or being short squeezed that we find in the last chapter.

Table 3: Score (using the score system):

Avg. Score	Foreign Country
1.86	6
Annualized	-216%

The average score is 1.86 (3 is a passing grade defined in my book Scoring Stocks). Four (out of 11) stocks have not been scored. If I scored them, I may not buy them.

There is not a single stock with meaningful insider purchase. I have encountered that the lowly-scored stocks with meaningful insider purchase appreciate more than the average. Most foreign companies do not have to list insider information.

There are too many foreign stocks in this group (not a single foreign stock among the best performers as described in the last chapter). I usually do not trust the financial statements of the smaller, emerging countries. If I skipped these six stocks, I would have saved a bundle. We cannot go back in time, but it is a strong guide for the future. I do not know why I still bought foreign stocks as they did not perform well in the last monitor. Luckily I did not place double bet on any of these losers.

Table 4: Sectors:

Sector	Tech	Miner	Health care, equip and drug	Misc.
No.	4	3	1	2
Annual. Return	-128%	-131%	-34%	-734%
Stocks	NTE,VELT, STEC,CRUS	SIM,IAG END	SIGA	BPI,HXM

Miners are not doing well in this period. Watch out for this sector as it flows with the global economy. Most miners are foreign companies. I do trust their financial data except from Canada and Australia.

Technology companies are not doing well. However, we have some technology companies included as the top performers as described in the last chapter. The only difference is most of the losers are smaller companies and most are foreign companies. I rate Tech a neutral. Buy those tech companies with high scores and good outlooks.

Performance

The combined annualized return of my big losers and big losers is 73%. It should be far higher as I placed multiple bets on many winners (four times on CSCO and two times on BSX, DGI and STRZA) and none for the losers.

Update I did another performance analysis in 1/2015 including all the stocks that had been screened but I had not bought. Except one from 25 stocks, they are either lowly scored, foreign companies and/or miners. Nine stocks had grade F from Blue Chip Growth. Surprisingly six of them had heavy insider purchases.

Conclusion

The data base of 11 stocks is too small to draw a conclusion. However, the conclusion of this monitor is very similar to the one I did with the larger database of about 200 stocks (vs. 50 stocks this time) 6 months ago.

Combine the results of the two chapters. My conclusions are:

1. The stocks with high scores perform better than those with low scores on the average.

2. Screens (searches) are monitored separately with about a total of 200 stocks and from about 20 screens. Buying candidates for being acquired has been profitable for this year and 2003.

3. From this monitor and the previous, foreign companies including those companies listed in the U.S. exchanges under perform the USA market.

4. Miners do not perform this time. It could be due to the so-called sector rotation. When the economy improves or this sector is recognized as being over-sold, most industrial metals would return to the former price levels.

5. The better performances from sector health care, medical equipment, drugs... are responding to the aging population.

6. My previous monitors had identified that foreign companies did not perform on the average. I still have several foreign companies this time. If I had omitted them, the return of this portfolio should be far better. I need to follow my recent results.

7. I bet less on the risky companies (most were small companies and /or had low scores) and bet more on better companies. It is profitable to bet on stocks that have higher appreciation potential.

8. Read articles on this topic. Here is one.

http://seekingalpha.com/article/3020666-are-you-making-these-5-common-investing-mistakes#comment-50228206

48   Performance monitor example

This article serves an illustration on how to do your own monitor. By the time you read this article, the findings could be outdated. In addition, it is based on my stocks actually screened and the number of stocks is too limited to draw a general conclusion.

I monitored the performance into two: one for short term and one for long term. Score 3 is my passing score for both short term and long term. This is an example and the date is 7/2015.

How score scores

	Avg.	< 3	3	4	5	6	7	>=8
Short	7%	2%	8%	11%	7%	14%	11%	-10%
Long	8%	4%	13%	14%	7%	21%	4%	-10%

Explanation
- The score system works if it is sequentially proportional to the return percentages. It is to some extent.

- From the table, we should use 3 as the passing grade for both short term and long term.
- Do not buy stocks when the score is 8 or higher. It is consistent from my previous monitors. Do not know why. I assume that when the stock is too good to be true, most likely it is not.
- When the stock scores between 3 and 7 inclusively, it is a buy.

How reliable is the score

As stated, it only applies to me for the time being. The reliability also depends on the size of the sample. The following shows the number of stocks.

	Total	< 3	3	4	5	6	7	>8
Short	747	397	113	97	69	41	27	3
Long	555	299	75	70	53	30	25	3

How fundamental metrics score

The following table shows us the predictability of the metrics.

Short Term: (7% return for the average)

Metric	Parm. 1	No.	%	Parm. 2	No.	%	Predict.
EY	>14	203	4%	<5	94	0%	Good
Blue Chip BC	A	150	7%	F	63	-4%	Good
BC Funda-mentals	A	191	14%	F	66	-11%	Good
Fidelity Analyst	Buy	150	10%	Sell	279	3%	Good
P/B	<1	162	1%	>2	333	9%	Bad
ROE	>25	180	9%	<2	110	4%	Good
GRT	<20	71	-4%	>25	685	6%	Good
P/CF	<20	179	8%	>30	99	5%	Good
Earn Gr Q-Q	>50%	227	6%	<5%	68	0%	Good
Sales Gr Q-Q	>25%	153	7%	<5%	154	0%	Good
Debt/E	<.1	172	15%	>1.5	69	2%	Good
RSI(14)	>60	85	9%	<40	33	-2%	Good
SMA 200%	>5	94	1%	<-5	19	-4%	Good

Long Term: (8% return for the average)

Metric	Parm. 1	No.	%	Parm.	No.	%	Predict.

				2			
EY	>20	28	3%	<5	77	-1%	Good
Blue Chip	A	99	8%	F	62	-4%	Good
Blue Chip Fund.	A	178	15%	F	65	-11%	Good
Fidelity Analyst	Buy	90	17%	Sell	208	4%	Good
P/B	<1	15	2%	>2	227	9%	Bad
ROE	>25	135	11%	<2	93	4%	Good
GRT	<20	67	-3%	>25	488	9%	Good
P/CF	<20	133	11%	>30	54	9%	Good
Earn Gro Q-Q	>50%	141	11%	<5%	68	0%	Good
Sales Gro Q-Q	>25%	97	8%	<5%	110	2%	Good
Debt/E	<.1	168	15%	>1.5	61	4%	Good
RSI(14)	>60	27	22%	<40	7	0%	Bad

Explanation

- I skip the metrics from various subscription services.
- The returns are used for comparison ignoring many yardsticks such as comparing to the market index and excluding dividends.
- P/B is not a good metric from my samples. RSI(14) is fine short term but not long term. However, due to the limited data on RSI(14), they are not conclusive. SMA-200% is not available for the long term as it is a new one for me.
- Short term is usually about 4 months and long term is about 12 months on the average; it is just a general guideline.
- Some data are both long term and short term by playing trick by not updating the stock prices of some data; some data could be eligible for both short term and long term as they are close in the specified ranges.
- The prediction of the metric is good if they're as expected.
- Your score is derived from the above metrics. Weigh more on the metrics with better predictability. Modify ('adapt') your scoring system based on your monitor.
- EY (E/P) is expected earning yield. GRT is earning growth rate.
- The stock has higher chance of appreciation if it is rated A in both the Blue-Chip composite score and its fundamental score, Buy in Fidelity Analysts' Opinion, ROE> 25%, GRT > 25%, Debt/Equity < 10% and Earning Growth > 50% for the long term. It is quite similar to the short term.

When you cannot find these stocks, relax the selection. I would start with Earning Growth > 30% as my primary metric.

Filler:

Joke of the century

To make America great again, we need to borrow money from China to contain China.

49 Debunk the myths

Buffett Mania

Traditionally, growth stocks have higher P/Es than value stocks, but the reverse is true today. As of 11/25/13, the expected P/Es (from finviz.com) of some randomly-picked stocks are:

Growth Stocks	Expected P/E	Value Stocks	Expected P/E
Cisco	10	Coca-Cola (KO)	18
Apple	11	Colgate-Palmolive (CL)	21
San Disk	12	Verizon (VZ)	14
Average	**11**		**18**

I suspect it is caused by Buffett and his followers coupled with low interest rates from bonds and CDs. KO, CL, VZ and many others belong to the stocks that Buffett would own. They all give dividends and have an edge such as brand name and monopoly. The above are only small samples of these stocks in the respective category. To me, it is a mild bubble and I name it Buffett Mania.

This mania will not continue as we're running out of these stocks to buy. I do not believe there will be opportunity to buy them at 50% discount (as Buffett preaches) unless we've a market crash. When a strategy is overused, they will not be effective. No exception.

The Reality

Warren Buffett is one of the premier investors in our generation. However, some of his practices are not applicable to today's market and/or to us, the retail investors.

Most of the money earned was for himself and not for the stock holders of Berkshire in the last three years. SPY, an ETF simulating S&P 500 index, offers greater diversity and has seen less volatility. If Buffett is such a hero in picking stocks, then those who constantly beat the S&P 500 Index by a sizable margin are better investor heroes, and there are many. We need to constantly scrutinize whom we listen to.

Performance Comparison

As of 11/1/2013, the average annualized return for the last 3 years:

BRKA	SPY
10%	11%

SPY gives an annual dividend of about 1.5% (about 1.9% this year) and BRKA does not. Not even beating SPY as a primer investor is just mediocre.

Why Buffett's current mediocre performance is important

I do not care how much money he made 10 years ago but what I will make in the next 10 years. Many have been utterly convinced by the many books written on his achievements many years ago. Are his strategies still relevant to us?

When Peter Lynch (managing the Magellan Fund, 5/1977 to 5/1990) lost his golden touch and he quit the job, I got my money out! Most investors did not even after experiencing several years of poor returns (compared to his previous incredible performance). The result was many years of mediocre return for the fund. Hence, Buffett's mediocre performance in the last three years matters and it could be the canary to his future performance.

Many of his teachings are still relevant and they are described in the next chapter. The following practices are to be debunked. I just want to seek the truth. Am I dumb on my part to argue with his success? Read the following with an open mind and decide it yourself.

Debunk the Myths

- 'Never sell.'

    The "Buy and Hold" strategy has been dead since 2000 for most. It is not a good strategy for experienced investors as the fundamentals of most companies change after several years and market timers can detect market crashes using market timing. Most books and comments that praise this strategy are based on data from before 2000. It may come back in the future such as a secular bull market that I predict in 2018.

    Buffett made big money in KO for the first 10 years of his ownership, but not a lot in the next 10 years. If he cashed in after 10 years of ownership and then bought another stock with similar performance, he would have made far, far more.

    I prefer to turn my portfolio to reflect the current market conditions and the companies' fundamentals that could have changed since the last time I reviewed them. Buffett's ownership in The Washington Post [Update: it was sold recently; he must have read this book ☺] was amazing then, but it could be too risky now if their paper does not take measures to stop the losing battle of paper publishing.

    Market fundamentals perpetually change! To illustrate, there were ten well-known department stores ten years ago mentioned on a TV show, and only Macy's survives; most others were acquired or bankrupted. The acquired may fare better. However, you need to analyze them again whether the combined company still fits your requirements and objectives.

There are so many examples to debunk the evergreen concept such as AIG, BlockBuster, HPQ and GE. The market is changing with new technology and competition. We cannot buy and sit back enjoying the appreciation and dividends.

I read an outdated but popular book by a very famous author. A very good portion of his recommended stocks have not survived. However, most stocks had great appreciation in the year after his recommendation.

If you do not sell, you do not have cash to buy stocks when the market is cheap.

He must have missed a lot of great companies like Apple as he did not use any of Apple's products. He did not buy Microsoft even Gates is his good friend. It is better to understand their products and their profit potentials, and make your decisions accordingly. He should depend more on his resources and his many analysts who should have diverse disciplines. Most highly-profitable stocks are not matured companies but small companies with innovative products.

- 'Rule #1. Do not lose money. Rule #2. Do not forget rule #1.'

If every stock bought is risk-free, the return cannot be that good. It is similar to buying Treasury Bills that have no loss in theory. However, holding Treasury Bills until maturity loses buying power due to inflation. Nothing risked means nothing gained. Our capitalist system punishes us for not taking risk, so is trading stocks.

Evaluate the ratio of "return / risk" to see whether the expected return is justified for the risk. If the chance to lose 50% is the same as gaining more than 100%, then the risk is justified. It is not a science, but probability theory and common sense are decent tools. In the long term it usually works. In addition, one's personal risk tolerance determines his/her investment methods.

- 'Margin of safety'.

There will be too few stocks to buy if everyone treats margin of safety as the first priority. It worked for Buffett before as few followed his 'margin of safety' practice. This is the herd mentality. However, it should work again if fewer folks are truly concerned about the margin of safety. However, most institution investors follow Buffett's preaching and they drive the market.

Most fund managers and analysts learn margin of safety in colleges. I do not expect we will have less folks following the theory on margin of safety. When you follow the herd, you will not beat the market. The margin of safety is equal to the difference between the stock price and the intrinsic value, which is quite easy to obtain from many web sites. From my experience using GuruFocus.com (a great site), margin of safety does not work for me.

Let me illustrate an example of my applying the right strategy to current market conditions. During a secular bull market (2018 according to my prediction), the market would favor momentum and growth over value and hence 'margin of safety' will not be appropriate.

- 'Think of Stocks as a Business'.

As an owner of many stocks, I do not have to run my portfolio like a holding company. I do not fire employees, do not have legal obligations, do not make day-to-day decisions, etc. I can sell the stock with a click of the button with no emotions and no legal liabilities attached. Do you really think your ideas on how to run the company will influence the management's decisions via your votes?

Running a business is very different from investing in a company. Do not be confused! Investors' only objective is to make a profit with least risk. The officers of a company are liable to frauds and negligence, which do not apply to the stock holders.

When a company bankrupts, most owners bankrupt too financially and mentally. The stock holder does not suffer the same at least not in the same degree. You may have many other assets, stocks and/or a job. You do not have to tell your loyal employees to leave. No lenders will call you unless you buy the stock on margin.

With an optimal portfolio of 30 stocks, where is the time to simultaneously run 30 companies responsibly?

- Buffett's portfolio is not diversified enough (especially in his early years). However, the portfolio under the insurance company might be.

  When he trades, he pays extra due to the huge volume. He usually buys the entire company and retail investors never run the company.

- Main brands represent mature companies that will give good dividends but usually have limited growth. When they do not perform, the stock will plunge. IBM is a recent example that Buffett owns. The Cloud technology is risky and not highly profitable at least for now. All these companies are having a hard time to protect the security of the data that are in the public servers and still figuring how to make money from this technology.

  The most profitable and riskiest companies are penny stocks. Buffett could reap the profits with their analytical skills. He chooses to stay away from them as they are too small for his portfolio.

- He may miss many of current strategies that work such as market timing, momentum strategy, technical analysis, insider trading, high tech companies, turnarounds and investing in small companies that proves to be the most profitable in recent years.

  During the peak or during the plunge, accumulate cash that is needed to purchase stocks at the bottom. Market timing is our tool. If it works more than 50% of the time, we should make good profits.

- Buffett avoids growth companies. He does not have Microsoft, Apple and Google in his portfolio. Google represents one of the most appreciated stocks in last 10 years. Google is expensive by the fundamental metrics. However, it is a growth stock with technology that Buffett may not appreciate.

Afterthoughts

- The holders of his company (actually it is a mutual fund to me) may have to pay a lot of capital gain taxes if they sell them.

- I doubled bet on BSX and it is one of my top performers in 2013. Even the company is in the same state I reside, but I have not attended any of their earnings meetings. How many of these meetings have you attended? If you believe the stock holder should run the company, you should attend these meetings. If so, I would be busy travelling around the country (and the world) with the 50 or so stocks I own.

- As of 3/1/14, all the news mentioned record earnings for Buffett. It is not a big deal as everyone buying SPY would have a record year. The fact is his fund does NOT beat SPY, which is a passive ETF without using his beautiful mind.

Links

The following is included for the printed book. Even for that, it is easy to access the web site http://ebmyth.blogspot.com.

Investor Hero:
http://tonyp4idea.blogspot.com/2011/11/no-more-investing-hero.html

Herd mentality:
http://www.tonyp4idea.blogspot.com/2011/12/fool-of-all-fools.html

Diversified:
http://tonyp4idea.blogspot.com/2011/09/diversification.html

From here on, most of these links will not be included for readers of hard copy. Get the links from http://ebmyth.blogspot.com/2013/02/links-for-hard-copy.html

#Filler

Buddhism's philosophy is great. It would ease a lot of pressure from investing. Japanese believed in it but they did not practice it. The Tsunami could be a bad deed deserves another bad deed which could be the many war crimes they had committed.

50   Preaching that works

Many of Buffett's preaching still works fine today. However, some need to be discussed further so we can use them effectively.

- Identify exceptional companies with durable competitive advantage.

    These are the companies with high profit margins such as Coke. Even Coke has Pepsi as its major competitor. These companies usually are matured companies giving generous dividends. They do not have to plow back all their cash into research and development. Very few if any high-tech companies and drug companies belong to the group. Most use the profits for building the next better mouse traps instead of giving out dividends. Should we ignore these companies? I do not ignore them, but Buffett would.

    Washington Post is one of these matured companies. However, the internet is changing all its advantage as most of us get our news analyses free from the internet. In addition, cutting down trees to make paper is not good for the environment. [Update. Buffett sold Washington Post recently.]

    Microsoft is in this category monopolizing PC operating system and Office, the most-used business software. I wonder why it is not in Buffett's portfolio and may be Gates could give him a good friendly pointer. However, Microsoft is losing its edge to Apple's products and potentially to Google's products now. Buffett still has not bought Apple and Google. He has missed these profit opportunities. According to Buffett, Microsoft, Apple and Google are not the companies with 'durable competitive advantage'. I have to disagree.

    There are many innovative companies that will not fit Buffett's 'exceptional criteria'. When they plow back most earnings to research / development, these companies do not have good net profits and they do not give generous dividends.

    To illustrate, BSX is one of them finding cures to chronic pains. I read an article on the company from my Sunday paper. Even I did not (and even today) really know how it worked, but I was excited enough to buy its stock two times without doing any research (not recommended) in Oct., 2012. As of 8/2013, it is up by more than 100%.

I will buy these 'exceptional' companies if I can find them. I will sell them when their price appreciation potentials have peaked or there are better stocks to buy.

- Get most info from financial statements.

    Today many web sites such as finviz.com or your broker's include most of the financial data and ratios. Buffett loses his edge as all these data are available to everyone at the same time. We do not have to read through the financial statements for these data. However, we do have to be careful:

    1. Ensure the ratios derived from these financial statements are up-to-date. Usually the company's web site provides the most updated data.

    2. Comparative ratios in the same sector. Many web sites provide this information. To illustrate, Price / Sale has different meaning between a super market and a drug company. The former makes money by selling a lot at low profit margins.

    3. It is still important to read the footnotes and 'extraordinary' items such as those one-time charges. Settling a major lawsuit could be a one-time charge.

    Success in investing today is not solely on how to get the information and understand the financial ratios, but how to separate the good data from garbage and how to evaluate all the immense data that are readily available from the net all over the world.

- Never sell.

    I have presented my opposing views on "Never Sell" philosophy in my last chapter. However, sometimes it has its merits. There are many companies that Buffett had/has incredible returns after holding for over 10 years such as Washington Post (sold recently), American Express and Coke to name a few.

    Very seldom I have stocks making over 300% as I usually sell them after they make over 100%. I keep my gainers longer in taxable accounts due to reducing capital gain taxes (not recommended to most). It is different style of investing and Buffett is a living example that his strategy works. We need to identify why this strategy works and whether it is still applicable to retail investors and to the current market conditions. Several thoughts:

1. These companies usually have been analyzed fully for its long-term appreciation potential. Do you have the time and the knowledge to do so?

2. He has great vision to see the real potential of a company. Do you have this vision?

3. Retail investors have more advantages than institution investors while institution investors have other advantages such as more thorough research. However, most institution investors can only trade on larger companies. We, the retail investors, should make full advantages available to us and avoid disadvantages.

Today commission costs are very low and there is no need to pay taxes on capital gains from non-taxable accounts initially and none in Roth IRAs. Comparing these expenses 20 years ago, some are not important today.

- Buy the stocks at 50% discount

   Stocks are manipulated to cause temporary price erosions. It was the same in early 2009.

   This strategy makes him and his teacher Graham a lot of money. As opposed to Graham, Buffett still holds these stocks longer even if they have not appreciated in one or two years. He seldom sells these stocks and many times patience pays off.

   My suggestion is some stocks will stay low forever for good reasons. It is better to repeat the same evaluation after they have been held for 6 months or so. Hold them if the fundamentals do not change for the worse. The stock prices of some bad companies could go to zero.

   It is similar to buy quality companies when everyone is selling in fear. The best profit opportunity is buying at the market bottom on quality stocks. Determining market bottom is impossible, but there are some hints that may help.

When a company has 2-billion-dollar cash and its market cap is 1 billion, most likely it is mispriced. There are exceptions such as a pending serious lawsuit or the market share has been reduced.

- Buy a good business with a good management at a discount.

    It is easier said than done. There are many companies on sale in 2000 and 2007. Need to separate gems from companies that will go bankrupt such as many internet companies in 2000. If the problem that causes the company to lose more than half of the value is temporary, then it could be a good buy. However, turnaround situation is not for a typical retail investor who most likely does not possess the knowledge, discipline and emotion to deal with turnarounds. Even the experts are expected to lose big on a few turnarounds.

    A good management is required for Buffett as he seldom wants to manage the company. Many companies go bankrupt because of frauds and / or poor management. It is a good sign that the owners have a good stake in their own companies. It is a bad sign when the CEO is overpaid compared to his peers and lives lavishly with huge loans from his company.

- Learn from mistakes.
    He made several mistakes as every investor did. He sold the businesses in re-insurance, airline, etc. and never made the same mistake again. Learn from how he deals with his mistakes.

- He does not follow hot fad such as the internet in 2000. I prefer to follow it, but have an exit plan and protect profits.

- Evaluate stocks with common sense. Mathematical models are for professors to have a job and they never resemble real life.

- Buffett has switched between bonds and stocks successfully. Most of the time, he was not the first one to exit, but he adapted to the market conditions better than most of us even with the technical analysis tools available today. He usually pays more than the market and/or bottom prices but it has turned out many times he was right.

- Buffett as a person has a lot for us to learn from. He is frugal and generous. Making money is his career and hobby, not because he loves to make money for worldly stuffs. For that, he should go to heaven one day.

- Buffett has his share of bad investing decisions such as buying IBM instead of buying Google, Microsoft and Apple.

- According to Buffett and Peter Lynch, they are misled more often than getting meaningful information by calling CEOs. In addition, most of us will not reach anyone important.

###

Search value stocks like Buffett

Buffett stresses on value and would like to buy these companies at 25% off their intrinsic values, which are quite hard to determine. There are many screens simulated on how Buffett finds stocks. You should paper test the screens and check the performances after at least 6 months. Here are some common parameters in these screens. I also recommend sell all stocks during market plunges.

- ROE. Check out the ROEs for the last 5 to 10 years, not just the most recent year.
- D/E. Low Debt/Equity.
- Profit Margin.
- Competitive advantage. The less competition, the better.
- Longevity. At least in business for 10 years.

From the above, Buffett cannot find too many stocks to buy during a bull market. He also ignores a lot of startups and high-tech companies. His portfolio should produce stable but not amazing performance.

In addition, he needs good managers who should be kind to his employees, paying back to the society and not using his company as his ATM besides business smart.

Using the Patriots franchise for illustration, the Sullivan family did not make money even on Michael Jackson's concert in New England while everyone made good money. After Kraft took over (paying a high price to many), the franchise turned around and became the most successful and profitable one under his helm.

Afterthoughts
There are so many books on Buffett. Glance through them in the book stores and pick up those strategies that fit your investing philosophy and style. Many of his techniques are not applicable to retail investors, so be selective. His yearly announcement reports show his insights, discipline and knowledge.

A joke, reality or a nightmare? I got a call from Buffett asking me to lead their stock research.

I asked him why for a nobody; you may be asking the same question. No kidding.

He told me that he should have read my book Scoring Stocks to buy Apple instead of IBM in May, 2013. It would save his company millions of dollars minus $10 for my book. Not to mention the market timing technique that had worked in the last two major market plunges.

I told him, "OK, I'll beat your mediocre returns of the last 5 years."
He said, "You can do better than that and at least beat SPY. If you do so, no one will be that stupid to leave my fund and pay the hefty capital gain taxes."

I told him, "I cannot beat the market as you are the market especially after your expensive fees. In addition, I do not know how to avoid day traders from riding my wagon in trading. Also most of my big profits were made in small stocks that your fund cannot trade besides owning the company."

I woke up trembling. I'm glad it is only a nightmare.

51   Newsletters and subscriptions

Why you do not see too many reviews on investment newsletters and subscriptions from the media? If it is a bad review, most likely
they will not advertise in the media. If it is a good review, they may have to face legal action if the vendor's subscription or newsletter does not perform.

I've been using investment newsletters / subscriptions for years. Many are priced reasonably and some are even free. While a lot of them are garbage, some are very good.

When you have a lot of money to invest and you're not using a financial adviser and/or not subscribing to any investment service, it could be a big financial mistake. You do not want to be penny smart but pound foolish. Very few have the knowledge and time to make use of the free financial data, guidance and articles from the web.

You need a computer, access to Internet and a spreadsheet in order to use most subscription services effectively.

I'm not going to compare specific services / newsletters, but I will include general pointers on how to select them. Yesterday's garbage could be a gold mine today if the subscription improves and/or the market conditions fit what they recommend.

First, you need to find out your requirements and how much time you can afford to use them. If you have $20,000 or less to invest, most likely your investment both in money and time will not pay off. Just buy an ETF and practice market timing described in this book. My pointers are:

- Newsletters giving you specific stocks to buy do not require much of your time. However, if they're successful, there will be too many followers buying the same stocks to drive up the prices of the recommended stocks at least temporarily. The owner of the subscription service and his insiders will buy the recommended stocks before you. I had several of this kind of newsletter, and so far I have not renewed any one of them due to the poor performances.

- If I found the Holy Grail in investing, do you believe I'll share it with you for $100 or so? I only will after I invested my findings first. My subscribers would push up the prices for me and then I unload them before them.

- If the volumes of the recommended stocks are small, they can be manipulated easily either by the newsletter owners and/or by your peer subscribers. The first ones to sell the recommended stocks win and the last ones to sell lose.

- I prefer systems that can find a lot of stocks by providing many searches (same as screens). However, it will take a lot of time to learn and test their performances that would require a historical database. Most likely, you need to further research on each stock screened. The screens would select a limited number of stocks for further analysis, so it will save you time.

From my experience, the best performance comes from the stocks that have been screened by more than one search especially for shorter term (less than 6 months). My theory is that they've been identified to many folks and hence their prices will be jacked up. It is more profitable to buy them ahead of the herd and sell them before the herd. In any case, research the stock.

- We all receive promotional mails that indicate their incredible performances such as tripling the money. Just ignore them. If it is that good, most likely they will keep them for themselves. Same for seminars to boost some penny stocks. Most likely the recommended stocks would rise initially to lure you and other suckers to move it. Watch out!

- A 'guru' told me that he made a big fortune in silver a month ago. Guess what? He also recommended selling it two months earlier and lost a lot of money in doing so. He is always right but he will not advertise the times he was wrong. We call it a double talk technique.

- There are free trial offers (or deeply discounted) for most subscription services. Take advantage of them. Some services require you to spend a lot of time, so ensure you have the time. Keep track of the performance yourself via paper trading. Do not trust their 'official' performances.

- Subscribe the newsletter to fit your style of investing. If you're a day trader, newsletters on long-term investing are not good for you. Some subscriptions handle all kinds of investing styles and you need to find the strategies and recommendations to fit your style.

- Newsletters on penny stocks are risky for most of us. They may show you a list of big winners but they do not show you their losers.

I define penny stocks as less than $2 (officially $5) and a market cap less than 100 M. However, I do buy stocks with prices around $2 in stock price or a capital cap less than 100 M. Actually I bought ALU at $1 but ALU's market cap then was about 2 billion at the time. The stocks with prices between $1 and $10 represent the most volatile stocks and few are real gems. They are routinely ignored by most analysts.

- There are many sectors like drugs, mines, insurance and banks that we cannot evaluate effectively ourselves. It is better to seek expert advices from specific newsletters. Check out their past performances and take advantage of the free trial offers.

- Remember there is no free lunch in life. The higher potential return of a stock is, the riskier the stock is. To me, all trades are educated guesses. The more educated the guesses are, the higher chance they will perform in the long run.

- Some newsletters / subscriptions save us time by summarizing the financial data by providing a value rank and a growth rank. When the market favors growth, you use the growth rank, and vice versa.

- Be careful on the commercials particularly from radio in selling to peoples' fears and their greed by overstating without necessarily telling the whole story. It is not possible to make 50% in covered calls consistently or making another gold rush from $400 to $1,800.

- TV financial shows usually exaggerate in order to sell their staffs. Analyze them before you act on the news.

- As a retail investor, most of us cannot afford to do extensive research. Many researches and market opinions are available in the internet free. Start to search for such information from your broker's site and financial sites such as SeekingAlpha.com, MarketWatch.com, CNNfn.com and Yahoo!Finance.com.

- Do not trust the performances of the newsletter providers. There are many ways to manipulate their performances.

- Most compare their performances with S&P 500. It is legal for investment newsletters to inflate their performance with dividends while comparing to an index without including dividends.

    To illustrate, for the last 10 years, S&P 500 has an average annual return of 1% on appreciation and 1.5% on dividends for a total return of 2.5%. Hence, the performance of a newsletter should compare itself to 2.5% not 1%.

- The performance of last 10 years (I prefer last 5 years) is more important than that of 25 years. Their method of stock evaluation / ranking hopefully has been improved since then. In addition, the last 10 years is a better prediction of the newsletter than the last 25 years as the weatherman finds out.

    More than one time, I found a popular subscription did not beat the S&P in the last 5 years but it did in the last 20 years. It could be that too many folks are using the same strategy.

- When the new major researcher takes over the subscription, s/he may not have the same expertise as the previous researcher.

- Ensure they change their strategies according to the current market conditions. For example, 5 years ago ADRs (U.S. listed stocks of foreign countries) perform far better than today.

- Few if any use real money for their portfolios, as they cannot cheat with real money. That's why you never achieve the compatible performance by following what the portfolio trades. Some cheat by using the best prices of the day. Some omit their losers. Do not trust any performance claims even from reputable monitor services unless the portfolios can be verified with real money.

    Some sample portfolios trade excessively and they may not fit your investment strategy not to mention the broker commissions and taxes.

- When a subscription service has several strategies (say 10 for illustration), it will advertise the strategies with the best returns for a specific time period.

- Today (12/8/2014) before the open TNH was down by about 6% and then by 12% at the end of the day. Cramer's site downgraded it at 9:45 am. Many of us can do the same at 9:45 after its big fall.

Contrary to not recommending investment services, here are very low priced or even free subscription services. By opening a small account with a broker, you can access their research. Check your current broker's website on evaluating stocks. AAII is a low-priced subscription.

###

Making full use of a subscription

Match your subscription to your style of investing. For example a value investor should not choose a subscription specialized in growth. Check the performance of the service in the last 5 years. Some perform great for the last 15 years but not any more due to too many followers.

Most subscription services including the free (as of this writing) Typically as in similar sites, Blue Chip Growth have four grades for each stock: Value, Growth, Timely and a combination of the three. Some have only two grades: Value and Growth.

When the market is favorable to value investing, select the grade Value such as in Early Recovery, a phase in the market cycle defined by me. To emphasize one grade over another, divide it by the opposing grade such as Value/Timely if it can be done (a letter grade can be converted to a number).

IBD

II use the composite grade of this popular service especially for day traders and short-term swing traders. It is more a momentum grade, but they do have a value grade. I evaluate their IBD50 stocks. Check out the recent performance of IBD50 as provided. It could be useful to have a second opinion of these stocks with another service.

Screen Basic under Screen Center. It lists the stocks with top IBD's metrics.

Leading sector under Screen Center. Basically it is the second and the third step of my Top-Down Investing strategy (the first step is market timing).

Next to the screened stock, click on the Stock-Checkup for a complete evaluation of the stock according to IBD.

GuruFocus

I use the screener to find stocks in my book Best Stocks. I found there are a lot of useful features I had not used. It will be a perfect system if they provide a historical database for testing the screens.

The idea is following the institution investors who drive the market. Besides this great concept, it offers many tools for analyzing stocks. It has a score system that has been proven. The following metrics are harder to find in other sites: F-Score, EV/EBIT, Shiller PE, DCF... Many metrics are compared to its industry and its history. They are displayed in an easy-to-read graphics.

Afterthoughts

- My friend told me he saw an ad that would show him how to make $500 a day for working a few minutes before the market opens. He is nice enough to share his 'discovery' with me. If it is as advertised, I would be the first one to sign up. If it really works, it will not work very soon. When a strategy is over-used, it will not work. Unfortunately, a fool is born every minute as the same ad had been here for a while.

- Currently I spend about $1,500 for all subscription services. I believe $200-$600 should cover the basic. To start, you can use your broker's web site for tools. Some have a lot of research for evaluating stocks and some even include searches. Try the biggest broker's research as they spend more on this area. Even if you do not trade with them, use their research by opening an account with the minimum balance.

- If the offer is too good to be true (like making $500 every day with little effort and little investing money), probably it is not. If they give you a free 50" TV for spending $299, most likely it is a trap with bait. Again, remember there is no free lunch.

  However, some baits are good like the free 30-day trial offer for an investment service or the free dinners I attended seminars on estate planning. It is part of the business cost. If I do not attend more than two dinners, eventually I would end up paying two free dinners for someone I do not even know. This book could be the best deal for your entire investment life if you invest time to read it, digest it and use the ideas that are applicable to you and the current market.

- Do not trust their claims and the past performance may not have anything to do with the current or future performance unless they are from reliable sources.

To illustrate how to monitor their recent performance, if they give you 20 stocks every week, save the prices and check their performance in the same period you usually hold the stocks. It has busted many well-advertised and very popular subscription services. I prefer to compare the performance to S&P 500 index. It is better to compare it both in an up market and a down market as some strategies amplify their performances by selecting riskier stocks.

- On 5/2013, I received an ad boasting how great its portfolio performs from a well-known subscription on investing. The cumulative return from 2001 to today is an impressive 308% beating the S&P 500's 43%. However, if you analyze it further, most of the big gains are made before 2009.

To prove it, I used their data and input their returns from 2009 to today. Their accumulative return is 37% while the S&P 500 is 66%. Current data has better predictive power than the older data.

The moral of the story:

1. Read any claim with skepticism. Test it yourself.
2. The recent performance has better predictive power than the older data.
3. When a strategy is over-used, it will become less effective.
4. The market conditions change from time to time. Some strategies work better than others in different conditions and different phases of the market cycle.
5. Most likely their return includes dividends while the S&P 500 index does not.

Fillers:

How celebrities and/or newsletter owners make money for themselves

To illustrate, a TV or talk host and his staffs know what stocks they want to promote in the next show. They may have bought these stocks before the show; is it legal? The viewers or listeners follow the recommendations to move the prices up. In two or three months later, these insiders dump the stocks and the stock prices come down.

52   This time is different

Today is really different.

Recently I read a classic book on investing. Similar to most other classic books, most ideas are not applicable to today's market. The author died more than 50 years ago. By my rough estimate, the ideas are 30% correct and 30% incorrect. The remaining fall into the grey area that they are only correct in specific market conditions and/or specific interpretations. Most correct ideas are now conventional wisdom and many have been repeated in this book. Some of the incorrect ideas are described as follows.

- Most of these books described strategies in investing and then selected examples to fit the strategies. Most of my examples are from my personal experiences. My bad experiences could be more beneficial to you by not repeating the same error.

- Tax laws have been changed since then. Roth IRA could be the best thing since slice bread if you're eligible. Check the Tax Avoidance chapter. This book has a link to the current tax law from Wikipedia to keep you updated with the current and future tax laws. Your tax lawyer or accountant is no substitution.

- Today most brokers' commission rates are so low that it makes some trading strategies more effective than before. My commission rate is $5 per trade (after some negotiation with the argument of frequency in trading) and one account is even supposed to be commission-free for a year via a special promotion. Your Dad may have paid over $300 for commission per trade.

- Tracking 'mispriced stocks' is less useful today than 50 years ago. Today these stocks are screened every day by investment subscriptions, fund managers and even retail investors. The extensively used P/E is only one metric among many to determine the value of a stock. P/B and ROE are not too effective as before.

   The only reason I can think of why the stocks are mispriced is via over-reaction by the media and manipulation. The media exaggerate in order to sell their viewership and most information is outdated. Most stocks are bargains during the market bottom. Lower prices than the historical prices do not mean better potential for appreciation.

Today, the real 'mispriced' stocks could be those who are losing the competitive edge of their major products, using high debts to boost up the earnings, having major lawsuits pending, etc. These stocks most likely do not appreciate.

- Retail investors have most of the financial information of a company and the economy at the same instance as the Wall Street experts. Actually we have more advantages. Our PCs are fast enough for our needs in evaluating investments and our spreadsheets can do most of the basic analyses. Indicated by any abnormal large volume of a stock from trading by fund managers, day traders could take advantage of it. Hence, they pay more to get in and get out of a stock.

- No one 20 years ago believed the bankruptcy of major companies such as Lehman Brothers, the old GM, etc. and losing most values of many companies such as Citi Group.

- We have new regulations, which are supposed to protect investors (from insiders' trading for example). However the government intervenes in the market by pumping up too much money to cause a non-correlation of the economy and the market. It seldom happened. When they stop this practice, the market will correlate with the economy.

    The chance of another 1987 crash is minimized with new regulations. We do not learn a lot from the 1929 crash as our market and its regulations are quite different from then.

- The economy may recover without employment recovery. Most jobs today can be outsourced. Big companies hire the best workers at the least costs in any country in the world. The world is getting smaller via better communication and more efficient transportation.

    Free trade and globalization make the world connected better and the participants should benefit. Without employment recovery, it would affect many sectors such as housing and retail. When one country is down economically, many other countries will be affected. Watching the economy of the USA alone is not enough today.

- Sir Newton and Irving Fisher lost a lot of their money in their investments, so their high IQs have nothing to do with investing. Even the Nobel-prize winners ran their hedge fund LTCM to bankruptcy. It also teaches us to diversify and the black swan could wipe out our entire savings if we bet all in one strategy or one stock.

  We have to change our strategy to adapt to the current market. The market 50 years ago most likely was not the same as the market today. Fewer lessons from 50 years ago are valuable than the lessons learned in the last 15 years.

- I have no intention of picking on the classic books such as Security Analysis written 60 or so years ago. It is a good read free in the book store. But I will not to spend $75 on a lot of obsolete info. It is a waste of paper on How to Get Information. I do not care much about senior security, margin of safety (not useful from my limited test), bonds (only for parking cash and reacting to the interest rate fluctuation), warrants and preferred stocks. Most financial ratios are readily available from free web sites such as finviz.com. Global investing is simple via today's ETFs. Market timing is never considered at their time.

- We do have new challenges and new tools.
  The big boys (mutual fund and pension managers) could manipulate the market. It could be a nice conspiracy theory that the blood-sucking big boys meet on the first full moon every month to determine the market direction and/or which sectors to rotate to. However, with today's internet, the big boys could drive the market fast and violently and the retail investors would likely follow.

  As high as 50% of today's trades are decided and executed by computers. When they act at the same time and in the same direction, the market would surge or plunge fiercely without warning.

  High speed trading could hurt us but also could benefit us. Sector rotation, ETFs, contra ETFs, options and day trading should be examined and understood (even if you don't participate) by today's investors.

  Dow Theory with emphasis on the Transport sector (including UPS today) loses some of its luster as a lot of products do not have to be shipped by rails such as the digitized music, ebooks and movies.

These are the tools and strategies that your Dad's generation did not use; not to mention those books written 50 years ago that did not have to deal with our challenges.

Conclusion

Technology and new regulations change our tools in investing. Your Daddy did not have today's powerful PCs, spreadsheets, internet, etc. The tax laws and regulations are changing every year. Read any book with an open mind and apply what works in today's market.

Today's market is influenced by the interest rate, aging population, population growths in different countries, globalization, China, wars, conflicts among countries, energy, technology, tax laws and regulations.

Links

Newton and his market loss:
http://www.cnn.com/2009/POLITICS/07/29/levenson.finance.regulation/

Irving Fisher:
http://en.wikipedia.org/wiki/Irving_Fisher

LTCM:
https://en.wikipedia.org/wiki/Long-Term_Capital_Management

Black swan:
http://en.wikipedia.org/wiki/Black_swan_theory

53 Hedge fund 101

LTCM, with two Nobel-prize winners, excellent supporting team and best technologies then, ran their hedge funds into the ground. Many hedge funds are closed due to frauds and/or poor performances.

The primary purpose is supposed to 'hedge' your investments from market plunges / dips. Since 2008, the government prints so much money, the market recovers and makes the hedges (shorts, derivatives, etc.) unnecessary. In reality, most hedge funds do not hedge.

Hedge funds get tons of press coverage as the Holy Grail of investing. The media need the advertising from this $2.5 trillion industry. It is similar to mutual funds but most tend to take more risk for better returns. Most require higher minimum investments and more restrictions such as requiring longer periods before withdrawal.

It could be the worst deal to their customers: 2% average up front and 20% average on your profit. It is more acceptable to me if the 20% is on profit over the S&P 500 or any relevant yardstick to the specific hedge fund.

Well, if they make a lot of money for you, it is not too much to object. However, most risk your money by betting big recklessly. When they win, they get 20% of your profit and they use you for advertising to lure other suckers. When they lose *your* money, they do not lose a penny. It encourages them to take big risks. I do not know any hedge fund (HF) manager who pays you back your losses.

An average mutual fund charges about 1.5% management fees. An average hedge fund charges 2% that would cover the expenses to run an office, market the products and research expenses. While the average mutual fund tries to beat S&P500 index or an index specific to the fund. The real compensation of an average hedge fund depends on the 20% of the profit.

You have better return by investing in a no-load index fund or a diversified ETF than an average hedge fund. To calculate the average hedge fund performance, you need to include the many hedge funds that are out of business.

After a hedge fund has failed, most fund managers just open another hedge fund (if they do not go to jail due to frauds) and give you all the excuse for losing your hard-earned money. Some lose their reputation but you need to check them out.

In 2011, the hedge fund industry did not beat the S&P 500 index fund after fees. I bet the hedge fund industry did not beat the market after 2011.

Some hedge fund managers learn modern portfolio theories from Ivy League universities and apply them in the hedge funds. Often their theories are wrong due to wrong testing procedures or they cannot be sustained in real life.

They usually invest in new companies and small companies where they would have big profits swing. They need to learn the business of the company they plan to buy the stocks, interview the owners, read between the lines, and double check whether the owners are telling the truth by talking to their competitors, vendors and customers. It explains the high cost of their research. For us, we just look at the transaction of the insiders to have the better research almost instantly with a low-cost subscription service. There is no need to travel to visit the company unless you want to.

Some use their specialty in certain sectors and that's fine. If they use derivatives, be careful and that's what resulted in our 2007 financial crisis. Derivatives could reduce the risk of the portfolio if they are properly used. If you still want to invest in them, ask for their methods and their historical performance. Very few hedge funds are good. When you find a good hedge fund, most likely it has been closed to new investors or its fees are outrageous.

The owner of a famous baseball franchise lost big money from a hedge fund that concentrated in the oil sector. Almost every ETF in this sector made good money that year. He still stayed with the hedge fund and had similar miserable return the following year. I did not blame his first mistake, but on his sticking with the same hedge fund after a losing year. It could be the hedge fund gave him a hard time to take his money out.

One hedge fund has a performance of 25% every year for a long period. The SEC, take notes and investigate whether they were using insiders' information. There are very few hedge funds with consistent performance beating the market after fees. If you find some, stay with them forever. One hedge fund was rated as the top fund and the next year it was out of business due to poor performance.

In 1980, this industry started with really capable fund managers and made good money for their clients. After that, every analyst wanted to open a hedge fund and most did not even beat the market after their expensive fees. Alternatively, just buy the ETF SPY and relax, instead of waiting for the hedge fund to wipe out your savings. This industry is not properly regulated.

Do not believe in any articles / ads praising how great the hedge funds are without knowing their credibility and their hidden agenda. The hedge fund indexes usually ignore the survivor bias of the bankrupted hedge funds and the early exits of many hedge funds.

Since the hedge funds very seldom keep the stocks more than a year, their capital gains would be short-term and hence would be taxed at higher rates than the long-term capital gains. In addition, most funds have 1-3 year lock-up periods and only allow withdrawals on the first day of each fiscal quarter.

Afterthoughts

- From WSJ, from 1999-2008, the hedge fund industry beats the S&P 500 by 13% a year. From WSJ, from 2009 thru July 2012, it lagged the market by almost 8%.

  In 2011, the average hedge fund lost money when the S&P 500 was flat. In 2012, the average hedge fund earned about 6% when the S&P 500 was up 13%. It is 'genius' to buy an ETF representing the entire market instead an average hedge fund.

- Now hedge funds can advertise.
  A pig wearing lipstick is still a pig. If you run 5 hedge funds, you will advertise your best fund. Advertising industry will benefit and eventually their investors in hedge funds will pay for this expense.

  http://finance.fortune.cnn.com/2013/07/10/sec-votes-to-let-hedge-funds-advertise/?iid=HP_River

- A hedge fund article from SA.

http://seekingalpha.com/article/584861-hedge-funds-are-they-just-smooth-operators?source=kizur

- Another hedge fund fraud.
  http://money.cnn.com/2013/07/25/investing/sac-capital-charges/index.html?iid=HP_LN

- Gold even managed by great hedge fund manager is down as of 7/2013.
  http://www.cnbc.com/id/100855708

- A famous hedge fund manager (so is the one on Sears) has big losses in JCP and shorting another company. It teaches us to diversify and be conservative.
  http://money.cnn.com/2013/08/26/investing/bill-ackman-sells-jcpenney/index.html?iid=HP_River

- Hedge funds must have a hard time in 2013. Hedging against a rising market is a fool's game. Another article.

- In 50 years, the $10,000 investment will grow to $1,170,000 assuming a 10% return a year. However, about $700,000 will be the cost of the typical mutual fund. It will be better to buy an ETF (far lower fee) and avoid market plunges described in this book.

Links
Modern Portfolio Theory:
http://tonyp4idea.blogspot.com/2012/05/modern-portfolio-theories.html

LTCM:https://en.wikipedia.org/wiki/LongTerm_Capital_Management
Hedge Fund: http://en.wikipedia.org/wiki/Hedge_fund

54 Modern portfolio theory MPT

Most fund managers learn modern portfolio theory from colleges. The theories are faulted. However, some gained Nobel prizes using the faulted theories - a bad reflection on today's silly Nobel Prize committee not to mention the silly award to President Obama for doing nothing but reckless spending. They do not invest with real money. I and many others have proved them wrong many times.

Walking randomly in the stock market postulates the price of a stock is already built-in, so there is no need to evaluate stocks. It is also known as the efficient-market hypothesis. Explain to me why as a group my stocks with high scores always beat my stocks with low scores for years. If you cannot find a functional scoring system, it does not mean all the scoring systems do not work. For the same reason, there is no need to take college courses to evaluate stocks if the prices are built-in.

When the professor writes equations on the board, he is dreaming and his fantasy world will never resemble reality. However, you need to waste time to 'learn' in order to get good grades. Without good grades from a prestigious college, you cannot get a good job.

The so-called modern portfolio theory is most likely based on wrong or insufficient testing parameters / assumptions. Unfortunately they're still supported by the Ivory Towers. All the students taking these courses should ask for refunds from these universities. Most likely these professors are still driving an old Toyota and have never made good money in the stock market besides in 'teaching', selling 'books' and/or running hedge funds to cheat you out of your money.

I'm still waiting for the counter arguments to prove me wrong. Professors, please drop me a line to defend yourself. So far, there is none.

Links
MPT: http://en.wikipedia.org/wiki/Modern_portfolio_theory

Efficient-market hypothesis:
http://en.wikipedia.org/wiki/Efficient-market_hypothesis

55   2011, the year stock pickers died

2011 is a year when stock pickers (particularly the value pickers) did not perform. The performances of AAII screens and the mutual funds I tested recently confirmed it. Most investment advisers / newsletters did not beat the market index in 2011. Check the performances of your investment newsletters such as Value Line and IBD. However, do not give them up. They may not perform for a short while but they will return back to the normal performance and hopefully sooner.

Most likely it is the result of the excessive printing of money.

The market was volatile with most of the gains in the first half of the year of 2011. Traders using technical analysis did better than the stock pickers based on fundamentals as they reacted to the trends.

From my limited data of about 250 stocks for a period of about half a year, I tested out which fundamentals do not work well in predictability in 2011. They were analysts' grade (Fidelity's summary grade of analysts for a specific stock), cash flow and the short %. Normally, the stocks with analysts' grade A (or above 8 from Fidelity's Advisor Opinions), cash flow (grade A from Blue Chip Growth) and shorter % (less than 5) would perform better than the average. Not this time. You can obtain most of these mentioned metrics from many other sources and most likely you reach the same conclusion for 2011.

I'm adjusting my search criteria accordingly for swing trades. I'm not buying a lot and waiting for the big dip that I expect it will come. However, when I see bargains, I'll buy them and wait for these stocks to recover.

My suggestion
Your fundamental metrics need to be checked whether they still perform in the current market. When they worked a year ago, it does not mean they will always work today.
Links
Stock pickers: http://www.tonyp4idea.blogspot.com/2011/11/no-more-investing-hero.html

56 Seeking Alpha

Seeking Alpha is a great site for investors. Here are my hints in using it.

- Use the portfolio function to enter all the stocks you own and/or the stocks you want to buy. When there are articles or news on the stock, you will be alerted in Portfolio of the main menu. It is handy to keep track of all news about your stocks. Its function is similar to Finviz.com and your broker may provide this function. Small stocks may not be covered.
- There are many good articles from the main page.
- Read articles by authors you selected to follow. There are many experts in their respective fields.
- Follow the authors with strategies similar to yours such as dividend income.
- From the main page, Market Performance via ETFs gives us which sectors are trending. It can be used for sector rotation.
- I enjoy articles on market timing and summary of the current market.
- Here is a good article: 60 Value Resources. http://seekingalpha.com/article/3485446-60-best-value-investing-resources-youd-be-crazy-to-miss

However, you have to watch out for the following:

- Promotion. Seeking Alpha is not set up as a charity organization. They are selling the products for their clients. Shamelessly I use it as a vehicle to sell my books. Some promotions are good if they are applicable to you.
- "Pump and dump". Be careful on small and/or low-volume stocks.
- One shorter made bad comments on EBIX that I owned. It turned out she did this all the time. EBIX has gained about 150% in a year.

57   Fidelity stock research

You have to be their customer to access all their research. If you are not one already, open an account with the minimal requirements and optionally buy a no-commission ETF from them. Their research is extensive and it could be the biggest bargain. Their StarMine (Analyst Opinions) has been proven to be a good predictor to me.

The following describes some of the features.

- Analyst Opinion. It is one of the major metrics I use in my proprietary scoring systems. From my limited database in 7/2015 and for short durations, the results are:

Short Term: (7% return for the average)

Metric	Parm. 1	No. of stocks	%	Parm. 2	No.	%	Predictability
Fidelity Analyst	Buy	150	10%	Sell	279	3%	Good

Long Term: (8% return for the average)

Metric	Parm. 1	No. of Stocks	%	Parm. 2	No.	%	Predictability
Fidelity Analyst	Buy	90	17%	Sell	208	4%	Good

- ETP (ETF to me).
- Key Statistics. Select the industry leader by comparing the metrics to its peers. They also compare their own metrics to the average of several years.

Research Reports and Financial Statements give us more information about the company. Ensure they are the most updated.

58   Institutional investors

Institutional investors include banks, hedge funds, insurance companies and mutual funds. They are important as they move the market, not the retail investors.

You want to follow them closely. When they buy specific stocks, buy the same stocks and vice versa. It is better to be one step before their action. Due to their large holdings, usually it takes a few weeks to load or unload the stock. Basically this is how day traders make money by jumping into their wagons. When you see a sudden surge in volume of a specific stock, there is a good chance the institutional investor(s) are trading.

GuruFocus.com indicates the stocks they are holding and their current trades. Finviz.com has similar information. IBD gives higher rating to the stocks that the institutional investors hold.

Normally the stocks owned by the institutional investors have larger market caps (over 1 billion) and most have stock prices over $10.

Once a while, their trades are not rational. When you act against them, you need a good reason and be patient.

I took advantages of them using Apple for illustration:

- Recommended in my book Scoring Stocks to buy Apple in June, 2013 (the publish date) while most of the institutional investors were dumping Apple. Apple scored very high.
- Recommended to sell Apple in my blog in Feb., 2015 when Apple was $132. It could make about $60 a share from June 2013.
- Took advantage of the correction making 12% for holding Apple in about 2 months.

59 The scents of a winner

During the beginning of Feb. 2014, I sold several winners expecting to pay zero Federal tax this year. Besides tax considerations, I expected a correction was coming.

I sold the following long-term gainers: MSFT (37%), CSCO (48%) and CAT 10%. As a group, they beat S&P 500 by a small margin.

The three sold winners are BSX, CAMP and USNA. I bought BSX (138% return) two times without looking at the fundamentals at all. I only have USNA (99%) and CAMP (282%) to compare and hope to find some common denominators.

Here is a table comparing the two. The metrics are around the time I bought the stocks.

	CAMP	USNA	Average
Return	282%	99%	
Bought on	12/24/12	01/28/13	
Sold on	01/08/14	02/12/14	
Days held	380	380	380
Screen	CAO	BF	
Fundamentals			
Expected E/P	39%	16%	28%
Earning growth	39%	16%	28%
ROE	40%	32%	36%
Total debt		0%	
Short %	5%	28%	
Technical			
SMA200%	13%	-10%	
RSI(14)	41%	50%	46%
Subscription			
Zacks	Average	Average	Average
IBD	Best	Average-	
Fidelity Analyst	Average-	Best	
Score			
My Score	46	26	36
P-Score	3	3	3

Explanation

The following tries to find any common denominators between the two winners. I leave out blanks in the average column where there is no common denominator. It is too small a data sample to draw a conclusion compared to my usual monitors.

Remember these metrics are for long-term holding of stocks (for me it is one year and one day).

- Screens.
  They are both selected from screens that have been proven winners. BF is the bottom fishing screen. CAO is the screen to search for candidates to be acquired.

- Fundamentals.
  Both have pretty sound fundamental metrics. Expected E/P (P/E in reverse), Earnings Growth and ROE are above their respective average.
  Short % is good if it is less than 10%. When it is above 25%, a short squeeze may be possible. The shorters of USNA made the wrong decision apparently.

- Technical.
  Technical indicators are great for spotting trend, but not in spotting bottom. When you hold the stock for a year, the short-term trend will do you no good.

- Expert advices.
  As in the table, all are not conclusive except the free Blue Chip Growth that is free at least for now. I used the Blue Chip Growth's Cash Flow grade.

- My Scores.
  I have two scoring system. Both stocks exceeded the passing grade (15) by a wide margin. "P-Score" is described in my book Scoring Stocks (passing grade is 2). "My Score" has been enhanced with the subscriptions services I am using.

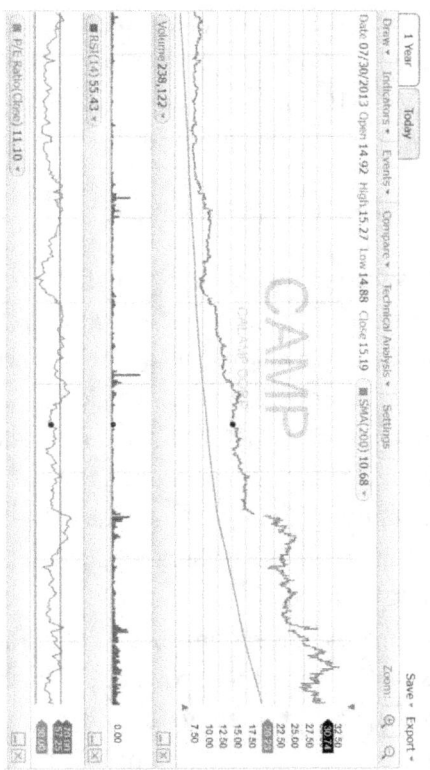

SMA-200 for CAMP. Soucre: Fidelity. Bring it up from your browser. Enter CAMP. Select Technical Indicator, then SMA, and enter 200 days.

Update

As of 4/2014, CAMP had a big plunge since I sold it. Lucky timing for me! I believe no stocks should double in a year. CAMP had returned 280% in just over a year. There are a few rare exceptions such as buying Apple and Netflix after their IPOs. I bought CAMP back after the big plunge. A fool and his money parted soon (no punch intended).

http://www.fool.com/investing/general/2014/04/25/why-calamp-corp-shares-plummeted-today.aspx

I traded LCC (U.S. Airline) making a big profit return in a month on two bets in 2013. I bought two more times in August, 2013 and as of 6/2014, it is over 163%. It scored 22 (passing grade is 15), so the scoring system works so far this time.

Common hints of a winner beside the above

- If you are a value investor and can afford to wait for 6 months or so, find stocks with bottom prices (with low P/E preferably). If you are a momentum investor, buy a stock on price trending upwards, but do not prepare to hold it for too long.
- Side with good management who can adopt and/or can turn around a bad situation. Remember, most of his/her staffs are usually puppets. If you do not have a visionary leader, the company will not do well. Steve Jobs had vision, but not too many in Microsoft today.
- For huge profits, invest in small companies that do not pay dividends as they need to plow back all incomes to research and development. It is too risky for me to invest in penny stocks though. I prefer companies that have a good niche such as a new technology, a new drug, etc. The best time is about 6 months after the IPO. By that time, the vision of the management and the marketability of the products and/or service are clearer. Most likely we have missed Microsoft, Google, Apple and Wal-Mart in that stage. However, in every decade or so, we have one or two such companies.

60   CALM, a short squeeze candidate

Cal-Maine Foods Inc. (CALM) has fallen from over $60 to $46 recently and it is my heavy bet. The open price today (12/15/2015) is $46.76. Readers might wonder I still recommend accumulating a falling stock. Simply put, the race is not over and this horse has a lot of potential (i.e. fundamentally sound). The payout would be huge as it has been ignored (the short float is over 55%).

Let me show you my evaluation process, so you may use it to enhance yours if you have one.

Currently, this stock was screened by my Short screen that spots fundamentally-sound companies with short floats over 35%. Most of the screened stocks deserve to be shorted, but I cannot find any justification for this stock.

Technically speaking

First, this stock has been hated as described by the following table with the exception of "Recom". Most data of this article are derived from the free Finviz.com on Dec. 15, 2015. The 'Conditions' are my personal preferences.

	Condition	Indicate	12/15/2015
Short Float	>35%	Short squeeze	55%
RSI(14)	<30%	Oversold	31%
SMA-20	<0	Short-term down	-13%
SMA-50	<0	Mid-term down	-17%
SMA-200	<0	Long-term down	-9%
Recom.	1 - Buy & 5 – Sell	3 – Neutral	2

Fundamentally speaking

Does this stock deserve the hatred? From the following table, it is a big NO.

	Condition	Indicate	12/15/2015
Forward P/E	>0 and < 20	Favorable	7
ROE	>20%	Favorable	40%
Profit Margin	>8%	Favorable	15%
EPS Q/Q	>15%	Favorable	418%
Sales Q/Q	>10%	Favorable	71%
P/FCF	<15	Favorable	12
Debt / Equity	<.5 (industry related)	Favorable	.05

One or two favorable metrics do not mean a 'Buy' or great fundamentals. However, all these metrics all yell 'Buy'. They are my major fundamental metrics that have recently proven in predictability.

I combine all these metrics and score CALM in 3 scoring systems plus PEY described below. As of this writing, CALM passes all my scoring systems with flying colors. Actually when stocks exceed the passing score by that much, I have a little concern; I cannot find problem with this stock.

	Passing Score	Score
P-Score	3	6
Short-term score	15	40
Long-term score	15	24
PEY	5%	23%

Explanation

- P-Score, Pow's Score. It uses the metrics available in the free Finviz.com with the exception of using Fidelity's Analyst Opinion instead of Finviz's "Recom". This score system is described in my book Scoring Stocks.
- The other two systems use additional metrics and/or scores I subscribe. I monitor these two scoring systems periodically and adjust the scores accordingly. Short-Term Score is used for holding stocks for less than 6 months.
- PEY, Pow's Earning Yield. It is similar to EV/EBIT (5 from GuruFocus or 1/5 = 20% for Earning Yield). Both consider debt and cash. The advantage of PEY is all the metrics are readily available for calculation if using Cash/Share instead of Short-term Liability. PEY also uses expected earnings.

Intangibles

From Seeking Alpha, enter CALM and you should find many articles. I do not find any alarms on CALM. Some farms that are affected by the bird flu will return if not already to production and eat into CALM's market. It is always a possibility that CALM will be infected by bird flu. However, with most chicken staying inside the farm and the extra precautions, the chance is slim. Let me have three scenarios as below.

Say if another bird flu (not in CALM) happens, the egg price would rocket and so is the profit of CALM.

Say if it happens to CALM, it will affect to the location involved only. As I stated, the management (they've been great) should have taken precautions to minimize the chance of bird flu.

Say if it happens in Hong Kong or another Chinese city, they will ban chicken from local farms and input them from the unaffected countries such as the US.

The egg price is returning to its normal price. Hence, the EPS will be lowered. With Forward P/E less than 7 and PEY greater than 23%, it has to fall a lot to cause any alarm.

Bonus metrics
From GuruFocus.com (a paid subscription), F-Score is 7 and Z-Score is 8; both are favorable.

Summary

This stock is technically unsound but fundamentally sound. It may still trend downward, but when it shoots up, it will be firework on display. Most value stocks are swimming against the tide, so we have to be patient for the market to realize its real value.

No one can identify the bottom precisely and consistently. I expect a short squeeze coming when the shorters cannot find more shares to short. The interest rate hike could trigger some covering of the shorts. The shorters are paying about 8% dividends. With this price, the risk is low and the potential appreciation is high. When one or two institutional investors move in, the price will surge.

The risk may not be the stock itself but the market in general. I expect a market plunge in 2016 as explained in my book Profit from Market Crash 2016. If the market crashes, I will add more shares of CALM. In the meantime, enjoy the generous dividend rate of 8.59% if there is no change in the stock price.

61 Politics and investing

This is a summary and some portions may be duplicated in other articles. You may ask why politics is discussed in this investing book. Politics has been proven to affect the market. For example, the market had reacted to the different stages of Quantitative Easing whose dates have been preset. The following is a more recent example.

I predicted 2015 would be a year with small profit and insisted on so even during the fierce correction in August. Why I was so sure? Very seldom the market is down in a year before an election year including 2007. The last occurrence was 1939, the year when WW2 started. Investing is a multi-discipline venture including statistics and politics. It may not always happen, but the probability is high for these years.

How to profit

2015 was a sideward market. The market reacted to good news and bad news. The strategy for sideway market is: Buy at temporary downs and sell at temporary peaks. Define 'temporary' according to your risk tolerance. I used 5% from the last peak or the market is 5% down for 'temporary down' and 10% for 'temporary peak'. In another words, I buy the stock when it is 5% down from the last peak and sell it when it gains 10% for this strategy. Be reminded that this strategy is opposite to market plunges, when you should exit the market totally (again depending on your risk tolerance).

The following are my purchases on 08/26/2015. I should have bought more stocks and one day earlier if I were not blinded by fears (a human nature) during this correction. Here is my proof for my buy orders. The four stocks were described as value stocks in a SA article and I did a simple evaluation. As of 12/31/2015, I sold all the four stocks except Gilead Sciences. The annualized returns are more impressive such as the GNW's 10% gain in one day.

Stocks	Buy Price	Buy Date	Return	Sold date
Apple (AAPL)	107.20	08/26/15	12%	10/19/15
Gilead Sciences (GILD)	105.94	08/26/15	-4%	
General Motors (GM)	27.69	08/26/15	12%	09/17/15

Genwealth Financial (GNW)	4.54	08/26/15	10%	08/27/15

There were similar examples in 2013 and 2014.

2016: Politics and the market

No one including all the Federal Reserve chairmen / chairwomen and all the Nobel-Prize winners in economics can predict market plunges. One chairman predicted a smooth market and a few months later the housing market crashed. Many predicted correctly market crashes by pure luck. One even received a Nobel Prize and became famous. However, you are glad to ignore his later predictions on the market.

There are at least two best sellers asking us to exit the market in 2009. If you followed them, you would miss all the big gains from 2009 to 2015. They did have a point. However, you cannot fight the Fed. The market had been saved by the excessive printing of money and hence created a non-correlation between the market and the economy. I bet these authors (famous economists and gurus) may have not made a buck in the stock market.

From their articles, they do not know the basic technical indicator. You only want react to the market when the market is plunging and not too early. That's why most fund managers cannot beat the market as most are not allowed to time the market. Buffett had mediocre returns in the last three years – I had warned my readers three years ago in my blogs/books. To me, the 'buy-and-hold' strategy is dead since 2000. The average loss from the peak for the last two market plunges is about 45%. Most charts depend on falling prices, so you will not save 45% and 25% loss is my objective.

Fundamentally speaking

The market in 2016 is risky due to the proposed interest rate hike, our record-high margin, strong U.S. dollar and the high expenses of the wars to start. Each reason could be a good-size article. Personally I try to maintain 50% cash and would flee the market if my technical indicator tells me so.

Politically (and statistically) speaking

The election year is the second best for the market, but it may not be this year. We seldom have three terms from the same political party. For that, I predict a win by the Republicans. Republicans are usually pro-business, but ironically the democratic presidency has better track record for better market performance.

The market has more than recovered since the day when Obama took office. The S&P500 performance under Republicans vs. Democrats since 1926 to 2014 is approximately:

Annualized return under Democratic presidencies: 13%
Annualized return under Republican presidencies: 6%

The market is riskier based on the above statistics. In addition, most likely we will have either a non-politician president or a lady president for the first time. The market usually does not favor to this kind of change.

Critical political issue for 2016

On our way back at about 4 pm on a Saturday, the bus was full of Spanish-speaking workers. I bet most are illegal workers working in the suburb such as our malls, the hospital and many restaurants. Why illegals? I bet most legal folks would get welfare instead of working in that shift. If they work, the state would take away the freebies such as health care in Mass. The illegals do not have this option. I do not think the politicians understand this. There is no need for building a border wall but punishing the employers. Before we do this, we need folks to take the jobs taken by the illegals today.

What will happen if the politicians turn the illegals to be legal? There will be nobody doing these jobs I predict. No one in the right mind wants these jobs as it is far better to collect welfare. Why politicians would make this stupid decision? They want to buy Hispanic votes as evidenced in the last two elections.

In addition, most politicians side with the welfare recipients. Since 40% of the population do not pay Federal taxes, the politicians have to satisfy their needs in order to buy votes. We should encourage folks to work, not the other way round. Representation without taxation is worse than taxation without representation.

Our high taxes, regulations and strong US dollar dampen our competitive edge.

Some political decisions/regulations that affect the stocks

Beside the presidency and the interest rate hike, there are many political decisions and regulations that affect the stocks. Just name a few here:
- The never-ending wars postpone our secular bull market beyond 2018.
- Solar City (SCTY). It depends on government energy credit.
- My Chinese solar panel stock evaporated when the US banned them from importing to the US.
- Any gun control measurement may affect gun stocks.
- Restrictions on cigarettes.
- France imposes extra taxes to foreign investors.
- Government bailouts on 'too big to fall' companies. I made more than 200% on Chrysler because of that.
- Corporate taxes boost the exodus of corporation headquarters to tax heavens for the US. It is the same for Chinese corporations.
- Infrastructure projects.
- Taking out the ban to export oil would increase the profits of oil companies.
- After the annexation of Crimea, the Congress restricted using Russia's rocket engines and gave new opportunity to the US companies in this area. Besides political consideration, Chinese rockets are the most cost effective.
- China's suppressing corruption affected Macau's casinos...

Summary
Politics affect the market. I predict a risky market in 2016.
Economy and religion also affect the market. Statistically speaking, the market is ahead of the economy by about 6 months. However, the current market is an exception. The correlation will return to normal.

Religions cause wars as the ones in the Middle East today. These huge expenses are consumption, not investing. It will not be good for most sectors of the economy especially in the long run.

Written in 1/1/2016.

62 GuruFocus

There are many interesting features in Gurufocus.com. It provides the recent stock picks from gurus. Gurus have evaluated the stocks and you just follow them. Gurus' picks and insiders' purchases could the best picks without doing a lot of work yourself. However, 2015 is not good for stock pickers including gurus. After using it for a while, I found it very useful and easy to use. It will not replace my production system in evaluating stocks but it will supplement and improve my system.

They provide a very comprehensive screener and several screens to simulate what gurus would pick. Check it out yourself. They do not have a historical database, so it will take a while to monitor the performances of the pick. A simpler way (also provided) is to check the performances of the gurus.

If you do not have any subscription, this one is recommended together with Value Line and Zacks. Try out the free offer to see whether it is useful to you. As with all vendor recommendations, I have not been paid by anyone of them except the free subscriptions and /or products for me to evaluate.

Besides no historical database, they have a choice on S&P 500, but not a choice on exchanges. There are many data including Exchange that can be displayed when the stocks are added to a portfolio. Gurufocus.com provides a lot of information on a specific stock and some are quite unique such as Piotroski's F-Score and the warning messages of a stock.

Filler

*** iPhone & drones ***

Almost 100% of drones are made in China. Should we check whether the Chinese have back doors in the drones? They could instruct the drones to take pictures or just use them to kill everything that moves. Hope it is a joke.

63 Piotroski's F-Score

The strategy is based on Piotroski's system. It has been doing very well until 2015. I first noticed it in AAII. The problem in AAII is it is very selective, so most of the time I do not find any stock. In addition, AAII recommends you to sell the stocks if they fail to meet the criteria. The following describes a strategy based on F-Score in a SA article:

"Here are the nine variables used to calculate the F-Score. Each variable gets scored a one (1) if the condition is met.

1. Positive (+) net income in the current year.
2. Positive (+) cash flow from operations in the current year.
3. Return on Assets [ROA] is higher in the current period compared to the previous year.
4. Cash flow from operations exceeds net income before extraordinary items.
5. Lower ratio of long-term debt to assets in the current period compared to the previous year.
6. Higher current ratio this year compared to the previous year.
7. Company did not issue new shares/equity in the preceding year.
8. Higher gross margin compared to the previous year.
9. Higher asset turnover ratio year on year.

Piotroski only selected stocks that scored 7 or above (maximum of 9)."

Gathering the above information is quite time-consuming. Gurufocus.com's (http://www.gurufocus.com/)
"All-in-one Screener" in GuruFocus includes the F-Score.

To illustrate, on 11/13/2013, I found the following 12 stocks: SGA, EXAC, ODC, FRS, ANEN, BGFV, LBMH, LDL, RUTH, LWAY, ITRN and GHIFF with the following criteria:

1. F-Score 8 or higher.
2. Market Cap between $100 M and $500 M.
3. Financial Strength between 7 and 10.

The market cap is selected as most big boys will not evaluate these stocks and they drive the market.

They provide a very comprehensive screener and several screens to simulate what gurus would pick.

My modifications

The modifications below are my suggestions with the following reasons:

- Most readers do not have GuruFocus. The modifications allow readers to obtain stock data from most financial sites including Finviz.com. The modifications resemble the original criteria.
- Add negative numbers. F-Score does not consider negative ratios.
- Adaptive criteria as described in the book. We replace the criteria that do not work in current market.
- Add ratios that are not available in Piotroski's era.

The first line is the original and it is followed by my changes (if any). Use Finviz.com.

1. Positive (+) net income in the current year.
   P/E is positive and less than 25: Add 1.
   P/E is zero or negative: Minus 1.

1. Positive (+) cash flow from operations in the current year.
   P/FCP is positive: Add 1.
   P/FCP is zero or negative: Minus 1.

2. Return on Assets [ROA] is higher in the current period compared to the previous year.
   ROA > 10: Add 1.
   ROA < 2: Minus 1.

3. Cash flow from operations exceeds net income before extraordinary items. Not used.

4. Lower ratio of long-term debt to assets in the current period compared to the previous year.

   Debt/Eq < .25: Add 1.

   Debt/Eq > .75: Minus 1.

5. Higher current ratio this year compared to the previous year.

   Current Ratio > 1.5: Add 1.

Current Ration < .8: Minus 1.

6. Company did not issue new shares/equity in the preceding year. Not used.

7. Higher gross margin compared to the previous year.

    Profit Margin > 15%: Add 1.

    Profit Margin < 5%: Minus 1.

8. Higher asset turnover ratio year on year. Not used.

Some metrics are not applicable to me or they are hard to find equivalent ratios. They are replaced with the next metrics.

1. Short Float < 5: Add 1.
   Short Float > 15 and < 25: Minus 1.
2. Sales Q/Q > 10: Add 1.
   Sales Q/Q < 2: Minus 1.
3. EPS Q/Q > 5: Add 1.
   EPS Q/Q < 1: Minus 1.
4. SMA50 > 10%: Add 1.
   SMA50 < -10%: Minus 1.

I called it FM-Score (M for modification). Need to adjust to specific industries. A supermarket turnover has low profit margin for example while a utility company has high borrowing cost.

Links
F-Score System:
http://www.investopedia.com/terms/p/piotroski-score.asp
SA article:
(http://seekingalpha.com/article/1806542-a-dividend-portfolio-built-using-the-piotroski-f-score)

Epilogue

This book was written for beginners and couch potatoes. However, the very basic investing knowledge is expected. This book has explained how to use the advanced strategies in my other books, but in very simple terms. There are many chapters that you should try them out. Many bonus chapters are your future reading. Thanks for reading this book and hope it will be beneficial to your financial health. If so, comment it in amazon.com.

There are many reasons you should write a review on this book:

- As of this writing (12/2015), I do not know any reviewers on all of my books. Some reviews were obviously written by friends and family members.

- How can a 50-page book have far more and better reviews than my 250-page book on Sector Rotation?

- I bet some reviews were written by my competitors or ones with strong bias against me being an Asian. I beg you to write an honest review.

- A best seller tells us to exit the market in 2009 when my book told you until recently using simple charts for similar period. They had so many excellent reviews from celebrities. If you followed this author, you would have lost a lot of money.

- I can take bad reviews, so I can improve. This book is about the size of three books. I bet you have got your money worth. It is organized as a reference book than a novel.

Discrimination me due to my last name is social injustice. So far, I donated all my profits to charities. Writing this book helps me more in investing than all the seminars and hundreds of investing books I read.

Bonus: Simple Techniques

For better security, use a two-factor login that should be available in most if not all brokers and most financial institutions such as your banks. To illustrate, after you have logged in, your broker sends a code to your phone to verify you are the rightful owner. Do not be a target of scams by showing your wealth. Do not click unknown web links. Do not lend money and do not give out your credit cards. Do not be greedy. Do not buy the products such as annuities recommended by marketeers, as these products are designed to make big money by them.

An ETF is a basket of stocks. For starters, just trade ETFs such as SPY (an ETF simulating S&P 500 stocks and the market to many), and you can skip the rest of the book. It has been proven, the SPY or VOO has beaten most funds by a good margin. That is why mutual funds are dying.

I prefer VOO which has an expense ratio of 0.03% vs. SPY's 0.09% as of 12/2022). For better diversification, I recommend RSP, an unweighted ETF of the S&P 500 stocks. MDY (0.22%), an ETF for midcap, is also recommended. The last 10 years had been great for SPY until recently. I do not know the next 10 years, and that's why I also recommend MDY together with VOO (or RSP). They represent a wide diversification. Most indexes take out the bad performers and include better additions every year, and hence you do not need to balance your portfolio except for market timing.

It only takes a few minutes every month (more often if the indicators are close to cross over) using the simplest market timing described in Chapter 5. When the market is not plunging, buy or keep SPY (or any ETF that stimulates the market); otherwise sell it. Do the opposite when the market is recovering. The techniques named Death Cross and Golden Cross are the best-kept secrets that have been proven in the last two crashes (2000 and 2008).

The following is from Portfolio Visual (https://www.portfoliovisualizer.com/backtest-portfolio#analysisResults). From 2000 to Nov., 2022 and including reinvested dividends, the portfolio consisting of 25% SPY, 25% RSP and 50% MDY returns (CAGR) 10% with a max drawdown of 51%.

Do not let the simple techniques that do not require any investing knowledge and time fool you. From 2000 to 2022 (today), it beat the market by a wide margin and I bet it beat most of the fund managers.

If you have less than $50,000 to invest, just buy ETFs. Improve your investing skills by reading investment articles from this book and your broker's website. For example, Fidelity has a lot of information for investors.

Subscription to AAII is recommended. When your portfolio grows more than $50,000, invest on a subscription such as Value Line, GuruFocus, Zacks or IBD (more for momentum traders). Initially, use the information for paper trading on value stocks, which is usually available from brokers.

For the long term, knowledge is most important in your investing life and experience comes next. Retail investors have a lot of advantages over fund managers. However, I advise you NOT to be a trader. Hence, you should ignore the 'fabulous' trade systems that claim to be very profitable. Statistically most amateur traders lose money as they cannot compete with experienced, disciplined traders.

How to start

I recommend trading ETFs first and when the market is not risky. You can skip the following if you do not have time for investing. The very basic terms such as ETF are not fully explained here; try Investopedia for terms you need to know. Otherwise, this book would be doubled in size and it would bore most readers. Investopedia, your broker's website (especially Fidelity) and AAII (requiring subscription) provide many excellent articles. Alternatively, buy a book for beginners.

Here are some freebies:
Click here for Morningstar classroom.
http://morningstar.com/cover/classroom.html
Click here for Vanguard.
https://investor.vanguard.com/investing/investor-education
Click here for Investopedia's Tutorials.
http://www.investopedia.com/university/
Click here for Yahoo!
http://finance.yahoo.com/education/begin_investing
Click here for Fidelity basic in investing.
https://www.fidelity.com/investment-guidance/investing-basics

1   Sample portfolio

It is a suggested sample. You need to tailor it to fit your personal requirements and your risk tolerance. In general, you should have an emergency fund for at least 3 months (6 months preferred). Many of our generation have one or even no layoff. However, I estimate the current generation will have 3 layoffs in their work life. It is due to automation, artificial intelligence, global economy, etc.

The rough estimate of stock holding in distribution between stock and bond is equal to 100 – Your Age. To illustrate in the following three portfolios, I use a 30-year-old, and hence he should have 70% in stocks and 30% in bonds (including gold, CDs and cash).

In addition, some sectors are better than others according to the market conditions. The following three portfolios are for regular, todays' market and one during a market crash. I use low-cost ETFs exclusively. ETF is exchange-traded funds. They are traded similar to stocks, but most are more diversified; their fees are usually lower than mutual funds.

ETF	Normal	Today (2/2021)	Crashing[5]
SPY[1]	40%	30%	0%
QQQ[2]	10%	10%	0%
VTIAX[3]	20%	5%	0%
LQD[3]	15%	20%	5%
GLD	5%	15%	15%
CD	5%	0%	0%
Cash	5%	20%	60%[6]
SH[4]	0%	0%	5%
PSQ[4]	0%	0%	15%

[1] VOO is a low-fee alternative to SPY.

[2] QQQ has more tech stocks.

[4] SH and PSQ are contra ETF to SPY and QQQ. They are shorting the corresponding index. When the market is recovering, switch them back to SPY and QQQ.

[5] Need to balance the allocations about two times a year as ETFs can grow or shrink. When the market crashes, rebalance it right away. All markets

will crash, and the last two (2000 and 2008) have an average loss of about 45%. Refer to the chapter "Simplest marketing timing".

[6] Today's low interest rate does not benefit us for CDs. I would leave the cash not invested and wait for the recovery to move back to stocks.

Of course, everyone's situation is different. If you are conservative, do not buy SH and PSQ. If you are afraid of inflation (especially due to the excessive printing of money), allocate more on GLD, a gold ETF.

Do not listen to financial news. They are used by institutional investors / analysts to manipulate the market. Many times they act the opposite from what they preach. This is the primary reason retail investors do not do better. With the GameStop incident, do not invest in most hedge funds. Buffett has proved the hedge funds with their high fees cannot buy an indexed ETF such as SPY.

The above is my recommendation. In the long run, it should work fine. Consult your financial advisor before taking actions. If you have more time, time the market as described (Death Cross and Golden Cross). If you are interested in investing, study the more sophisticated techniques described in my book "Art of Investing 2nd Edition".

Link
Best Vanguard ETFs https://www.youtube.com/watch?v=mSEyghlZchQ

VTI or VOO: https://www.youtube.com/watch?v=v7staXdVE8c

#Filler: Simple measures to reduce net security.
Do not click any links from unknown sources. Some seem to be ok but not.
MalwareBytes, for checking viruses, is free for download (they do not pay me). Personally, I use a Chromebook for my financial transactions and a two-factor login for my stock trading.

#Filler "How to make a 50% return"

https://www.youtube.com/watch?v=eEto5nEkf1Y

#Filler Buffett, the person.
https://www.youtube.com/watch?v=w-eX4sZi-Zs

2   Investing for 'lazy' folks

You have better things to do than investing or you do not have the time, the desire to learn and/or expertise in investing. You should be better off to buy ETFs.

I recommend the following 4 ETFs. If you have $100,000 to invest, buy $25,000 for each recommended ETF. Consult your financial advisor before taking any action. The recommended ETFs should have a large market cap (the ETFs themselves and not the stocks they hold) and have a high volume.

Most returns started on July 1 and ended on July 1 the following year; this article is written on July 20, 2021. All are annualized returns for easy comparison. Fees, commissions and dividends have not been included; you can add the dividend yield and prorate it for YTD return.

Symbol	Name	YTD[1] Return	1 Year[2]	5 Years[3]	Bear[4]
IWF	Russel1000Grow	30%	34%	40%	-33%
QQQ	QQQ	30%	46%	42%	-31%
VTI	Vang. Viper Tot	34%	22%	42%	-35%
VUG	Vang. Growth	37%	33%	41%	-32%
Avg.		31%	34%	41%	-33%
SPY[5]		34%	21%	39%	-35%
Beat[6]		-9%	60%	6%	7%

[1] The start date is 1/4/2021 and the end date is 7/1/2021.
[2] The start date is 7/1/2020 and the end date is 7/1/2021.
[3] The start date is 7/1/2016 and the end date is 7/1/2021.
[4] The start date is 1/2/2008 and the end date is 4/1/2009. My estimates.
[5] SPY is the ETF for the S&P 500 index. It is used as a yardstick.
[6] = (Avg. − SPY) / SPY. Again, it does not include fees, commissions and dividends.

Comments:
- The YTD is the only period that this portfolio does not beat SPY (the market to many). It could mean the market could be changing the favorite from growth stocks to value stocks. However, 31% return is far above the average of the market.

- The one-year return beats the market by 60%.
- The 5-year return beats SPY only by 6%, but the return of 41% is nothing to sneeze at.
- All except Vanguard's Viper Total are ETFs for growth stocks. Hence, I expected it would not beat the market, but it still did by 7%.
- You can time the market using the techniques described in this book as often as you can. When the indicator tells you to exit, you can sell these ETFs and reenter the market when it recovers. Riskier investors can buy contra ETFs such as PSQ and SH instead of holding cash when the market is down.
- At least once in a year review the selection. Use ETFdb.com for information. If you do not have time, it is fine skipping the review. When you switch ETFs, taxes should be considered.
- Most ETFs replace some stocks periodically to ensure better appreciation potential.
- I prefer VOO due to lower fees (about .03%) fee over SPY (about .06%) for long-term investors and SPY for short-term investors due to lower spread (difference between ask price and sell price) as a larger fund.

3 Simplest analysis of ETFs

Evaluate an ETF
ETFs are a basket of stocks according to the market, a specific sector, country or a specific theme.

Yahoo!Finance used to give the P/E of an ETF. Try to get it from ETFdb.com. Enter the symbol of the ETF such as XLU, and then select Valuation. If it is below 15 and above zero, it could be a value ETF. Also, if the current price is lower than its NAV, it is sold at a discount (or premium vice versa). Compare its YTD Return to SPY's.

Alternatively, get similar info from http://www.multpl.com/. In addition, this website provides the following metrics: Shiller P/E, Price/Sales, and Price/Book.

From Finviz.com, enter the ETF symbol. If SMA-20%, SMA-50% and SMA-200% are all positive, most likely the ETF is in an uptrend. To illustrate, SMA-200 is Simple Moving Average for the last 200 trading sessions (no trading on weekends and specific holidays). The percent is how much the stock price of the ETF is above the SMA. If the percent is negative, it means the stock price is below the SMA.

If your average holding period of your stocks is about 50 days, SMA-50% is more appropriate to you. If RSI(14) > 65, it is probably oversold; if it is < 30, it is probably under-sold (indicating value).

In addition, ensure the ETF's average volume is high (I suggest more than 10,000 shares), the market cap is more than 300 M, and it has low fees. Most popular ETFs have these characteristics. Beginners should avoid leveraged ETFs.

How to determine if the sector has been recovered
It is easier to profit by following the uptrend of an ETF using the above info. It is hard to detect when the bottom of an ETF has been reached. If SMA-20%, SMA-50% and SMA-200% are all positive, most likely the ETF is in an uptrend or it has recovered. It does not always happen as predicted, so use stops to protect your investment.

Link: Fidelity ETF https://www.youtube.com/watch?v=tUsFTN7iDcQ
Vanguard offers many low-cost ETFs.

An example

First, determine whether the market is risky. Most beginners should not invest in a risky market. Advanced investors can bet against the market or a specific sector by buying contra ETFs or puts.

Next, you want to limit the number of sector ETFs by selecting those that are either in an uptrend or hitting bottom (bottom is hard to predict). Personally, I prefer sectors with long-term uptrends (indicated by articles found in many websites including cnnfn.com and Seeking Alpha.

For illustration purposes only for deteriorating market conditions, I would select the following ETFs: SPY (simulating the market based on large companies) and XLP (consumer staples). XLP should perform better than XLY (consumer discretionary) during a recession as those products are the necessities.

Technical indicators such as SMA-50 (Simple Moving Average for the last 50 sessions), SMA-200 and RSI(14) are obtained from Finviz.com and the rest are obtained from Yahoo!Finance.com. After you buy the ETF, use a stop loss to protect your investment. For example, the biotech sector moved up for many months until it crashed in 2015. Change the stop loss value every month to protect your gains in this case.

As of 2/5/2016	SPY	XLP (staples)	XLY (discreet.)
Price	190	50	71
NAV	192	50	73
• Technical			
SMA-50	-4%	0%	-7%
SMA-200	-6%	2%	-7%
RSI(14)	44	50	36
Other	Double bottom at $186		
• Fundamental			
P/E	17	20	19
Yield	2.1%	2.5%	1.5%
YTD return	-5%	0.5%	-5%
Net asset	174 B	9 B	10 B

Explanation
- The figures may not be identical among websites due to the dates they are using.
- XLY has the best discount among the 3 ETFs as most investors believe a recession is coming.

- XLP has less down trend among the 3 ETFs as expected.
- XLY is more undersold among the three as expected.
- Double bottom is a technical pattern that indicates the stock would surge upward.
- SPY has a better value according to its P/E.
- XLY's dividend is the least among the three as they have more tech companies in the ETF. They have to plow back the profits to research and development.
- XLP has the best YTD return among the three.
- As long as the asset is above 500 M (200 M for specialized ETFs), it is fine and all three pass this mark.

There are many metrics such as Debt/Equity not readily available from most websites. Many sites list the top holdings of a specific ETF. Just average the metrics of the top ten or so of its stock holdings.

Links
Fidelity ETF: https://www.youtube.com/watch?v=tUsFTN7iDcQ

#Filler: Illogical logic
If we do not test for the pandemic, we would have zero increase in this pandemic. Some silly folks buy this argument. What happens to the once-great country?

Filler: The problems of the U.S.
1. Our political system. We waste time arguing between the two parties. There is no long-term planning, as the other party could claim the credit. Same as corporations' CEOs who care about their yearly bonuses.
2. The politicians have to satisfy their voters. Today give them free cash by jacking up the printing press. And ignore the long-term consequences.
3. We have to protect our workers, our environment... Hence, we cannot compete with many countries.
4. We have spent too much on the military and ignore our crumbling infrastructure.
5. Historically no country can rule the world forever.
6. We blame China, but ignore how hard-working Chinese are.

An example

This example evaluates RING, a gold miner, using ETFdb and Finviz that are free from the web. The data is from July, 6, 2020.

Bring up ETFdb and enter RING in the search. There is basic info that are important to me: Sector (gold miners), Asset Size (Large-Cap), Issuer (iShares), Inception (Jan. 31, 2012), Expense Ratio (0.39%) and Tax Form (1099).

They fit all my requirements. The expense ratio is higher than most ETFs that simulate an index such as SPY. I try to trade ETFs using Tax Form 1099 in my taxable accounts. The large cap created about 8 years ago by a reputable company is good.

Select "Dividend and Valuation". P/E of 17.39 is fine in a rank of 11 in 27 in a similar group of ETFs. As in my books, I stated it is hard to evaluate miners. I buy this ETF primarily to fight the possibility of inflation and the potential depreciation of USD. The dividend rate of 0.52% (0.70% from Finviz) is in the low range of the scale; it is fine for me as dividend is not my concern.

There is more info from this website. For simplicity, bring up Finviz:
- The short-term trend is up (SMA-20% = 8% and SMA-50% = 7%).
- The long-term trend is up (SMA-200% = 26%).
- It is close to overbought (RSI(14) = 64%; 65% to me is overbought).
- It is -4% from 52-w High. It has performed well from the YTD, Last Year, Last Quarter, Last Month and Last Week.
- It almost doubled in price from mid-March this year.
- Avg. Vol. is fine.

From ETFdb, check the Holding. It has 39 stocks, so it is quite diversified for this industry. The two top holdings are NEM (19%) and ABX (18%), which is listed as GOLD in NYSX. I also consider buying these two stocks in addition to RING. You can estimate the other metrics that are not available by averaging these two stocks. Here is my summary:

STOCK	NEM	GOLD
Forward P/E	20	25
Debt / Share	0.31	0.24
ROE	17%	22%
Sales Q/Q	43%	30%
EPS Q/Q	389%	254%
SMA50	2%	4%
RSI(14)	59%	60%
Insider Trans	-13%	N/A
Fidelity's Equity Summary Score	6.1	6.8

4   Simplest ways to evaluate stocks

Beginners should trade ETFs only. This chapter is for the readers who are ready or getting ready to trade stocks. In general, ETFs are diversified, less volatile than trading stocks. However, stocks offer higher profit but higher risk.

Many stock researches have already been done recently and some are available free of charge. I have no affiliation with Fidelity except I retired from it. You can open an account with them with no balance. Their Equity Summary Score is one of the best indicators; I check out **value** stocks with scores higher than 8. Concentrate on fundamental metrics such as P/E for long-term holds, and momentum metrics for short-term holds. Add criteria to limit the number of screened stocks. Finviz.com is a free screener.

Several sources

The popular ones are Morningstar, Value Line, The Street and Zacks (currently free for rankings of individual stocks). If they are not free, check out whether they are available from your local library. I have 3 simple ways to evaluate stocks starting with the simplest. In addition, read the articles on the selected stocks from Fidelity, Finviz, Seeking Alpha and many other sources for further evaluation.

Fidelity

Select only stocks that have Fidelity's Equity Summary Score 8 or higher. There is tons of information about a stock. Once in a while I did not agree with this score such as SHOP and ZM that scored high in August, 2020. Include the following for your analysis.

A modified stock selection based on a magazine article

Most metrics are available from Finviz except EV/EBITDA.

9. Forward P/E (expected earnings and not based on the last twelve months). It should range from 5 to 15 (10 to 25 for high tech stocks). EV/EBITDA (from Yahoo!Finance) is a better choice as it includes the debts and cash than P/E; it would be more effective if it uses forward

earnings. If you do not use EV/EBITDA, ensure Debt/Equity is less than 0.5 except for the debt-intensive industries.

10. ROE (Return of Equity) measures how well the company uses the capital. I prefer stocks with ROE greater than 5%.

11. Volatility. Conservative investors should select stocks with a beta of less than one (i.e., less volatile).

12. Insider Transactions for sales (i.e., negative) should be less than 5%. If it is -5%, most likely the insiders are dumping it.

13. Compare the metrics such as P/E and Debt/Equity to its five-year average and its competitors (available in Fidelity).

14. Momentum. Check out the SMA-50 (actually SMA-50%) and SMA-200. Ideally, they should be positive. SMA-50% is especially important for stocks you do not want to keep for a long time.

15. Check out articles on the stock as some recent events (for example a new lawsuit) have not been included in the metrics.

16. Compare the trend of the sector this stock is in. Under Finviz, enter the related sector ETF.

Summary
The sources are Fidelity (Equity Summary Score and various comparisons), Finviz and Yahoo!Finance (for EV/EBITDA). Value stocks should be held longer.

Category	Score / Metric	Value /Momentum
Score	Fidelity's Equity Summary Score	Both
Value	EV/EBITDA	Value
	P/E cheaper compared to 5-year avg.	Value
	P/E cheaper compared to its sector.	Value
	Insider Purchases	Both
Safety	Debt/Equity	Value
	Compare it to its sector.	Value

Momentum	50-SMA%		Momentum
	200-SMA% (for long term holds).		Value
Articles	Check out latest events		Both
Market	No purchase if market is risky.		Momentum

A simple scoring system using Finviz

Bring up Finviz.com and then enter the stock symbol.

No.	Metric	Good	Bad	Score
1	Forward P/E[1]	Between 2.5 and 12.5, Score = 2	> 50 or < 0, Score = -1	
2	P/ FCF[1]	< 12, Score = 1	>30 or < 0, Score = -1	
3	P/S[1]	< 0.8, Score = 1	< 0, Score = -1	
4	P/ B[1]	< 1, Score = 1	< 0, Score = -1	
	Compare quarter to quarter of last year			
5	Sales Q/Q	> 15%, Score = 1	< 0, Score = -1	
6	EPS Q/Q	> 20%, Score = 1	< 0, Score = -1	
			Grand Score	
	Stock Symbol Date[2]	Current Price	SPY	

Footnote

[3] Negative values for Sales (due to accounting adjustments), Equity and Book are possible but not likely.

[4] The last row is for your information only. SPY is used to measure whether it will beat the market by comparing the return of this stock to the return of SPY.

The Score

Score each metric and sum up all the scores giving the Grand Score. If the Grand Score is 3, the stock passes this scoring system. Even if it is a 2, it still deserves further analysis if you have time. You may want to add scores from other vendors. To illustrate on using Fidelity, add 1 to the score if Fidelity's Equity Summary score is 8 or higher. Monitor the performance after every 6 months or so to see whether this scoring system beats the market.

Very basic advice for beginners
Beginners should stick with U.S. stocks with Market Cap greater than 800 M (million), Debt/Equity less than .25 (25%) except for debt-intensive industries such as utilities and airlines and Forward P/E between 5 to 20 (25 for high-tech companies). These metrics are all available from Finviz.com, which is free.

Do not have more than 20% of your portfolio in one stock (unless it is an ETF or mutual fund) and do not have more than 30% of your portfolio in one sector.

For more conservative investors, buy non-volatile stocks whose beta (available from Yahoo!Finance) is less than 1. Beta of 1 represents the market (the S&P 500 index). For example, a stock with beta 1.5 statistically fluctuates more than 50% of the market and hence it is very volatile.

Try paper trading to check out your strategy and your skill in trading stocks. If your broker does not provide one, use a spreadsheet to record your trades or check the availability of simulator.investopedia.com.

Link: Buy stocks/ETFs: https://www.youtube.com/watch?v=4vjkeC_4EmU
https://www.youtube.com/watch?v=wMxj6iB92ZA

#Filler: Silence is golden

I am glad I did not give advice to a friend who had to decide whether to take a lump sum payment or an annuity. The correction in March, 2020 would wipe out a lot of his portfolio if he took the lump sum payment. No one would share his profits when the predictions are correct, but the blame if it does not materialize.

It is the same in investing that nothing is certain. With educated guesses, we should have more rights than wrongs especially in the long run.

5   Simplest market timing

Why market timing
Before 2000, market timing was a waste of time. However, after that, we have had two market plunges with the average loss of about 45%. It sounds harder to time the market than it actually is. We have a simple technique to detect market plunges and when to reenter the market. Our objective is reducing the loss to 25%.

Market timing depends on charts; the following describes how to use chart information without creating charts. Most charts will not identify the peaks and bottoms of the market as they depend on data (i.e., the stock prices). However, it would reduce further losses. It is simpler than it sounds. Just follow the procedure below.

The first part of this technique detects potential market plunges, and the second part advises you when to start reentering the market. It applies to individual stocks too. It also works to detect the trend of a sector (entering an ETF for the specific sector instead of SPY) and a specific stock.

Step-by-step procedure
When the market timer indicator (Death Cross) described next tells you to exit the market, sell SPY (an ETF simulating S&P 500). Do not forget to buy back SPY or similar ETF such as RSP, when the indicator (Golden Cross) tells you to return.

My experiences in 2000s
Basically I did the same as the above with some adaptations. I worked for a mutual fund company and they did not allow me to trade stocks effectively. However, I was allowed to trade sector funds offered by the company. Every two months, I switched to the sectors with the best performances for the last month. When most sectors were down for the last month, I rotated them to the money market fund. In March or April, 2000, I switched to traditional sectors from high-tech sectors (better to switch to market money funds). During that time, I bought stocks that had enough cash to last more than two years judging by their burn rates. The indicators should do a better job.

How to detect market plunges without charts (similar to <u>Death Cross</u>)
7. Bring up Finviz.com.
8. Enter SPY (or any ETF that simulates the market) or RSP, equally-weighted SPY.

9. If SMA-200% is positive, it indicates that the market plunge has not been detected and you can skip the following steps.
10. The market is plunging if SMA-50% is more negative than SMA-200%. To illustrate this condition, SMA-200% is -2% and SMA-50% is -5%.
11. Another hint: B/S (buy sell ratio) is negative, specially it is more negative than last week.
12. Conservative investors should sell most stocks starting with the riskiest ones first such as the ones with negative earnings, high P/Es and/or high Debt/Equity. Obtain this info from Finviz.com by entering the symbol of the stock you own.
13. Aggressive investors should sell all stocks. Extremely aggressive investors should sell all stocks, buy contra ETFs such as PSQ, and even short stocks. I do not recommend beginners to be aggressive.

Example
As of 2/12/2022, the following are from Finviz.com.

ETF	SMA-200	SMA-50	SMA-20	Death Cross?
SPY	-0.8%	-4.2%	-1.7%	Yes (Step #4)
RSP	-0.5%	-1.9%	0.4%	Yes (Step #4)

Both ETFs indicate the market is a confirmed crash from my indications using a technique similar to Death Cross. However, they are quite close, and we should keep an eye on these numbers. In this case, SMA-20 has not been used. If it is a false alarm, the Golden Cross would indicate it and you should return to equity; it could be quite common in volatile markets. The futures indicate that on Monday (2/14/22) the market would plunge further. Another test is using SMA-350: When the current price is below SMA-300, it is a crash. SMA-20 has to be more negative than SMA-50 and it has not been used here.

Simple chart example. Bring up StockCharts.com and enter SPY. It indicates Death Cross occurred on around March 20, 2022.

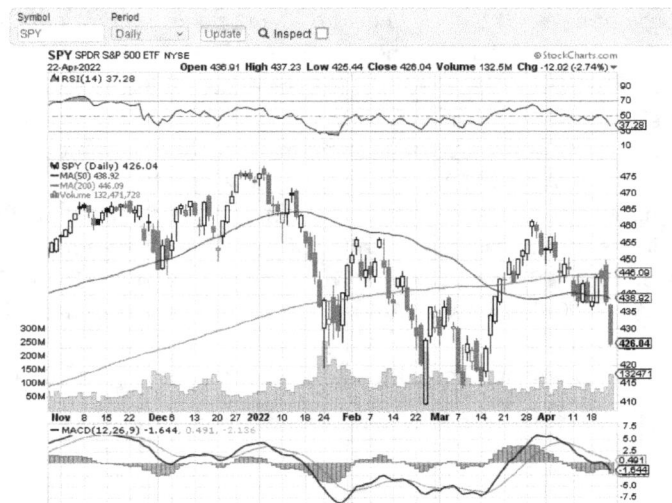

When to return to the market (similar to Golden Cross)

Use the above in a reversed sense to detect whether the market has been recovering. However, when the SMA-200% turns positive, I would start buying value stocks (low P/E but the 'E' has to be positive, and/or low Debt/Equity).

6. Bring up Finviz.com.
7. Enter SPY (or any ETF that simulates the market).
8. If SMA-200% is negative, the market is not recovering, and you can skip the following steps.
9. Sell all contra ETFs and close all shorts if you have any.
10. Market recovery is confirmed when SMA-50% is more positive than SMA-200%. To illustrate this condition, SMA-200% is 2% and SMA-50% is 5%. Commit a large percent of cash (or all cash for aggressive investors) to stocks. If you do not know what to buy, buy SPY or an ETF that simulates the market.
11. Another hint: B/S (buy sell ratio) is positive, specially it is more positive than last week.

How often should you check the market timing indicators?

Do the above once a month. When the SPY price is closer to SMA actions percentage, perform the above once a week. The charts and data for market timing described in this book are based on SMA-350 (Simple Moving Average) that is more preferable than this simple procedure, but it requires some simple charting.

Nothing is perfect

If the market timing is perfect, there would be no poor folks. The major 'defects' are:

- It does not detect the peak / bottom as it depends on past data. However, it would save you a lot during the crash.
- It is hard to determine whether it is a correction or a crash.
- From 2000 to 2010, there was only one false signal. The indicator tells you to exit and then tells you to reenter the market shortly. In most cases, you do not lose a lot. After 2010, we have more false signals.
- The market may not be rational or may be influenced due to specific conditions such as excessive printing of USD. If you do not mind charting, use SMA 350 (or 400) using SPY. Buy when the price is above SMA-350 (or SMA-400), and sell otherwise. SMA-400 reduces the number of false signals, but it is not nimble.
- I do not recommend Bitcoin but agree with most of thinking of this YouTube. https://www.youtube.com/watch?v=a5J8gMrEZxg

6 Rotate four ETFs

We can beat the market by rotating one ETF that represents the market such as SPY and cash via market timing. Aggressive investors can add SH or PSQ (contra ETFs) to the four to have better returns during market plunges.

During a market uptrend, rotating the following four ETFs could be more profitable than staying with SPY (or any ETF that simulates the market). Be warned that a short-term capital gain in taxable accounts is not treated as favorably as the long-term capital gain; check current tax laws.

The allocation percentages depend on your individual risk tolerance. You can use indexed mutual funds. Compare their expenses and restrictions. Some mutual funds charge you if you withdraw within a specific time period.

Select the best performer of last month (from Seeking Alpha, cnnFn, or one of many ETF/mutual fund sites). Add a contra ETF such as SH to take advantage of a falling market for more aggressive investors. Add sector ETFs to the described four ETFs such as XLY, XLP, XLE, XLF, XLU, IYW, XHB, IYM, OIL and XLU to expand your selection.

ETFs	Money Market	U.S.	International	Bond
Fidelity		Spartan Total Market	Spartan Global Market	Spartan US Bond
Vanguard		Total Stock Market	Total International Market	Total Bond Market
My choice	Fidelity	SPY	Vanguard	Fidelity
Suggest %				
During Market plunge	90%	0%	0%	10%
After plunge	10%	60%	20%	10%

Explanation

- The above are suggestions only. If your broker offers similar ETFs, consider using them.
- Check out any restrictions of the ETFs and commissions.

- 4 ETFs (one actually is a money market fund) are enough for most starters. They are diversified, low-cost and you do not need rebalancing except during a market plunge.
- The percentages are suggestions only. If you are less risk tolerant, allocate more to a money market fund, CD and/or bond ETF.
- Have at least 10% allocated to the money market fund for safety.
- When the market is risky, reduce stock equities (i.e., increase money market and bond allocations).
- The symbols for Fidelity ETFs are FSTMX, FSGDX and FBIDX.
- The symbols for Vanguard ETFs are VTSMX, VGTSX and VBMFX.
- If you are more advanced, use additional sector ETFs to rotate. Also buy long-term bond funds (such as 30-year Treasury) when the interest rate is 10% or more.

#Filler: Glad to be an investor

After watching the following YouTube video, I am glad my parents did not push me to play piano and also glad I do not have any musical gene. How can I compete with this kid?

https://www.youtube.com/watch?v=yf0B4rVoq44

Also, glad not into some life-threatening professions such as surgical doctors, soldiers, fire fighters, etc. I can make mistakes in investing from time to time without suffering from the consequences. With the uptrend market for most of the last 50 years, most investors should make good money. Thank God.

#Filler: Where common sense is not common sense

Excessive printing of money is not a long-term solution. Servicing the huge debt weakens our competitiveness. The politicians just want to buy votes today and finance their campaigns. Our next generations have to pay for these huge debts.

#Filler: Cayman Island
Most global corporations are making fun of our tax system. Moving the "headquarter" to low-tax countries such as Cayman Island with a mailbox, a bank account and/or an office that has never been used is a norm. The profitable Boeing has negative tax liability. What a shame!

7 Simplest technical analysis

When the stock, the sector that the stock is in and the market are all above its SMA-N averages (Single Moving Average for the last N sessions), most likely the stock is trending up.

5. Bring up Finviz.com from your browser.
6. Enter SPY. Write down the SMA-200 (Single Moving Average for 200 sessions). Positive numbers indicate that the trend for the market is up.

    However, the market could be peaking or overbought. Be careful when SMA-200 is over 5% and / or RSI(14) is over 65%. RSI is a metric on overbought / underbought.
7. Enter the sector ETF the stock is in. Write down the SMA-50. Positive numbers indicate that trend for the sector is up.

    However, the sector could be peaking or overbought. Be careful when the SMA-200 is over 10% and / or RSI(14) is over 65%.
8. Enter the stock symbol. If your average holding period of the stocks is 200, use SMA-200 and so on. I recommend SMA-200 for holding value stocks long term and SMA-50 for momentum stocks. Write down the SMA-N for your stock. Positive numbers indicate that the trend is up. However, the stock could be peaking or overbought. Be careful when the SMA-200 (or SMA-50) is over 25% and / or RSI(14) is over 65%.

If the above three criteria and the fundamental criteria are satisfied, most likely it is a good buy. If you buy sector ETFs or mutual funds only, you can skip step #4. In any case, use stop loss to protect your investment.

8 The best strategy

The best-kept secret in investing is to buy a weighted ETF. I use SPY as an example here. This ETF is well diversified as it keeps all 500 stocks in the S&P 500 index. The ETF has a higher position (in percentage) on stocks with higher market cap. The stocks with higher market caps usually grow the market cap by having good management and good products. The bad stocks are deleted from the index periodically.

The second best-kept secret is using simple market timing as described in this book to reduce the losses in market crashes.

It is very hard to beat this strategy. You do not need any knowledge in investing, and you only spend a few minutes every month to time the market. The market is risky when the metrics show you so such as the price is close to the simple moving average in using SMA-350 method; in this case you time the market more frequently.

9 Don'ts for beginners

- Do not use leverage: options, margin and leveraged ETFs.
- Do not short stocks.
- Buy low and sell high.
- Buy value stocks. Sell profitable stocks after a year and losers before holding 12 months for favorable tax treatments in non-retirement accounts. Be a turtle investor.
- Limit momentum trades.
- Use stops to protect your portfolio.
- Do not follow 'experts' blindly (most have their own agenda).
- Do not trade penny stocks (i.e., stocks less than 200 M and/or price less than $1 to my definitions).
- Venture into momentum trading when you have knowledge and time. Avoid trading systems that are available.
- Do not day trade. Most beginners lose most of their money.
- Do not take classes / seminars that promise you big money - if it works, they will give out their secrets.
- Be selective on investing subscriptions. If they give you a handful of stocks to thousands of subscribers, most likely the actual performance will not be good. Check their past performances that use real money.
- Beginners (even some experts) miss many opportunities by only buying blue chips and/or the companies they know.
- Do not buy stocks making new lows, as there could be another bottom.
- Buy stocks on their way up, especially when the market is in an uptrend with low inflation and low interest rates.
- Do not buy products from financial planners and/or promoters but pay them for advice. Avoid annuities and some insurance products unless you have good reasons. If the promoter gets a 10% commission or a 2% front-loaded mutual funds (and some may switch funds annuity making him 2% richer every year), run as fast as you can.

Link
Common mistakes: https://www.youtube.com/watch?v=zkNueyFs8zQ

10   Summary

The following improves the odds of success but there is no guarantee.

Risky Market?

Bring up Finviz.com. Enter SPY. If both SMA-50% and SMA-200% are both negative, do not invest especially when SMA-50% is more negative than SMA-200%.

Evaluate value stocks from others' researches

Gather a list of stocks from screens and/or recommendations from magazines. Use researches that are free. Value stocks should be kept for at least 6 months. In six months or so, evaluate the bought stocks again to see whether you want to sell the stocks. Some other sites may provide free trial or one-time evaluation: IBD, GuruFocus, Zacks and Morningstar. Fidelity requires an account but there is no minimum position.

Name	Pass Grade
Fidelity's Equity Summary Score	>=8
Value Line[2]	Timeliness > Average
	Proj. 3-5 yr.% > 5%
VectorVest[1]	VST > 1 and RV > 1

[1]   Should be available from your local library.

[2]   Free for limited number of stocks and free trial.

Evaluate stocks

Bring up Finviz.com and enter the stock symbol.

Metric	Passing Grade
Forward P/E	Between 5 and 20 (25 for tech stocks)
P/FCF	< 15 and ratio is positive
Sales Q/Q	>10
EPS Q/Q	>15

Intangible Analysis

Bring up Finviz, Fidelity, Yahoo!Finance or Seeking Alpha (fewer articles now) and enter the stock symbol. To prevent manipulation, the stocks should have larger cap (> 200 M) and higher daily average volume (> 10,000 shares).

#Filler: The Ten Commandments of Investing.
http://www.investopedia.com/articles/basics/07/10commandments.asp

- Set goals. * Personal finances in order. * Ask questions. * Do not follow the herd. * Due diligence. * Be humble. * Be patient. * Be moderate. * No unnecessary churning. * Be safe. * Do not follow blindly.

- My additions: * Diversify. * Study market timing. * Protect your losses and profits. * Monitor your screens and your metrics. * Be emotionally detached from investments.* Learn from mistakes. * Stay away from bubbles. * Be socially responsible.

Appendix 1 – All my books

- Art of Investing (highly recommended combining most of my books on investing). It has over 500 pages (6*9), double the size of an average investing book. Similar books: Using Fidelity. Using Finviz.
- Sector Rotation: 21 Strategies and Shorting Stocks and ETFs have more specific chapters on the topic.
- Using Profitable Investing Sites. Investing Lessons.
- Best stocks for 2023.
- "Nuclear War with China?"
- Books for today's market: Profit from Coming Market Crash.
- The following books are in a series: Finding Profitable Stocks, Market Timing and Scoring Stocks.
- Books on strategies: Trading System, Swing (Rotation + Momentum), ETF Rotation for Couch Potatoes, Momentum, SuperStocks, Dividend, Penny & Micro Stock, and Retiree.
- Books for advance beginners: Be an expert (highly recommended), Introduce, Investing for Beginners, Beat Fund Managers, Profit via ETFs, Buffett, Ideas, Conservative and Top-Down.
- Miscellaneous: Investing Strategies. Buy Low and Sell High. Buy High and sell Higher. Buffettology. Technical Analysis. Trading Stocks.
- Concise Editions and Introduction Editions are available at very low prices and are competitive with books of similar sizes (50 pages) and prices ($3 range).

Most books have paperbacks. Links and offers are subject to change without notice.

Best stocks to buy for 2023

We care about performance only. Not considering dividends and fees, my last three books in this series have beaten the SPY (the market to most) by huge margins. "Best stocks" series. A new book may be published on Dec. 15 every https://www.amazon.com/dp/B0BQCLCZP9

Performances of the primary lists of my last five books in this series:

Book	Stocks	Return	Ann.	Beat RSP by
Best stocks to buy for 2022	10	4%	4%	153%
Best Stocks to buy as of July, 2021[4]	8	5%	13%	487%
Best Stocks for 2021 2nd Edition	10	42%[3]	52%[3]	220%
Best Stocks for 2021	4	29%	44%	118%
Best Stocks to Buy from Aug, 2020	14	45%	45%	3%

		9	25%	32%	196%[2]
Avg.		9	25%	32%	196%[2]

Sector Rotation: 21 Strategies

- On 5/26/2020, I searched for "Sector Rotation" under Amazon's Book. They are listed in the same order except my book Sector Rotation: 21 Strategies.

Book	Date	Size[1]	Kindle $[1]	Hard $
Sector Rotation: 21 Strategies	**05/2020**	**425**	**$9.95**	**$24.95**
Super Sectors	09/2010	289	$26.39	$49.95
Dual Momentum Investing	11/2014	240	$40.40	$42.20
Sector Investing	05/1996	260		$29.94
Sector Trading Strategies	08/2007	164	$26.39	$16.66
The Sector Strategist	03/2012	225	$26.39	$44.96
ETF Rotation	10/2012	125	**$9.95**	**$14.99**
Optimal... Sector Rotation	07/2015	80		$44.07

[1] From Amazon on size and prices as of 5/25/2020.

My book won in all categories except the price for hard copy in one. However, my book won as the lowest cost per page by a wide margin. In addition, as of 5/2020 I bet that no author besides me made over 4 times using sector rotation starting the amount more than his yearly salary then.

- I have **21** strategies in sector rotation while most books have only one. It ranges from simple rotation of a stock ETF and cash for beginners to many advanced strategies for experts. Most other books have one or two strategies.
- Andrew, a contributor on Sector Rotation article at Seeking Alpha, said, "Great stuff, Tony. It's great to meet experienced traders such as yourself. I had a browse through the book and think your method is a little more refined than mine."
- "You have written the book in a way that makes good and logical sense." Bill.
- Do not be fooled by past performances. Just check the recent performance of the top 50 stocks selected by IBD in the last five years. The mediocre result (hopefully it will change) could be due to too many followers and/or there is no evergreen strategy. I seldom heard the fantastic results from the followers of O'Neil, our greatest chartist. The adaptive strategy of this book shows you how to select the most profitable strategy for the current market.
- I switched most (if not all) my sector funds in April, 2000 from technology sectors to traditional sectors (better to money market fund). We can reduce losses by spotting market plunges and the sector trend.

Shorting Stocks and ETFs

Recent performances.

Stocks	Short Date	Close date	Duration	Return	Annualized
ACVA	06/10/21	09/29/21	111	22%	72%
CCL	07/14/21	09/29/21	77	-8%	-36%
CENX	09/17/21	09/29/21	12	3%	105%
CLOV	09/16/21	09/29/21	13	10%	291%
CSPR	09/16/21	09/29/21	13	33%	917%
EOSE	09/15/21	09/29/21	14	10%	261%
MILE	07/22/21	09/29/21	69	53%	279%
NCLH	07/27/21	09/29/21	64	-5%	-27%
REAL	06/04/21	09/29/21	117	22%	68%
UAVS	06/04/21	09/29/21	117	41%	127%
Average	07/30/21	09/29/21	61	18%	206%
RSP	S&P 500			0%	

It is for education purposes and I am not responsible for any errors. As in most parts of this book, commissions, dividends and fees (interest for shorts) are not included, and hence the returns are less than specified. They are real and all trades for the period.

Stocks	Short Date	Close date	Duration	Return	Annualized
BBIG[1]	09/30/21	11/19/21[1]	50	35%	258%
BFLY	09/30/21	11/18/21	49	14%	107%
EOLS	11/10/21	11/17/21	7	10%	523%
FLDM	10/13/21	11/18/21	36	14%	147%
MKFG	10/27/21	11/18/21	22	-9%	-149%
PAVM[1]	10/20/21	11/19/21[1]	30	34%	413%
TSP	10/05/21	11/18/21	44	-11%	-91%
VRM	10/13/21	11/17/21	35	13%	135%
Average	10/14/21	11/18/21	34	13%	168%
RSP	S&P 500			4%	

Appendix 2 – Art of Investing

Art of Investing consisting of 15 books in 1. Besides saving money and your digital shelve space, it gives you quick reference and concentration on the topic you're currently interested in. It covers most investing topics in investing excluding speculative investing such as currency trading and day trading. It has over 500 pages (6*9), about the size of two investing books of average size.

The 15 books

Book No.	Amazon.com
1	Simple techniques
2	Finding Stocks
3	Evaluating Stocks
4	Scoring Stocks
5	Trading Stocks
6	Market Timing
7	Strategies
8	Sector Rotation
9	Insider Trading
10	Penny Stocks & Micro Cap
11	Momentum Investing
12	Dividend Investing
13	Technical Analysis
14	Investing Ideas
15	Buffettology

The book links are subject to change without notice.

"How to be a billionaire" is for beginners and couch potatoes, who can use the advanced features of this book in the simplest and less time-consuming techniques. Most advance users can skip this section unless they want to use some of the short cuts described.

We start with the basic books Finding Stocks, Evaluate Stocks, Trading Stocks and Market Timing. You can select and start with one of the many styles and strategies in investing such as swing trading and top-down strategy. Many tools are described in other books such as ETFs, technical analysis, covered calls and trading plan.

Many books start with "Why" to lure you to read more and are followed by "How" and then the theory behind the book.

If the book you're reading is beneficial to you, imagine how it would with 850 pages.

Most readers' comments are on "Debunk the Myths in Investing", which this book is originally based on. As of 2018, I did not know any of the commentators on my books.

"I skipped ahead to his chapter book 14 (of "Complete the Art of Investing"), Investment Advice just to get a feel of his writing style. His research is phenomenal and doesn't overwhelm with big words or catchy "sales-like" tactics.

I truly believe this ordinary man, Mr. Tony Pow, has a gift of explaining his experience as an investor without the bull crap of trying to make you buy his stuff. He seemingly just wants to share his knowledge, tips, and clarity of definitions for the kind of folks like me who want to understand something FIRST before jumping in with emotions of trying to make a boat load of money. I like the technical analysis side he brings.

Mr. Tony Pow talks about hidden gems in his book; well....quite frankly, he is a hidden gem. Thank you and I will also post my comments about this author to my Facebook page!" – JB on this book.

"Excellent book, recommend to all investors... great knowledge. It has fine-tuned my investing strategies... Your book is hard to set aside, as I read it all the time learning good techniques and analysis of stocks, ETF... Since I purchased your book in March, I have underlined, highlighted and placed tabs on top of pages for quick reference." – Aileron on this book.

"Tony, I just finished reading your 2nd edition. It's my pleasure to report that I found it most interesting. You're welcome to use this blurb if you like:

Debunk the Myths in Investing is an all-encompassing look at not only the most salient factors influencing markets and investors, but also a from-the-trenches look at many of the misconceptions and mistakes too many investors make. Reading this book may save not only time and aggravation but money as well!"

Joseph Shaefer, CEO, Stanford Wealth Management LLC.

"Tony, Great work!" from James and Chris, who are portfolio managers.

"'Debunk the Myths in Investing' is a comprehensive book on investing that deals with many aspects of this tense profession in which with a lot of knowledge and a bit of luck (or vice versa) one can greatly benefit...

Therefore 'Debunk the Myths in Investing' is an interesting book that on its 500 pages offer a lot of knowledge related to investing world and many practical advice, so I can recommend its reading if you're interested in this topic."
- Denis Vukosav, Top 500 Reviewers at Amazon.com.

"490 pages (Debunk) of a genius's ranting and hypothesis with various theories throughout, written light-heartedly with ample doses of humor...Yes, the myth of not being able to profitably time the market is BUSTED...

One might ask... Why is he giving away the results of his hard-earned research for only $20? He states that his children are not interested in investing and wants to share his efforts with the world." - Abe Agoda.

"Excellent book, recommend to all investors... great knowledge. It has fine-tuned my investing strategies... Your book is hard to set aside, as I read it all the time learning good techniques and analysis of stocks, ETF... Since I purchased your book in March, I have underlined, highlighted and placed tabs on top of pages for quick reference." - Aileron on this book.

"Great stuff, Tony. It's great to meet experienced traders such as yourself. I had a browse through the book and think your method is a little more refined than mine."
"Your strategy is very rules based and solid. I sometimes envy people who have developed something like this."

Making 50% in one month
I claim to have the best one-month performance ever for recommending 8 or more stocks without using options and leverage. My following return is 57% in a month or 621% annualized. They are slightly different as I calculated the average from the averages of three different accounts. The average buy date is 12/26/18 and the "current date" is 01/28/19.
The performance may not be repeated. I will use the same screen for the coming years and even the expected 10% (or 120% annualized) is very good.

I used the same screen for searching stock candidates. I spent a total of about 20 hours from Dec. 15, 2018 to Jan. 5, 2019.

Stock	Buy Price	Sold or Current Price	Buy date	Sold or Current date	Profit %	Profit % Ann.	Status
CHK	2.13	2.99	01/03/09	01/18/19	40%	982%	Sold
MNK	16.41	21.45	01/03/19	01/25/19	31%	510%	Sold
MNK	16.43	21.45	01/03/19	01/25/19	31%	507%	Sold
NNBR	5.68	8.58	12/26/18	01/28/19	51%	565%	
NNBR	5.72	8.58	12/26/18	01/28/19	66%	727%	
ESTE	4.35	6.45	12/26/18	01/18/19	48%	766%	Sold
LCI	4.61	8.29	12/21/18	01/28/19	80%	767%	
MDR	8.01	9.13	01/08/19	01/28/19	14%	255%	
YRCW	3.29	5.78	12/21/18	01/28/19	76%	727%	
YRCW	3.26	5.78	12/21/18	01/28/19	77%	742%	
ASRT	3.56	4.18	12/26/18	01/28/19	17%	193%	
UTCC	7.13	11.00	12/26/18	01/28/19	54%	600%	
YRCW	2.92	5.78	12/26/18	01/28/19	98%	1083%	

Best one-year return
I claim to have the best-performed article in Seeking Alpha history, an investing site, for recommending 15 or more stocks in one year after the publish date without using options and leverage.

https://seekingalpha.com/article/1095671-amazing-returns-velti-alcatel-lucent-alpha-natural-resources

Your choice for your next book
I was surprised that one told me $25 is a lot for an investing book. It could be less than a taxi cab to the airport attending a seminar, and the time is peanut comparatively.

"Art of investing 2nd Edition" should be your first choice. If you are short-term trading, I recommend "Sector Rotation: 21 Strategies" and "Shorting Stocks /ETFs 2nd Edition". These books together with "Using Fidelity" and "Using Finviz" share many articles.

A new book every Dec. 15 with a July update (not a promise) is my selections on stocks. So far, the returns of the selected stocks are phenomenal. "Best stocks" series. A new book may be published on Dec. 15 every https://www.amazon.com/dp/B0BQCLCZP9

Appendix 3 - Our window to the investing world

The paperback version of this chapter can be found in the following link.

http://ebmyth.blogspot.com/2013/11/web-sites.html

- **General**
  Wikipedia / Investopedia /Yahoo!Finance / MarketWatch / Cnnfn / Morningstar /CNBC / Bloomberg / WSJ / Barron's / Motley Fool / TheStreet
- **Evaluate stocks**
  Finviz / SeekingAlpha / MSN Money / Zacks / Daily Finance / ADR / Fidelity / Earnings Impact / OpenInsider / NYSE / NASDAQ / SEC / SEC for 10K and 10Q (quarterly) reports required to file for listed stocks in major exchanges.
- **Charts**
  BigCharts / FreeStockCharts / StockCharts /
- **Screens**
  Yahoo!Finance / Finviz / CNBC / Morningstar /
- **Besides stocks**
  123Jump / Hoover's Online / FINRA Bond Market Data / REIT / Commodity Futures / Option Industry
- **Vendors**
  AAII / Zacks / IBD / GuruFocus / VectorVest / Fidelity / Interactive Brokers / Merrill Lynch /
- **Economy.**
  Econday / EcoconStats / Federal Reserve / Economist /
- **Misc.**
  Dow Jones Indices / Russell / Wilshire / IRS / Wikinvest / ETF Database / ETF Trends / Nolo (estate planning) / AARP /

Appendix 4 - ETFs / Mutual Funds

What is an ETF
ETFs have basic differences from mutual funds: 1. Lower management expenses, 2. Trade ETFs same as stocks, and 3. Usually more diversified but not more selective than the related mutual funds such as NOBL vs FRDPX.

The major classifications of ETFs are 1. Simulating an index such as SPY, QQQ and DIA, 2. Simulating a sector such as XLE and SOXX, 3. Simulating an asset class such as GLD and SLV, 4. Simulating a country or a group of countries such as EWC and FXI, 5. Managed by a manager(s) such as ARKK, 6. Betting a market or sector to go down such as SH and PSQ, and 7. Leveraged (not recommended for beginners).
Fidelity: Index ETFs (https://www.fidelity.com/etfs/overview).
Wikipedia on ETF (http://en.wikipedia.org/wiki/Exchange-traded_fund).

List of ETFs
ETF database (Recommended): http://etfdb.com/
ETF Bloomberg: http://www.bloomberg.com/markets/etfs/
ETF Trends: http://www.etftrends.com/
A list of ETFs. Seeking Alpha.
http://etf.stock-encyclopedia.com/category/)
A list of contra ETFs (or bear ETFs)
http://www.tradermike.net/inverse-short-etfs-bearish-etf-funds/
Misc.: ETFGuide, ETFReplay
Fidelity low-cost index funds:
https://www.youtube.com/watch?v=zpKi4_IJvlY
Fidelity Annuity funds with performance data.
http://fundresearch.fidelity.com/annuities/category-performance-annual-total-returns-quarterly/FPRAI?refann=005
ETFs vs mutual funds; https://www.youtube.com/watch?v=Vmz0CzlQvHk
Three ETFs: https://www.youtube.com/watch?v=MVi2RhpffuU

Other resources
Most subscription services offer research on ETFs. IBD has a strategy dedicated to ETFs and so does AAII to name a couple. Seeking Alpha has extensive resources for ETF including an ETF screener and investing ideas. So is ETFdb.

Not all ETFs are created equal
Check their performances and their expenses.

When to use or not to use ETFs
I prefer sector mutual funds in some industries, as they have many bad stocks such as drug industry, banks, miners and insurers. Most mutual funds cannot time the market.

When you believe a sector is heading up (or contra ETF for heading down), but you do not have time to do research on specific stocks, buy an ETF for the sector; it is same for the market.

Half ETF
Taking out half of the stocks that score below the average in an index ETF could beat the same full ETF itself. I call it HETF (half the ETF). You heard it here first.

To illustrate, sort the expected P/E (not including stocks with negative earnings) in ascending order and only include the stocks on the first half. Add more fundamental metrics. It will take a few minutes.

Disadvantages of ETFs
- When you have two stocks in a sector ETF one good one and one bad one, the ETF treats them the same. Stock pickers would buy the one that has a better appreciation potential.
- Sometimes the return could be misleading due to stock rotation. To illustrate this, on August 29, 2012, SHLD was replaced by LYB in a sector fund. SHLD was down by 4% and LYB was up by 4% primarily due to the switch. Unless you sell and buy at the right time (which is impossible), your return would not match the ETF's returns due to the replacement.
- Ensure the performance matches the corresponding index; it is hard due to excluding dividends.

Advantages of ETFs
- We have demonstrated that you can beat the market by using market timing. Between 2000 and Nov., 2013, you only exit and reenter the market 3 times and the result is astonishing.
- It is easy to rotate a sector vs. buying/selling all of the stocks in this sector. Rotating a sector is the same as trading a stock.
- The risk is spread out, and your portfolio is diversified especially for a market ETF or buying three or more ETFs in different sectors.
- Periodically the bad stocks in most funds are replaced by better stocks.
- Eliminate the time in researching stocks.

Leveraged ETFs

I do not recommend them. Some are 2x, 3x and even higher. They're too risky for beginners. However, when you are very sure or your tested strategy has very low drawdown, you may want to use them to improve performance. Most leveraged ETFs and contra ETFs have higher fees.

My basic ETF tables

I include some contra ETFs, mutual funds and Fidelity's annuity. Some of these may be interesting to you. Most Vanguard's ETFs have lower fees.

ETFs and funds come and go. Some ideas and classifications are my own interpretation. Refer to ETFdb for updated information. Not responsible for any error. Check out the ETF or fund before you take any action.

I prefer VFINX over SPY for the lower fees; both simulate the S&P 500 index. The stocks in the ETF can be either equally weighted or weighted by market caps. The latter is more like using momentum strategy, as the rising stocks usually have larger market caps. The index usually kicks out some poor-performing stocks and replaced them with better stocks. These ETFs are suited for long-term investing without constant reviews.

Table by market cap:

Category	ETF	Mutual Funds	Fidelity's Annuity	Contra ETF	Alternate
Size:					
Large Cap	DIA			DOG	
	SPY			SH	VOO VFINX RSP FXAIX
	QQQ			PSQ	FNCMX
	RYH				
Blend	IWD	BEQGX			
Growth	SPYG	FBGRX			FSPGX
Value	SPYV	DOGGX			FLCOX
Dividend	NOBL	FRDPX			
	VYM				
Mid Cap			FNBSC	MYY	
Blend	MDY	VSEQX			
Growth		STDIX			
		BPTRX			
Value		FSMVX			
Small Cap			FPRGC	SBB	FSSNX
Blend	IWM	HDPSX			
Growth		PRDSX			FECGX

Value		SKSEX			FISVX	
Micro	IWC					
Multi						
Blend		VDEOX				
Growth		VHCOX				
Value		TCLCX				
Total					FSKAX VTI	
Bond						
Long Term (20)	VLV	BTTTX		TBF		
Mid Term (7 – 10)	VCIT	FSTGX				
Short Term (1 – 3 yrs.)	VCSH	THOPX				
Total	BOND	PONDX				
Corp Invest Grade	VCIT	NTHEX				
High Yield (junk)	PHB	SPHIX				
Muni	MUB	Check state				
Special situation						
Buy back	PKW					

Table by sectors:

Sector	ETF	Mutual Funds	Fidelity's Annuity
Banking[1]		FSRBK	
Regional	IAT		
Biotech	IBB	FBIOX	
	XBI	Large	
Consumer Dis.	XLY	FSCPX	FVHAC
Consumer Staple	XLP	FDFAX	FCSAC
Defense + Aero	PPA		
Finance	KIE	FIDSX	FONNC
	IYF		
Energy	XLE	FSENX	FJLLC
Energy Service		FSESX	
Farm	DBA		
Gold	GLD	FSAGX	BAR
Gold Miner	GDX	VGPMX	
Health Care	IYH	FSPHX	FPDRC
	VHT	VGHCX	

House Builder	ITB	FSHOX	
Industrial	IYJ	FCYIX	FBALC
Material	VAW	FSDPX	GSG
	IYM		
Natural Gas	UNG		
Oil	USO		
Oil Service	OIH	FSESX	
Oil Exploration	XOP		
Real Estate	VNQ	FRIFX	FFWLC
REIT	VNQ		
Retail	RTH	FSRPX	
	XRT		
Regional bank	KRE	FSRBX	
Semi Conduct	SMH		
Software	XSW	FSCSX	
	IGV		
Technology	XLK	FSPTX	FYENC
	FDN	FBSOX	
		ROGSX	
Telecomm.	VOX	FSTCX	FVTAC
Transport	XTN		
	IYT		
Utilities	XLU	FSUTX	FKMSC
Wireless		FWRLX	

Footnote. [1] Also check Finance.

Table by countries outside the USA:

Country	ETF	Mutual Funds	Fidelity's Annuity	Alternate
Australia	EWA			
Brazil	EWZ			
Canada	EWC	FICDX		
China	FXI	FHKCX		
EAFE	EFA			
Emerging	VWO	FEMEX	FEMAC	FPADX
Europe	VGK	FIEUX		
Global	KXI	PGVFX		
Greece	GREK			
India	INDY	MINDX		
Indonesia	EIDO			
Latin America	ILF	FLATX		
Nordic		FNORX		
Hong Kong	EWH			

Japan	EWJ	FJPNX		
S. Africa	EZA			
S. Korea	EWY	MAKOX		
Singapore	EWS			
Taiwan	EWT			
Turkey	TUR			
United Kingdom	EWU			
Foreign:				
Combination				
Intern. Div.	IDV			FTIHX
Small Cap	SCZ			
Value	EFV			
Europe	VGK			

#Filler: Honey, my book can play music.
https://www.youtube.com/watch?v=HxGT5z6d-GA&list=PLMZa6mP7jZ2b1otqG4tfbgZpLEdh6YiNF

www.ingramcontent.com/pod-product-compliance
Lightning Source LLC
Chambersburg PA
CBHW071445220526
45472CB00003B/670